MILITARIZED
GLOBAL
APARTHEID

GLOBAL
INSECURITIES
A SERIES EDITED BY
CATHERINE BESTEMAN
AND DARRYL LI

MILITARIZED

IZED

GLOBAL

APART

HEID

CATHERINE BESTEMAN

Duke University Press

Durham and London 2020

© 2020 DUKE UNIVERSITY PRESS
ALL RIGHTS RESERVED
PRINTED IN THE UNITED STATES OF AMERICA
ON ACID FREE PAPER ∞
DESIGNED BY AIMEE C. HARRISON
TYPESET IN MINION PRO AND IBM PLEX MONO
BY WESTCHESTER PUBLISHING SERVICES

Library of Congress Cataloging-in-Publication Data
NAMES: BESTEMAN, CATHERINE LOWE, AUTHOR.
TITLE: MILITARIZED GLOBAL APARTHEID / CATHERINE BESTEMAN.
OTHER TITLES: GLOBAL INSECURITIES.
DESCRIPTION: DURHAM : DUKE UNIVERSITY PRESS, 2020. | SERIES: GLOBAL INSECURITIES |
INCLUDES BIBLIOGRAPHICAL REFERENCES AND INDEX.
IDENTIFIERS: LCCN 2020017122 (PRINT) | LCCN 2020017123 (EBOOK)
ISBN 9781478010432 (HARDCOVER)
ISBN 9781478011507 (PAPERBACK)
ISBN 9781478013006 (EBOOK)
SUBJECTS: LCSH: EMIGRATION AND IMMIGRATION—ECONOMIC ASPECTS. | DEVELOPED
COUNTRIES—EMIGRATION AND IMMIGRATION—GOVERNMENT POLICY. | DEVELOPED COUNTRIES—
EMIGRATION AND IMMIGRATION. | DEVELOPING COUNTRIES—EMIGRATION AND IMMIGRATION.
CLASSIFICATION: LCC JV6038 .B478 2020 (PRINT) | LCC JV6038 (EBOOK) |
DDC 331.6/21724—DC23
LC RECORD AVAILABLE AT HTTPS://LCCN.LOC.GOV/2020017122
LC EBOOK RECORD AVAILABLE AT HTTPS://LCCN.LOC.GOV/2020017123

In recognition that our contributions are vastly different in scale, size, and scope, I note that this modest book is inspired by and indebted to Cedric Robinson's reflection on his masterful *Black Marxism*:

AS A SCHOLAR IT WAS NEVER MY PURPOSE TO EXHAUST THE SUBJECT, ONLY TO SUGGEST THAT IT WAS THERE.

—Cedric Robinson, *Black Marxism: The Making of the Black Radical Tradition*, xxxii

CONTENTS

THE ARGUMENT

O n Tuesday, April 21, 2015, three major stories in the *New York Times* included an article about the disastrous loss of over eight hundred lives in the Mediterranean when a ship filled with hopeful migrants sank on April 18, an article about the arrest of six young Somali Americans in Minnesota who were suspected of attempting to join isis, and an article about the hundreds of thousands of "missing black men" across the country who are in prison. These seemingly disparate stories about normal topics of the day in 2015—the upsurge in the number of refugees attempting to reach Europe, security fears about immigrants, and the disproportionate incarceration of Black men in the United States—reflect an emergent new world order in which race and mobility feature as primary variables for which heightened security and militarization are the answer. This book attempts to sketch out some dimensions of this new world order, a militarized form of global apartheid.[1]

Militarized global apartheid is a loosely integrated effort by countries in the global north to protect themselves *mobility* against the mobility of people from the global south. The new apartheid apparatus takes the form of militarized border technologies and personnel, interdictions at sea, biometric tracking of the mobile, detention centers, holding facilities, and the criminalization of mobility. It extends deep into many places from which people are attempting to leave and pushes them back; it tracks them to interrupt their mobility, stops them at certain borders for detention and deportation, pushes them into the most dangerous travel routes, and creates new forms of criminality. It stretches across most of the globe, depends on an immense investment of capital, and feeds a new global security-industrial complex. It draws on and remakes historically sedimented racial formations that are highly localized but articulated with global imaginaries of race and racial difference. Because the new apartheid relies on and nurtures xenophobic ideologies and racialized worldviews, it recasts the terms of sovereignty, citizenship, community, belonging, justice, refuge, and civil rights and requires the few who benefit to collectively and knowingly demonize and ostracize the many who are harmed. It is at its most visibly militarized in Israel, and also in Australia, Europe, and the United States, where it serves the purpose of guarding hegemonic whiteness.

A new form of imperialism—security imperialism—is emerging from and shoring up global militarized apartheid. Security imperialism is expressed in the policies and practices used to identify and contain "risky" people throughout the globe, accompanied by interventions to securitize space for militaristic and economic domination. These emergent imperial formations are spatial and technological rather than territorial, and they are taking shape through projects that racialize and incarcerate people while securing cosmopolitan class privilege and capitalist extraction across borders. They tether the concept of security to militarization and make the militarization of everyday life normal.

ON VOCABULARY

Throughout this book I use "the global north" to mean the U.S., Canada, Europe, Israel, Australia, New Zealand, Russia, the Gulf Cooperation Council countries (United Arab Emirates, Bahrain, Saudi Arabia, Oman, Qatar, Kuwait), and East Asia (Japan, South Korea, Singapore, China, Hong Kong, and Taiwan). This list overlaps considerably with the group of states identified by political scientist and Pentagon consultant Thomas Barnett as "the Functioning Core" interconnected through globalization (which he defines as "network connectivity, financial transactions, liberal media flows, and connective security") in his influential "The Pentagon's New Map."[2] Barnett argues that the Functioning Core should initiate U.S.-led military occupations in the areas he identifies as "The Non-Integrating Gap," places he identifies as existing outside of globalization and that constitute the greatest security threats in the world today: "the Caribbean rim, virtually all of Africa, the Balkans, the Caucasus, Central Asia, the Middle East and Southwest Asia, and much of Southeast Asia," in addition to Central America and most of the countries in South America. Of additional concern to Barnett are the places he identifies as "Seam States"—Mexico, Brazil, South Africa, Morocco, Algeria, Greece, Turkey, Pakistan, Thailand, Malaysia, the Philippines, and Indonesia—that buffer the Non-Integrating Gap from the Functioning Core. He promotes a strong U.S. military presence in the Seam States as a strategy to control mobility and secure the Functioning Core against terrorism. I lead with Barnett's argument not because of his influence in anthropology—he has none, so far as I can tell—but because his model is a potent expression and extension of the homeland security doctrine that has redefined U.S. militarism, militarization, and policing since 9/11 and reshaped security regimes and security empires across the world as part of the global war on terror.

With some exceptions, Barnett's Non-Integrating Gap and Seam States roughly correspond to the global south of this book. But, as will become clear, I do not accept his reasoning about their similarities or why they should be grouped together for heuristic analytical purposes. In their book about why the global south is a harbinger of political futures in the global north, Jean and John Comaroff define the global south as "a polythetic category, its members sharing one or more—but not all, nor even most—of a diverse set of features. The closest thing to a common denominator among them is that many were once colonies, protectorates, or overseas 'possessions,' albeit not necessarily during the same epochs."[3] As they emphasize, the line between the north and the south is not definitive: it "is at best porous, broken, often illegible."[4] Following the Comaroffs, my use of the generalizing phrase "global south" is not meant to imply unity or homogeneity, or—central to my argument—that the global south is in any way disarticulated from the global north. It is also not meant to overlook class divisions that pervade the global south as well as the global north, including the presence across the global south of global cities and the existence of a global class of cosmopolitan elites who share the control of wealth, capitalist interests, access to political power, and the ability to move freely. (Of particular interest is China, which is one of the world's largest exporters of migrants, with a massive internal migration system of its own, as well as a rising status as a premier global financial lender and capitalist investor, with, some argue, imperialist designs.) Nevertheless, also central to my argument is the claim that it is possible to theorize in general terms an emerging militarized, hierarchical relationship governing the management of migration and labor mobility from those countries I identify as the global south to those countries I identify as the global north, and that this relationship has historical antecedents.

Similarly, the global north, as used in this book, reflects Michel-Rolph Trouillot's understanding that while globalization has been a fragmented process, the beneficiaries have been North America, Western Europe, and Asia—a list to which I have added Australia/New Zealand, Israel, the GCC states, and Russia. Trouillot's discussion of "fragmented globality" captures the differentiated labor markets that constrain the ability of people in the global south to participate in and benefit from globalization equally with the global north.[5] The central argument I pursue throughout this book is how the "fragmented globality" described by Trouillot is a racialized process with deep historical roots and persistent innovations, which is now being weaponized through militarized security bordering innovations.

ON SOMALIA

Because the outlines of the new world order of militarized global apartheid began to take shape for me through my long association with people from Somalia, I open this book with a short tour through recent Somali history because it contains many of the themes developed in later chapters. Twentieth-century Somali history includes a consistent pattern of foreign interventions and incursions, beginning with the colonial era and continuing with the impact of Cold War–influenced foreign aid, through the 1980s, when Somalia became the second largest recipient of U.S. economic and military aid in Africa and built the largest army in Africa.[6] Foreign support enabled Somalia's dictator Siyad Barre to utilize militarized authoritarian measures to maintain power, culminating in a bombing and strafing campaign in the 1980s against communities in northern Somalia that were contesting his leadership.

In 1990, following the fall of the Berlin Wall, the U.S. Congress acknowledged Barre's record of human rights abuses and voted to withhold further funding for his government. His government collapsed within a month, and the militias that deposed him turned against each other to fight over which could lay claim to the state and its resources, including foreign aid.[7] The number of people displaced in this catastrophe during 1991–93 tells a grave story of the aftereffects of U.S. support for a brutal dictator: nearly a million people fled Somalia, about 2 million were internally displaced, and at least a quarter million were killed.[8] As refugees poured out of the country, foreign armies moved in, accompanied by foreign NGOs, humanitarian agencies, and multilateral governance institutions attempting to reinstitute governing structures in the standard form of the Westphalian nation-state (e.g., political order based on the principles of state sovereignty and nonintervention by states in the internal affairs of other states, the basis of the contemporary international order of separate, legally equal, territorially bounded nation-states). Their efforts met with repeated failure, leading scholars, humanitarians, and journalists over the subsequent decades to regularly name Somalia "the worst humanitarian crisis in the world," "the most ignored tragedy in the world," "the most failed state," the most corrupt nation on earth, and, simply, "the world's most dangerous place."[9] Somalia became the poster child for trendy political descriptors: "failed state," "mission creep," "protracted refugee crisis."

As Somalia's instability persisted and Somalis continued to flee across the border into Kenya, the Dadaab refugee camp complex in Kenya became the largest in the world. In the years since Dadaab's creation in 1991, and despite (or because of) ongoing interventions by the UN, the African Union, the EU, the U.S., Ethiopia, Kenya, Turkey, and some of the GCC states, which provided humanitarian and development aid, backed particular militia factions, and attempted to engineer a new government through sponsoring twenty peace conferences, Somalia never achieved stability. The immediate post-collapse violence by warring militias competing for territory during the 1990s was followed by another calamitous explosion of violence in 2006 that destroyed a brief period of relative calm when Ethiopia, with U.S. military support, invaded to overthrow the nascent Islamic Courts Union (ICU) government. The invasion prompted the consolidation of Al-Shabaab, a militant group dedicated to opposing foreign intervention in Somalia. The instability created by the invasion, the overthrow of the new government, and Al-Shabaab's violence contributed to a famine, producing another massive flow of refugees and internally displaced people during 2006–12. By the beginning of 2012, Somalia was more insecure than ever before. Al-Shabaab responded to its designation as a terrorist group by the U.S. in 2008 with a pledge to target Western operations within and outside of Somalia and by allying with Al-Qaeda. Many scholars argue that although U.S. foreign policy toward Somalia after 9/11 was oriented toward quashing terrorism, it in fact enabled Al-Shabaab to emerge as an effective anti-Western terrorist group.[10]

The vast majority of Somalis were left to manage in a devastated environment characterized by violence, famine, and insecurity. In addition to ongoing attacks by Al-Shabaab, repeated incursions by Kenyan troops, and the contested presence of African Union troops, the U.S. began bombarding Somalia with airstrikes—at least 110 drone strikes, airstrikes, and raids in Somalia between March 2003 and November 2018, with a record high of forty-six strikes in 2018 and then fifty-two in 2019—to kill suspected members of Al-Shabaab. Such strikes also caused civilian casualties, displacements, and generalized terror.[11] Somalis still stranded in Dadaab have few options, especially following the 2018 U.S. travel ban against Somalis and immigrants from six other countries, popularly known as the Muslim ban.

The point of recounting this history is to demonstrate that over the past several decades Somalis have experienced a succession of foreign interventions by governments based in the global north whose aim has been to reorient Somalia to their economic and political desires, using increasingly militarized means. The results have been disastrous for Somalis, many of whom found themselves incarcerated in insecure camps, fleeing drone attacks, enduring war-related famines, and impounded by barriers to their legal ability to move. Somalis fleeing Al-Shabaab's violence move to Kenya but are then forced to move from the camps when insecurities flare or their refugee status is revoked; they move between Nairobi and the refugee camps when xenophobic ethnic cleansings sweep Nairobi; they make their way north to get on leaky boats in often-thwarted attempts to cross the Mediterranean; or they make their way south to South Africa, where they face periodic xenophobic violence that leaves them maimed or dead.[12] Their search for safety over the past two decades reveals some of the contours of the global system of militarized apartheid that I aim to describe in the following chapters.

Returning to Barnett's model, from the vantage point of my Somali acquaintances who live within Barnett's Non-Integrating Gap, the poverty and insecurity of the Gap looks like an intentional creation of the Functioning Core—a series of militarized borders, proliferating border walls, imprisoning refugee camps, detention centers, tightly policed and dangerous border crossing zones, violent interventions by militaries and agents of the global north, and regions made unsafe by the rise of militias in response to those interventions.[13] While Barnett, much like Thomas Friedman before him, defines the Gap as globally disconnected—which for Barnett is a condition to be remedied through U.S.-led military intervention—those who live within the Gap might see its insecurity as produced by a combination of militarized interventions by the global north (in support of friendly dictators, to overthrow unfriendly dictators, for resource extraction, and for other corporate interests of the global north) and militarized containment (closed borders, refugee camps, deportations, and detentions of unauthorized border crossers) designed to thwart the border-crossing mobility strategies of residents forced out of the Gap by such interventions.[14]

Their search for security is hardly unique; the global south houses the vast majority of the world's refugees and displaced people—those threatened by climate change, poverty, and war. Barnett's understanding of the Non-Integrating Gap, much like Friedman's earlier definition of "turtles" (by which he meant those countries that resist joining capitalist globalization), mistakenly presumes that the poverty and insecurity in these regions is due to their global disconnection. But the view from the south reveals this to be a myopic argument that ignores global connections that pervade the global south through transnational emigration and diasporas as well as myriad global military, corporate, and NGO interventions.[15]

The life strategies pursued by my Somali acquaintances demonstrate the shortcomings in the available scholarly vocabulary for describing the structures that shape transnational connections and diasporic networks that originate in Barnett's Non-Integrating Gap; the existing vocabulary fails to adequately capture the encounters through which people from the Non-Integrating Gap engage the rest of the world. For the Somali diaspora, "transnational" is inadequate because their connections are not necessarily made between and through national entities or frames; rather, for example, they are made between refugees incarcerated in camps in Kenya and people living in stateless southern Somalia, between refugees living with few civic rights in South Africa and refugees in UNHCR refugee camps, between refugees in camps in Kenya and refugees in camps in Tanzania. The nationalist frame is almost completely irrelevant in the lives of Somalis except for the fact that national governments from the global north, in the name of their own security, regularly intervene in Somalia or to contain Somalis, through attempts either to impose new governmental structures that continually prove irrelevant to people living in Somalia or to impose new security regimes through proxy armies, alliances with warlords, drone strikes, or travel bans. And one of the primary ways in which the nationalist frame is made consistently relevant for Somalis seeking security is through militarized border controls that other nations wield against their ability to move, in effect incarcerating them in zones of profound and enduring insecurity.

Somalia is but one example of the effect of policies in the global north that incarcerate and traumatize people in the global south in the name of security and profit in the global north. In the globalized contemporary, the emergence of a system of militarized apartheid used by wealthy and powerful countries in the global north against people from the global south is the signature form of globalized structural violence of our era. Other scholars have used the phrase "global apartheid" to describe the historic and current world order, arguing that from the age of exploration to the age of imperialism to the colonial era to the age of the Cold War to the age of neoliberalism and the Washington Consensus to the current moment, the global north has been engaged in projects of racialization, segregation, political intervention, mobility controls, capitalist plunder, and labor exploitation of people in the global south.[16] While terms like *imperialism*, *globalization*, and *transnationalism* have been helpful for highlighting many important dimensions of these global processes, the term *apartheid* shifts the frame to capture the use of race and nativist language to structure mobility, belonging, class inequality, elimination, and extermination, as well as the relevance of border controls and the hierarchical modes of excluding or incorporating racially delineated people into a polity for labor exploitation. My argument builds on this perspective by acknowledging the significance for this emergent world order of new forms of militaristic border security, containment, and empire building.

ON RACE

Race is a human creation constructed in particular locations in particular historical time periods for specific reasons linked to the creation of hierarchies that benefit particular social groups at the expense of others. It is both a structure and a process; it is both specific to localities and global in scope; it is iterative and constantly reinvented; and it is rooted in the particular history of European imperial expansion and the development of capitalism.

Roger Sanjek defines race as "the framework of ranked categories segmenting the human population that was developed by western Europeans following their global expansion beginning in the 1400s."[17] Cedric Robinson goes back further in time, locating the creation of racialism in premodern Europe, arguing that capitalism and racialism co-emerged in feudal Europe through internal ordering structures that later "permeate[d] the social structures emergent from capitalism."[18] In his view, "The tendency of European civilization through capitalism was, then, not to homogenize but to differentiate—to exaggerate regional, subcultural and dialectical differences into 'racial' ones. As the Slavs became the natural slaves, the racially inferior stock for domination and exploitation during the Middle Ages, as the Tartars came to occupy a similar position in the Italian cities of the late Middle Ages, so at the systemic interlocking of capitalism in the sixteenth century, peoples of the Third World began to fill this expanding category of a civilization reproduced by capitalism."[19]

Racialism and capitalism emerged together in Europe through processes that created forms of differentiation in concert with emerging regimes of ownership, control of property, and profit-seeking. Fundamental to the emergence of racialism in Europe and its global spread through the centuries of imperialism, the slave trade, and colonialism is the centrality of white supremacy. "White supremacy is the unnamed political system that has made the modern world what it is today," writes philosopher Charles Mills in his opening sentence of *The Racial Contract*, in which he theorizes the Racial Contract as a set of agreements among white people that racial hierarchies that benefit white people and ensure white hegemony should remain the norm and be defended on the global stage politically, juridically, rhetorically, and philosophically.[20] "The general purpose of the Contract is always the differential privileging of the whites as a group with respect to the nonwhites as a group, the exploitation of their bodies, land, and resources, and the denial of equal socioeconomic opportunities to them. All whites are *beneficiaries* of the Contract, although some whites are not *signatories*."[21] The Racial Contract is not only global, Mills argues, but foundational to modernity. The modern world was "expressly created as a racially hierarchical polity, globally dominated by Europeans," at its most visible just prior to World War I when about 85 percent of the earth was claimed by Europe as "colonies, protectorates, dominions, and commonwealths."[22] Leading European political philosophers like Hobbes, Locke, Rousseau, and Kant all took the Racial Contract for granted in their theories about humanism and democracy, in which equality only applied to white men, Mills notes. Thus, the canon of Western political philosophy emerged within a set of assumptions that accepted white supremacy and a racialized ordering of the world as a given, assumptions that extend through contemporary theorizations of liberalism, modernity, development, and humanitarianism.

Paul Farmer's seminal work on structural violence in Haiti offers a striking example in his devastating portrait of how Haiti's treatment by the global north following the 1791 slave revolt amounted to centuries of apartheid policy in the form of unjust trade blockades, the draining of resources, support for dictators, and the unequal barring by the United States of Haitian as opposed to white immigrants.[23] The revolution in Haiti had "filled the liberal world in its entirety with horror and scandal," offering them an object lesson in the importance of ensuring global white hegemony, writes Domenico Losurdo, in his crisp argument that the golden age of liberalism in the U.S., England, and France was fundamentally a project to consolidate white supremacy. The history of liberalism is uncontestably conjoined with the history of imperialism and colonialism—a history of racialized segregation, white supremacy, and resource extraction that underpins the current iteration of global apartheid.[24]

European liberalism emerged in the context of historic connections among white settler colonialism in the Americas, the transatlantic African slave trade, and the East Indies and China trade in the late eighteenth and early nineteenth centuries, connections that colonial studies scholar Lisa Lowe argues have been obscured in much historical scholarship by the separation between the liberalism archive and the imperial archive.[25] Reading these archives together allows Lowe to track the "intimate connections" among colonized indigenous peoples, enslaved people, and indentured Asian labor, through which Anglo-American liberal government created racial classifications to facilitate the management of labor throughout the globe. Centuries of dependence on the removal of indigenous people and their replacement with enslaved Africans led British colonizers concerned about slave revolts in the Caribbean to import Asian laborers, who were treated as a separate race from enslaved Africans. Their servitude was part of Britain's move from mercantile colonialism to a system they called "free trade" in East Asia, but managed through imperial rule over populations Britain viewed as unfit for self-governing. Britain did not colonize China, but rather extended what Lowe calls "imperial governmentality" through its management of trade routes and control of port areas, which allowed Britain to manage the "free" movement of labor in the form of indentured workers sent from China to the West Indies. As Britain moved from colonial repression enacted through violence to liberal governance through which populations were categorized and racialized, the management of imperial trade routes that were developed to connect production, manufacturing, and consumption allowed Britain to penetrate markets against the interests of local rulers (such as with the opium trade, which directly opposed Qing sovereignty) and to oversee the movement of people. Older forms of domination—enslavement, plantation agriculture, trade monopolies—could be accommodated within liberal ideas of free trade and British maritime dominance, adding additional layers to imperial power. By "conceptualizing the intimacies between settler colonialism in the Americas, transatlantic slavery, the East Indies and China trades in goods and people, and the emergence of European liberal modernity," Lowe shows how the basic assumptions of liberal modernity—freedom, wage labor, free trade, representative government—emerged directly from, were shaped by, and continue to reflect "Europe's colonial imperative."[26]

Europe's "colonial imperative" depended on normalized racism to maintain white autonomy and superiority in the global arena. Historians Marilyn Lake and Henry Reynolds document the circulation of books and articles during the nineteenth and early twentieth centuries among leading politicians in the U.S. and Britain and the British dominions of Australia, Canada, New Zealand, and South Africa about how to ensure white supremacy in their respective countries. Following Britain's success at opening markets for Asian labor, Chinese and Indians migrated to other parts of the world in massive numbers: 50 million migrants left China and 30 million left India. Chinese migrated to Australia, New Zealand, the Pacific, and the North American West, as well as throughout Southeast Asia; Indians migrated to labor in South Africa and to replace formerly enslaved people in the Caribbean.[27] As their numbers grew, white North Americans in the West and in the British dominions became agitated with fears about being overrun by Asian migrants and losing their right to self-govern on behalf of the white population. Lake and Reynolds document their response in the letters, speeches, and friendships formed between politicians in these far-flung places who shared strategies and supported each other's efforts to maintain whiteness as their central identity and power. Britain itself drew a clear distinction between those countries in its empire it viewed as fit for self-government (the white settler colonies of Canada, Newfoundland, the colonies in Australia, New Zealand, and the Cape of South Africa) and those Crown colonies in Africa, Asia, the Caribbean, and the Pacific deemed unfit for self-rule. The self-governing colonies insisted on their right to manage immigration any way they wished, including their right to block British subjects, such as Indians, from immigrating. "The imagined community of white men was transnational in its reach, but nationalist in its outcomes, bolstering regimes of border protection and national sovereignty," they write.[28] The writings that circulated among the political elites in these places entrenched "the emergent racial dichotomy between whites and non-whites and the related understanding that democracy was a privilege reserved for whites."[29]

Indian migration within the British empire to the Union of South Africa and Canada shows how this worked. South African authorities concerned about the growing presence of Indians engineered ways to discriminate against both contracted Indian workers and Indian elites through various laws that were meant to encourage them to return to India through disenfranchisement, taxes, prohibitions on property ownership, requirements for biometric registry, and the denial of legal recognition for Hindu and Muslim marriages. Within this process, identification of those targeted written into law and policy shifted from "Asiatics" to "Indians," reflecting the emergence of national identity within the bureaucratic efforts of the Union of South Africa to manage migration. This process "enabled a recoding of the racialized logic of the state as a naturalized logic of nationality,"[30] leading to new efforts within white settler British colonies to correlate race and nation in order to preserve whiteness. Just after the turn of the twentieth century, Indian migration to Canada prompted the country's first passport requirement—"a technology that nationalizes bodies along racial lines."[31] Drawing on the Canadian case, Radhika Mongia argues that "control over mobility does not occur after the formation of the nation-state, but that the very development of the nation-state occurred, in part, to control mobility along the axis of the nation/race. In this way 'nationality' comes to signify a privileged relation between people and literal territory."[32] A fundamental political commitment to white supremacy thus weaves through these histories of imperial and colonial connections.[33]

Similarly, in their corrective critique on silences about race in globalization scholarship, anthropologists Deborah Thomas and Kamari Clarke describe how modern processes of globalization have utilized and reconfigured "deeply embedded social hierarchies and prejudices rooted in a past characterized by territorial concepts of belonging and notions of civilization that both generated and were generated by racial inequalities."[34] They see globalization and racialization as simultaneous and mutually constituting processes, in which "the new transnational political economy . . . has worked through the persistence of an old racial order organized through socially entrenched divisions of labor in which a global working class not only remains in place (as compared to capital, which moves) but also remains segmented along racial, gender, ethnic, and national lines."[35]

The shared insistence on racial hierarchy by the United States, Britain, and British dominions had a dramatic global effect. Lake and Reynolds describe the reverberations in China, India, and Japan of the repeated and insistent performance of white solidarities and kinship across the British empire and the U.S. from the 1870s to the early 1900s: the overthrow of the Qing Dynasty by men seeking to push China to become a modern, racially unified nation in order to confront American and British imperialism; Gandhi's rage that Britain refused to intervene against the appalling treatment of British subjects from India working in South Africa and the demand in India for immediate political reform to create equality with Britain; Japan's fury about the treatment of Japanese immigrants in white settler states and the refusal of those states to accept a racial equity clause in the founding Covenant of the League of Nations following World War I; and the rise of militant forms of nationalism in Japan and elsewhere in reaction to such racial exclusions.[36]

In short, constructions of race and racialized hierarchies created within European feudalism and mercantile capitalism and exported globally through European imperialism and colonialism shaped the creation of modern liberal democracies throughout the world. As the following chapters make clear, these racialized hierarchies are now finding new life within the post-1989 rise of global neoliberalism through processes that differentiate beneficiaries of flexible capital (the global north and the global cosmopolitan elite) from those populations in the global south held in place by border and mobility controls as the global working class. Barnett's presumption that the incorrectly named Non-Integrating Gap lies outside of globalization not only reflects a misperception of the contemporary era but is historically unsupported as well. Later chapters track how these globally connected processes of colonialism, decolonization, and neoliberal globalization unfolded in different parts of the world through the creation of locally specific racialisms within enduring hierarchies.

Throughout these discussions, the argument remains attentive to the malleability of racism—that racism is a process that creates and colonizes difference for its own purposes, using its own essentialisms, even when the categorical constructions embraced by racists are absurd. Take the example of the "coloured" racial category in South Africa, which was created for an explicitly racist purpose as a buffer group to include everyone who the state claimed did not conform to the definition of "whites," "Africans," and "Indians." The coloured category thus included people from widely varied backgrounds, from descendants of the Cape's indigenous populations to people of mixed-race, Malay, and Chinese heritage. The current global war on terror has effected a similar logic in the creation of "Muslim" as a racialized category subject to racist rhetoric, xenophobia, and specific exclusions. As Ghassan Hage has argued,

> Islamophobic classifications vaguely and continuously fluctuate between the Arab, the Muslim, and "Islam," between the racial phenotypes, the ethnic stereotypes, and the religious generalizations. That is, from the perspective of the racializing subject, it is unclear where the Arab and the Muslim begin and end, where they are separate and where they fuse and where they even go beyond to delineate anyone who in the eyes of the Western racists looks like a "third world person." Both racists and the police, on the lookout for potential "Muslim terrorists," have killed or captured South Americans, Africans, Sikhs, Hindus, Greeks, Southern Italians, and many others. Keeping to the vagueness of racist thought is crucial since it conveys something important about the imaginary nature of the experience itself. Nor is this vagueness, in fact, a problem from a practical perspective. Racists have always managed to be exceptionally efficient by being vague. It could even be said that vagueness, empirical "all-over-the-placeness," contradiction, blocking-of-the-obvious, and even sometimes a totally surrealist grasp of reality, are the very conditions of possibility of the maximal efficiency of racist practices.[37]

Islamophobic classifications that target Muslims as a racialized category to be surveilled, feared, and caricatured have a global reach, promoted through political rhetorics honed in the global north and exported across the world through popular culture and warfare. "The impact of a racialized Islam is a global one," writes Junaid Rana, enlivening border militarization and security regimes around the world, as we shall see.[38]

ON APARTHEID

Before turning to the argument of the book, a very brief review of South Africa's iconic apartheid system, in place from 1948 to 1990, sets the framework. South Africa's apartheid system reflected its particular goals of perfectly aligning race and class and creating a labor regime responsive to the specific needs of industrialized capitalism. Apartheid on a global scale takes inspiration from the original South African model, while accommodating demands for the flexible modes of accumulation inherent to neoliberal capitalism and the creation of a multiracial cosmopolitan elite whose mobility is relatively unfettered because of their class standing. While there are differences between how global apartheid is unfolding in a context of global neoliberalism and how South African apartheid was linked to industrialized capitalism, the global form iterates the South African model to a striking degree.

Apartheid is a legal edifice that mandates, constructs, and enforces the supremacy of one racial group over another. In South Africa, the apartheid system supported by the National Party after its political victory in 1948 systematized white supremacy through policies and laws designed to manage the "threat" posed by Black people by incarcerating them in zones of containment while enabling their controlled and policed exploitation as workers, upon whose labor South Africa was dependent.[39] The set of policies that came to constitute apartheid in South Africa did not appear in 1948 as a newly designed model of social order; rather, it reflected and expanded colonial-era practices of racial identification and segregation, land dispossession of indigenous people, the restriction of voting rights to white people, divide-and-rule governance practices for Black people, and the exploitation of Black workers—all fundamental components of colonial intervention and control in South Africa that preceded the rise of the apartheid state under the National Party.[40] Apartheid was yoked to white Afrikaner nationalism; apartheid's architects saw their task as a modernist project of statecraft to ensure the system of white supremacy that they believed was their legal (and divinely mandated) right.[41]

Apartheid as a comprehensive, official social system and national policy developed through an unfolding series of policies, laws, and reforms over decades, as the South African government continually refined various dimensions of white supremacy, Black containment, and labor control through legislation, policy, evolving bureaucratic practice, and new security technologies. Although based in a legal edifice, apartheid is also always a process that is continually renewed and refined through law, policy, bureaucracy, and daily engagements. As Deborah Posel explains in her cogent analysis of apartheid's first two decades in South Africa, it was not a "single, coherent, monolithic project," but rather evolved as a mix of dogma and "radical provisionality" to maintain white supremacy in response to shifting contexts and contestations.[42] Over the four decades of its formal existence in South Africa, apartheid's architects continually introduced various tweaks and reforms, as well as altering certain racial categories (allowing for exceptions to rigid racial restrictions for Japanese and African Americans, for example) to manage some of the external and internal pressures produced by the construction of a legal edifice of white supremacy. Apartheid's adaptability and flexibility was part of its strength, but also a reflection of the enormous work it took to manage the internal contradictions of a system built on hierarchy, exclusion, and oppression.

In brief, South Africa's apartheid order emerged through the creation of mutually exclusive legally defined identities, the sorting of those identities into geographically demarcated areas through mandated residential racial segregation, and the assignment of those identities to different locations in the hierarchical social order. This was accomplished through the creation of four distinct official racial categories (African, Coloured, Indian, and White) into which every single individual was placed, a process accompanied by the delineation of race-based geographical areas and the removal of people rendered "out of place"—because their state-assigned racial identity was not consonant with their residence—in order to create residential zones of racial homogeneity. The removal of people of color from newly designated white space affected 3.5 million Black South Africans, making this process "one of the largest mass removals of people in modern history."[43]

A particularly devious component of the apartheid racial landscape was the creation of new independent "homelands" for Black South Africans identified by the state as "Africans," which enabled their disenfranchisement from areas legally defined as white under the fiction that those in the African racial category could belong to and exercise political rights within their homelands.[44] Created to be ethnic enclaves for Black Africans, the homelands justified the political disenfranchisement of Black Africans from white South Africa and were intended to (re)tribalize Black South Africans, co-opt a resuscitated and traditionalized African leadership, and fragment Black opposition by nurturing distinct ethnic identities: Zulus were assigned to KwaZulu, Xhosa to Transkei or Ciskei, Shangaan to Gazankulu, and so forth. Black South Africans reassigned through removal to one of the homelands found themselves in small, overcrowded, remote, fragmented geographical areas that were far from life-sustaining. Homelands offered little to support their residents: they were infertile places devoid of the modern amenities, education, infrastructure, health care, and service delivery that white South Africans enjoyed, governed through structures and authorities emplaced and managed by the apartheid regime. While the apartheid government promoted the homelands as spaces of cultural authenticity and native belonging for Black people, in reality they functioned as population dumps and labor reserves from which men and women were drawn into white South Africa to work in the mines, on farms, and in domestic service to create profit and comfort for white South Africans.[45] South Africa's famous mines depended on African labor drawn from the homelands, as well as from neighboring countries, whose extraordinarily poor wages reflected the prohibitions under which they had to offer their labor. African workers were housed in cramped dormitories and forbidden to bring their families; they were not allowed to organize or find paths for upward job mobility; and they were prohibited from settling permanently in their places of employment. Their wages were not intended to support their families left in the home-lands, who were instead supposed to be self-sufficient but also responsible for the reproduction of the labor force and the care of the elderly. Influx control policies allowed into white South Africa only those African workers required by South African employers, but the demand for labor was so great that by 1950 58 percent of the African population lived either permanently or part-time in white areas. By 1960 the number had climbed to 63 percent.[46]

The legal presence of all Black workers in white South Africa was con-tingent on employment. Because the South African economy was heavily dependent on Black workers—"Black life remained the condition of white prosperity," writes Deborah Posel—the government issued passes to Black workers that identified them as employees, and without those passes their presence in white space was illegal.[47] The pass system regulated Black mobil-ity and ensured employer control over workers. The purposeful impover-ishment of the homelands and their taxation by the apartheid government ensured a labor supply of Black people who had to seek employment from white people outside the homelands, but as noncitizen guest workers, they lacked the right of democratic participation extended by the state to their white employers.

Black South Africans, of course, refused to comply with removals, border controls, mobility controls, and the pass system, relentlessly moving into white spaces, establishing squatter communities, moving through white spaces without passes, resisting efforts to remove them back to homelands, and, in general, challenging constraints on their mobility and civic rights. The militarized security apparatus required to maintain racial segregation; monitor borders and mobility; catch, detain, and deport people who violated pass laws and residential zoning laws; protect white neighborhoods against Black mobility; watch, police, and supervise the movements of Black people in white territory; and monitor the activities of anti-apartheid activists was not only extraordinarily costly but ultimately unsustainable.

In sum, "apartheid" as it unfolded in South Africa evolved around five key elements. These elements, I argue, are now taking shape systemically on a global scale through a constellation of policies and laws, many of which have roots in white settler and European colonialism and imperialism. To review, apartheid relies on an essentialized cultural logic that ties people to place through racial and nativist ideologies and discourses (translated globally: just as KwaZulu was for Zulus, Mexico is for Mexicans, Germany is for Germans, Japan is for Japanese, and so forth). Second, ethno-racialized groups and their respective territories created through apartheid practices are unequal because the territories inhabited by people of color are disenfranchised and impoverished by design in order to ensure white supremacy. Third, the delineation of territorial belonging is reinforced by a bureaucratic system of identity documentation (such as passports and visas) and mobility controls that perpetuate racialization. Fourth, in addition to being a system of identity management, racial segregation, and white supremacy, apartheid is also, critically, about the control and exploitation of the labor of people of color. And fifth, because apartheid is exploitive, unfair, and unjust, its maintenance requires a massive, pervasive, continually responsive, and expensive militarized security apparatus. Across all five elements is the role of the state in sanctioning, through law and policy, racial oppression as apartheid's distinguishing feature. As we shall see, a number of specific models of racialized management originating in South Africa's historical experiments with mandated racial hierarchies were adapted in other places for similar purposes, including concentration camps, the pass system, guest worker programs, and biometric registries for risky or undesirable populations.

THE BOOK

To build my argument that we are living in an age of militarized global apartheid, the following chapters show how the contemporary iteration of a racialized world order and a hierarchical labor market dependent upon differential access to mobility on the basis of origin replicates each dimension of apartheid. Chapter 1 offers a set of observations about the co-creation of racialized nativisms in different parts of the world over the past century, with particular attention to the centrality of whiteness to American, European, and Australian governance and national identities, and racial purity to Middle Eastern and East Asian countries. Chapter 2 turns to the question of plunder. Along with imperialist and military interventions, the expansion of systems of "capitalist plunder" engineered by agents of the global north into the global south renders localities in the global south unsustainable or unpromising for ordinary life and provokes out-migration, forcing people from the global south to confront the apparently contradictory demand for their labor and the militarized borders of the global north in their search for security, employment, and a sustainable life.[48] Containment regimes such as refugee camps, detention centers, and offshore holding facilities designed to interrupt the mobility of those displaced by plunder, military intervention, and other factors are detailed in chapter 3, which focuses most specifically on the effects of policies that criminalize unauthorized immigrants in the U.S. and the EU. Chapter 4 investigates how the global north allows for the controlled and policed border crossing of laborers, even while investing in ever-new forms of containment, drawing attention in particular to the huge importation of labor in Israel and GCC and East Asian countries. Chapter 5 chronicles the massive investments by the global north in militarized border technologies that reach far beyond their territorial borders to manage the movement of people from the global south, both to contain those considered "undesirable" or expendable in detention centers or refugee camps far from the borders of the global north, as described in chapter 3, and to create an exploitable labor force, as described in chapter 4. It also suggests the emergence of new security empires built on regimes of militarism and surveillance that link risky people across borders with risky domestic subjects. Chapter 6 offers reflections on what the demise of apartheid in South Africa might suggest about the global future. The chapters bring different parts of the world into focus—more attention is given to the criminalization of migrants in the EU and the U.S., while the discussion of imported labor turns more to the GCC states and East Asia—but the intention is to build, step by step, a complex and layered portrait of our emerging world order.

Before moving on, it is important to acknowledge that this book takes a much more global and overarching view than the usual focus on nuance that anthropologists typically embrace. This is purposeful. I wish to make visible a totalizing system coming into existence, in the same way that apartheid came into existence: piecemeal, uncoordinated, accretive, iterative, through resonating logics and systemic resonances. I am not suggesting militarized global apartheid was conceived and implemented by a singular group of actors making decisions in common and controlling the world. I am suggesting that an overarching set of logics founded in capitalism, racism, and militarization is moving the world toward a particular overarching structure of mobility controls that, even while the local expressions may be different, nevertheless form part of a broader pattern. One of my goals is to identify and map out these patterns in order to locate weaknesses, points of contradiction, and failures where resistances against militarized global apartheid and new political imaginaries might find success.

Similarly, this broad-brush portrait is not intended as a homogenizing project of the global south. The experiences of people in the global south are not interchangeable or identical. In making a case that the emerging security apparatus across the global north is creating a new militarized global apartheid based on racism I am not arguing that people from the global south experience the apartheid apparatus in the same way. Emplacement matters.[49] Modes of mobility matter. Context matters. History matters. The local significance of Blackness, for example, is made through local meanings and struggles in each place.[50] My effort to highlight a broad, global agenda on the part of the global north to incarcerate, contain, and police those from the global south is not intended to ignore these truths. To the contrary, the diverse accounts about how people from the global south encounter, endure, trick, struggle against, overcome, or get killed by their encounters with the security regimes of the global north reveal the contours across the world of the militarized global apartheid apparatus, but it is these contours and not the diversity of experiences of those struggling against those contours that are the focus here. Just as Black South Africans contested segregation and apartheid throughout the twentieth century, migrants all over the world act in defiance of militarized apartheid, insisting on their right to mobility, demanding political representation and recognition, working with collaborators to build movements demanding justice. The focus of this book is not on their agency; it does not address the creative, persistent energy of people subverting, challenging, overcoming, manipulating, or slipping through the imperial webs of control. Again, this is intentional. The strategies, agency, emotional lives, heartbreaks, and victories of the mobile have been thoroughly plumbed by ethnographers, including myself. Instead, the book responds to challenges by postcolonial scholars to locate and analyze imperialism and to the reminder by Shahram Khosravi of "migrants' fundamental right to opacity, that is, that not everything [about their migratory experiences] should be seen, explained, understood, and documented."[51] My decision to avert my gaze from their lives should not be mistaken for disinterest or ignorance—quite the contrary. My hope is that by bringing the structures of imperialist oppression into relief, those of us committed to a saner, healthier, hopeful world in which people have the opportunities they need for fulfillment and joy can find targets to aim for and dismantle.

CHAPTER ONE

BELONGING

The barbarians were at the door, which was bad enough,
but they were also claiming that "our" home could be theirs.
—MICHEL-ROLPH TROUILLOT, "THE ANTHROPOLOGY OF
STATE IN THE AGE OF GLOBALIZATION: CLOSE ENCOUN-
TERS OF THE DECEPTIVE KIND"

More than two decades ago Akhil Gupta and James
Ferguson wrote about the efforts by political elites
and anthropologists alike over the past century to
tie people to place, thus enabling the illusion that cultural
identity roots people in particular geographical places
where they are imagined naturally to belong.[1] Tying people
to place through the simultaneous creation of cultural
identities linked to nation-state membership informed the
idea of immigration and influx control, making mobility
seem dangerous, pathological, and threatening to the consolidation of nationalist identities within politically delineated territorial borders. As Noel Salazar and Alan Smart
note, while mobility is nothing new,

What is different in modern times is that human mobility needs to be framed in relation to the global political system of nation-states, who set and control the parameters of (trans)national movements and prefer relatively immobilized subject populations. The development of travel documents (not in widespread use until the First World War) and controls at ports of entry and other checkpoints mark how governments categorize the rights to mobility across well-defined territories. Seeing it as a threat to their sovereignty and security, a disorder in the system, a thing to control, modern states have preoccupied themselves with the ordering and disciplining of mobile peoples—be they nomads or pastoralists, gypsies, homeless people, runaway slaves, or labor migrants. . . . In a world that is perceived to be in constant flux, control over people's mobility potential and movement has become a central concern for projects of management and governance.[2]

Over the past century states in the global north have been crafting nationalist identities for citizens while building mechanisms to police cross-border movements of citizens and noncitizens as a critical expression of sovereignty. Such identities took shape within historic struggles over European imperialism and colonialism across the globe—struggles that racialized populations and produced racialized categories of enslaved people, indentured laborers, and indigenous peoples, as discussed in the introduction. Racial differences took shape in particular localities in conjunction with place-specific hierarchies and conditions of colonial or imperial relationships, but place-specific racial logics were connected through what Lisa Lowe calls an "Anglo-American settler imperial imaginary."[3] Consequently, over the past several hundred years a central component of nationalist identity formation has been the role of race and, in different places and with different iterations, white supremacy in structuring membership, belonging, and hierarchies of inclusion and exclusion.[4]

As is well known, the consolidation of nationalist identities occurred through the promotion by elites of particular ideologies, discourses, and cultural understandings about who belonged to the nation-state by virtue of descent and birth (and thus who did not), political processes of exclusion, and the creation of the passport used by countries to clearly brand those who belong and to exclude those who do not.[5] The study of nationalism as a politically and ideologically engineered project has generated an enormous amount of scholarship that will not be reviewed here, except to note that in the white settler colonial states of the United States, Canada, Australia, and

New Zealand (as in South Africa), in the colonizing states of Europe, and in the new nation of Israel the process of consolidating a nationalist identity connected to political membership was a specifically and lethally racialized project.[6] Along with the genocides, removals, and eliminations of indigenous peoples, white settler societies built liberal democracies fundamentally based on whiteness (and in the case of Israel, Jewishness), and the racial hierarchies worked out through European colonialism shaped racialized national identities in Europe.[7] These historical trajectories created the basis for the global pattern of white supremacy that currently regulates mobility.

WHITE SETTLER AND COLONIAL STATES

In his masterful comparative study of white settler colonialism in the U.S. and South Africa, George Frederickson writes, "The assumption that America was meant to be a homogeneous white nation, inhabited chiefly by members of the Anglo-Saxon and closely related 'races,' was strongly established by the time the Constitution went into effect."[8] The very first legislation to define the qualifications for citizenship (the Naturalization Act of 1790) restricted citizenship only to free whites, whose mobility into the U.S. remained unfettered, a law that was reaffirmed in the Nationality Act of 1870 and the Naturalization Act of 1906, and which remained on the books until 1952 (with piecemeal exceptions for the naturalization of people of African descent in 1870, for Chinese in 1943, and for Filipinos and Indians in 1946).[9] This policy obviously required the government to create rules to define who could qualify as white and to use such racial categories to determine political enfranchisement.[10] The centrality of whiteness to American identity targeted minorities within the country as well as immigrants: with the end of slavery following the Civil War and the extension of citizenship to African Americans, white males enacted racial segregation laws and strategies to disenfranchise African Americans as part of the ongoing consolidation of whiteness as the bedrock of American identity. Chinese immigrants were subject to the first exclusion law in 1882 in response to rising anti-Chinese sentiment in the West following the Gold Rush. As the number of Chinese immigrants fell, racist exclusions and violence against Japanese residents surged in line with their growing success as farmers and business owners. Even though Japanese immigration was basically disallowed through an agreement with Japan, the 1913 Alien Land Act targeted Japanese farmers in seven states by forbidding landownership and long-term leasing of land by anyone ineligible for U.S. citizenship—namely, all immigrants not considered white, including people of Japanese origin.[11] By 1917 Congress had succeeded in passing legislation that in effect created "Asian" as a racial category by denying entry to anyone with origins from territory stretching from Japan to Afghanistan.

After fears of an Asian influx were controlled through these exclusions, the 1924 Johnson Reed Act responded to growing anti-Semitism with immigration prohibitions favored by white men influenced by the eugenics movement. National origin quotas emplaced in the 1924 Act used the 1890 census as the basis for determining quotas for entry, thus prioritizing immigrants from Northern Europe, whose numbers were greater in that era, in order to restrict Jewish and Southern European immigrants. Excluded from the basis for quotas was everyone from the Western Hemisphere (who were at the time considered white), those already ruled ineligible for citizenship (all Asians except for those from the Philippines, which became a U.S. territory in 1898), and those descended from indigenous and African (enslaved) ancestors. After the United States acquired the Philippines as a territory in 1898, Filipinos became U.S. nationals with immigration but not citizenship rights, becoming the only Asian immigrants allowed entry after 1924, in response to a demand for labor after earlier exclusions had halted the labor supply from China, Japan, and India. When male Filipino immigrants began organizing for labor rights and courting white women, anti-Filipino sentiment moved the U.S. government to grant the Philippines independence and to set a national quota for Filipino immigrants that was the lowest in the world. Filipinos were basically barred from entry after 1935 in response to rising hostility to their presence in the western U.S.[12] "The central element of this hostility was the ideology of white entitlement to the resources of the West," explains historian Mae Ngai.[13]

White supremacist ideology was baked into the rationale of the U.S. Border Patrol at its creation in 1924, an organization embraced by white supremacists as providing legal opportunities to wield violence against Mexican migrants.[14] As geographer Joseph Nevins explains in his history of U.S. immigration, "One cannot divorce the Border Patrol's founding in 1924 from an era when eugenics was the rage. In this regard, its founding was about, among other things, maintaining Anglo racial domination."[15]

Mexicans, who were considered white for the purposes of the 1924 national origins quotas law, although still subject to a visa requirement for entry to the United States, became a separate race subject to restricted entry in 1930, which Ngai identifies as the emergence of racialized Mexicans as "iconic illegal aliens."[16] Mexican immigrants still did not face legal barriers to naturalization, but hardly any actually were naturalized, due in part to the racist structures of exclusion they experienced.[17] Although 4.6 million Mexican immigrants came to the U.S. as agricultural workers from 1942 to 1964, racist practices of segregation, Jim Crow–like restrictions, and the lack of protections afforded to agricultural workers in the New Deal ensured they were never viewed as part of the American working class or the national body.

Thus, throughout the first half of the twentieth century, the color bar for entry used against Asians and others deemed nonwhite mirrored the color bar previously used against African Americans and indigenous peoples who were already in the U.S. Immigration law had become a tool for crafting new racial categories.[18] As Ngai summarizes: "The national origins quota system proceeded from the conviction that the American nation was, and should remain, a white nation descended from Europe. If Congress did not go so far as to sponsor race breeding, it did seek to transform immigration law into an instrument of mass racial engineering."[19]

Immigration reform in 1965 seemed to offer an opportunity to deracialize immigration policy. It eliminated national origin quotas and instated in their place a system for admittance that gave every country an identical quota, with preferences for desired occupations as well as family members of people living in the United States. While immigration reform enabled a surge of immigration from Asian countries (although immigration from Africa remained tiny until the 1990s), it restricted immigration from Mexico (subject to quotas for the first time) and thus contributed to ongoing tensions about illegal aliens, since Mexicans without entry visas continued to immigrate in response to strong employer demand. Public debate about the potential dangers of Mexican "illegals" thus persisted, provoking additional reforms over the next two decades to tighten immigration controls, securitize the U.S.-Mexico border, enhance deportation capacity, fast-track removals, and criminalize undocumented Mexican workers.

Despite the legal and social transformations signaled by immigration reform as well as other progressive legislation intended to interrupt the history of white supremacy in the U.S. (such as the Voting Rights and Civil Rights Acts), ensuring white supremacy nevertheless remained an ongoing political project in subtle as well as overt ways. White politicians consistently worked to enact laws and policies with racist effects and to dismantle the antiracist possibilities to which the Immigration, Voting, and Civil Rights Acts aspired. Following upon the earlier history of Jim Crow laws and police brutality visited upon African Americans during the decades of struggle for civil rights, more recent policies included lending and real estate practices to entrench residential racial segregation and impoverish Black neighborhoods, the rise of a system of mass incarceration that disproportionately imprisons people of color, the disproportionate removal of Black men from mainstream society and enfranchisement as convicted felons who face ever more exclusions from social entitlements, and the impact on Black political participation of surgically racist efforts to deconstruct the Voting Rights Act.[20] Historic and ongoing efforts to segregate, police, and disenfranchise African Americans influenced how immigrants were racialized historically through law and in the popular imagination, as post-1965 immigrants from Southeast Asia, South Asia, Latin America, Africa, the Middle East, and the Caribbean were confronted by the Black–white racial binary that defined U.S. political belonging from the time of its creation as an independent nation.[21]

The post-9/11 identification of Muslims as security threats worthy of state surveillance and immigration exclusions is the newest iteration of the use of immigration law as a racializing tool. The so-called Muslim ban introduced by President Trump and upheld by the Supreme Court in 2018 bars immigrants from Somalia, Syria, Yemen, Iran, and Libya, in addition to North Korea and Venezuela. Earlier versions of the ban also included Iraq, Sudan, and Chad. President Trump repeatedly called for a "total and complete shutdown of Muslims entering the United States," as well as a system of surveillance to track Muslims already living in the U.S. Such discriminatory rhetoric and policy provokes fear and anti-Muslim acts of bigotry and racism, which by 2018 reached record numbers in the U.S. (as well as in the UK).[22]

In short, immigration control in the United States has long been used as a tool for crafting a racialized nation that prioritizes and centers whiteness. Because race is such a flexible social category, immigration control can be used to shape the contours of whiteness by variously targeting immigrant populations through racializing discourses and policies that place them firmly outside of whiteness. Resurgent white nationalism in the U.S., abetted and revealed by Donald Trump's presidency, reflects these deep historic commitments.

Canada, Australia, New Zealand, and Western European countries enacted similar racial logics of exclusionary citizenship, through genocide and removals of indigenous colonized peoples in the cases of Canada and Australia, through ideologies of racial superiority, and, after the end of colonialism, through laws that racially restricted citizenship in Europe. European colonialism was marked by what Ann Laura Stoler has called "a distinct colonial morality" explicitly oriented toward identifying, managing, and marking "the racial and class markers of being European." This process "emphasized transnational racial commonalities despite national differences. Not least, it instilled a notion of Homo Europæus for whom superior health, wealth, and education were tied to racial endowments and a White Man's norm."[23]

The former British dominions of Australia, Canada, New Zealand, and the colonies in South Africa took the "White Man's norm" as their defining feature as they crafted nationalist identities within the British empire that were emphatically oriented toward producing and protecting whiteness. Australia's founding as a commonwealth was marked by the expulsion of Pacific Islanders brought to work the cane fields and the implementation of immigration restrictions against those categorized as nonwhite, setting the course for subsequent legislation to ensure Australia remained white. In their chapter titled "White Australia Points the Way," historians Lake and Reynolds write that "at the beginning of the twentieth century, Australians drew a colour line around their continent and declared whiteness to be at the very heart of their national identity. . . . Their policies reflected and would in turn shape new racial solidarities across the world."[24] Australia's unabashed course proved influential to the other British dominions in Canada, New Zealand, and South Africa, who watched Australian immigration laws with interest and fell in lockstep behind Australia's militant refusal to consider Japan's proposal to include a racial equity clause in the 1919 founding Covenant of the League of Nations, despite Japan's defense of Australia in World War I. Alongside the Australian colonies, New Zealand had restricted Chinese immigration in the late nineteenth century, followed by even more draconian laws that, in turn, encouraged Canada, citing New Zealand's laws as precedent, to pass legislation in 1923 that "gave the Minister of Immigration complete discretion to refuse any application for entry, allowing for the virtual prohibition of Asian migration. . . . The Act of 1923 had the effect desired by White Canada."[25]

Furthermore, the creation of reserves for indigenous peoples in Canada provided a model of great interest to white South African authorities, who came to Canada in the 1920s to learn about Canada's reservation system, which they utilized as a template for creating South Africa's homelands. A few years earlier, South Africa had modeled its South African Land Settlement Act of 1912 and 1913 after Canada's Dominions Land Act of the 1870s, which restricted indigenous people from acquiring property or trading off the reservations, denied them voting rights, and established a "kind of pass system for exit and re-entry to reserves."[26]

In sum, ensuring white supremacy lay at the heart of the self-governing British dominions in Canada, Australia, New Zealand, and South Africa, as well as the United States. The laws, exclusions, and rhetoric promoted by these countries' leaders offered an object lesson to the rest of the world in racism, drew a global color line between those identified as white and those they categorized as nonwhite and inferior, and helped incubate transnational racial awareness and solidarities as well as nationalist movements in other countries in response to the exclusions and humiliations perpetrated on a global scale by white supremacists.

While Britain allowed its dominions to determine their own immigration policies as part of their right of self-government, a relatively open approach to immigration characterized its relationship with its other colonies. But following the end of European colonial rule and the emergence of a global political order based on mandatory nation-state citizenship, European states like Britain and France that had extended citizenship to some of the colonized began curtailing that policy, constructing instead a new regime of mobility controls. From the 1940s to the 1970s, former colonial subjects began moving to the formerly colonizing countries of Europe in response to the huge demand for labor to repair the war-ravaged continent.[27] Men and women from British colonies in the West Indies held rights in the British empire and began arriving in Britain after the war, as did Algerians, who held French citizenship, in France. Although Europe had long experienced and struggled over internal ethnic differences, historian Rita Chin argues that postwar immigration was perceived "as qualitatively different—a new kind of diversity."[28] By the late 1950s, hostility toward the new arrivals in the UK had grown so significant that quotas and visa requirements were emplaced after 1962 on immigrants from India, the Caribbean, East Africa, and Hong Kong. Following the unexpected arrival in the UK of East African Asians after Kenyan independence in 1967, the government again narrowed the requirements for entry of former colonial subjects, and then, under Margaret Thatcher, "abolished the categories of citizens of the UKC and British subjects, as well as the principle of jus soli, which had granted automatic citizenship to anyone born on British soil. It also created a new definition of citizenship exclusive to the United Kingdom."[29] England and France, as well as the Netherlands and Germany, introduced a variety of measures to encourage immigrants to return to their countries of origin, including by placing restrictions on citizenship for the children of immigrants. Chin notes the efforts by Western European governments to couch their anti-immigrant restrictions in cultural rather than racial terms, calling upon concepts like national belonging and heritage to justify excluding formerly colonized subjects. The rise of the far right in French national politics over the past few decades has included a notable shift in lexicon whereby those with Arab origins came to be called "Africans" or "foreigners" rather than French, a lexical shift accompanied by growing and visible expressions of racism in the job market, the private housing market, and welfare services.[30]

What this brief overview reveals is that at the very moment that former colonies were transitioning to independence and gaining political freedom, former colonizers were working to ensure the hegemony of an international structure to control population movement, to enforce the national conferral of citizenship as the only form of internationally recognized political belonging, and to make certain that they could retain whiteness—couched in the language of European heritage—as a key factor in determining who would be allowed to cross their borders.[31]

This orientation deepened in the 1980s and 1990s, with the implementation and expansion of the Schengen Agreement, which enabled the free movement of people within participating European Union countries while assigning responsibility for the management of EU borders to EU border states.[32] Gaining entry to the area covered by the Schengen Agreement is managed through a hierarchical visa process that is reflected in entry policies for the U.S., Canada, and Australia as well. These countries offer documented entry to a selection of prescreened immigrants through a variety of pathways, including one or more of the following: "winning" a visa through a lottery system (fifty thousand of which are available annually for the U.S. to highly screened immigrants from throughout the world who have applied through U.S. embassies in their home countries); receiving approval to enter through family reunification programs; receiving entry as vetted and approved refugees; and/or receiving entry on temporary tourist, student, guest worker, or professional worker visas.[33] But the logics that determine visa categories and thus the ability to gain entry reflect a racialized global hierarchy. It is not by chance that the EU visa system defines as "negative" countries— those countries whose citizens require visas to enter the EU—all the countries in Africa, most of those in the Caribbean, all the poorer Latin American and Asian countries, and most of the Muslim countries.[34] The terminology of negative countries replaced the previous vocabulary that identified such countries as the "black list," in contrast to the "white list" of countries that did not require a visa to enter the Schengen zone. The criteria for placement on the black list and the white list is opaque, as is the route through which a country on the black list might be moved to the white list.[35] Taken together, the countries on the negative list cover over 80 percent of the world's non-European population, with the effect of denoting "suspicion, mistrust and fear toward all nationals from the 'negative' countries (countries whose population are predominantly poor, Black, and/or Muslim)."[36] Similarly, the U.S. visa waiver program applies only to European countries as well as Australia, New Zealand, Japan, Taiwan, South Korea, Brunei, and Chile.

For people who arrive without a visa at the border of the EU, the Dublin Agreement of 2003 expanded the responsibility of EU border states by mandating that asylum applications must be submitted at a migrant's first port of entry, where the applicant must remain while the claim is being processed, thereby denying migrants the ability to take advantage of the Schengen Agreement's free movement policy and ensuring the burden of asylum management falls to border countries.[37]

African migrants became the initial focus of EU border-making practices along Europe's southern border, closely followed by concerns about Muslims from North Africa and the Middle East, which rose to a fevered pitch with the so-called migration crisis of 2015. The EU's concern with targeting Africans and Arabs for exclusion may be "understood to be nothing less than yet another re-drawing of the global colour line," writes Nicholas de Genova, citing Étienne Balibar's charge that Europe's border fortification efforts constitute a "European apartheid."[38] Chapter 3 will discuss Europe's border-management practices in greater detail; the central point here is to note the racialist orientation of these practices.

Following the formation of the EU and the inauguration of the Schengen Agreement, Europe's border states along the Mediterranean began investing in surveillance and monitoring equipment and negotiating individual agreements with North and West African countries to catch unauthorized migrants. Spain heavily fortified its North African enclaves of Melilla and Ceuta, forged agreements with Morocco to interrupt migrant routes, and initiated joint operations with Senegal to close down sea passages from West Africa to Spain, while introducing, for the first time, visa requirements for people from Arab and African countries.[39] Italy introduced patrols to interrupt migrants making their way across the Mediterranean from Tunisia and Libya. The EU created Frontex in 2004 to coordinate EU border policing efforts, and EUROSUR, the European Border Surveillance System, a few years later to track and apprehend unauthorized migrants using drones and radar before they even reach the EU border. The EU allocated 60 percent of its Home Affairs budget to managing migration during 2007–13, in addition to the large amounts spent by border states on patrolling, monitoring, and detaining immigrants, and the budget allocated to Frontex expanded from €19.1 million in its first year of operation (2006) to €84.9 million by 2012.[40] Because these huge expenditures originated from the very small number of Africans attempting to cross the seas to reach Europe in the 1990s and early 2000s, when African migrants in Spain constituted less than 1 percent of clandestine migrants entering the country, anthropologist Ruben Andersson asks, "Why have such massive efforts been expended to target black Africans in the borderlands, and what racial and colonial legacies underpin these efforts?"[41] Andersson notes that the idea of the clandestine African migrant only emerged after the 1970s, when the oil crisis, the impact of structural adjustment policies on contracting African economies, and a reduction in fishing resources due in part to overfishing by European and Asian corporations pushed African farmers and fishers to begin looking north for work, "in the European countries that had largely been responsible for their economic predicament and whose borders now came with a 'no entry' sign attached."[42] The massive investments in patrolling and controlling African mobility into Europe has created an "illegality industry," he argues, that reacts to and deepens Europe's fears of being overrun by brown and Black people.

Europe's border countries stand as the border guards of the EU not only because of policy agreements that position them with this responsibility, but also because of deeper histories of racial ambiguities internal to Europe. The EU border countries of Spain, Italy, and Greece have long felt themselves marginal to the European project, and they comply with EU mandates and directives to demonstrate their eagerness to belong.[43] Spain's history in connection with the expulsion of Muslims (sometimes referred to as a "purifying" process in Spain) profoundly shaped Spanish self-identity as marginal to the "real" Europe, endangered by its proximity to African and Arab connections. After Spain joined the European Economic Community, rejecting Africanness became a cultural, political, and intellectual preoccupation—an orientation made even clearer by media characterizations of African residents being held in detention centers in the Spanish enclaves of Ceuta and Melilla in North Africa as wild barbarians.[44]

The Balkans also complicate the racial boundaries of Europe—the Balkans are a source of labor for Europe and home to people who are both European and Muslim, and who thus occupy a position of "off-white" or not-quite-white identity in relation to white Europe, suggests Nicholas de Genova.[45] De Genova argues that the turn to the language of "crisis" after 2015 in reference to growing numbers of Muslims trying to reach Europe is about racial order—clarifying that Europeanness is really about simplifying Europe's racial complexities and consolidating a clear understanding of whiteness as central to European identity.[46]

Anthropologist Verena Stolcke argues that immigration policies in postcolonial Europe reflect a fear of losing a fabricated sense of nationalist cultural integrity, a concern rooted in a belief that immigrants embodied such profound difference as to be culturally incommensurable: "Contemporary cultural fundamentalism unequivocally roots nationality and citizenship in a shared cultural heritage," she writes, arguing that "in the modern world of nation-states, nationality, citizenship, cultural community, and the state are conflated ideologically."[47] Although Stolcke privileges cultural over racial identity, in each case nationalist identities emerged through a "White nation fantasy," the entitlement felt by white citizens of settler societies—racists and multiculturalists alike—that they held the right to define the nation.[48]

The most recent indication of this sense of entitlement is the resurgent popularity of white nationalist political rhetoric in many European and white settler colonial countries, such as Pauline Hanson's One Nation movement in Australia, Geert Wilders's Party for Freedom in the Netherlands, Marine Le Pen's National Front in France, Austria's Freedom Party, the Sweden Democrats, and, as noted above, Donald Trump's white nationalist base in the U.S. Elections of candidates from far-right parties in Germany (Alternative for Germany), Poland (Law and Justice Party), and Italy (Lega Nord) have dramatically increased in recent elections, and extreme-right parties in Austria, Finland, Italy, and Poland have ministers in the government.[49] The alt-right (or white nationalist) obsession with the post-1965 liberalization of immigration law in the U.S. mirrors the right-wing *Herrenvolk* politics of contemporary Europe "that reserved social democracy solely for the white majority."[50] The contemporary nativist discourse in these countries about who belongs and whose entry should be barred is rooted in the specific history of white supremacy and follows the apartheid logic of using race to construct hierarchies of belonging and exclusion.[51]

In addition to race and geography, class preferences play an important role: entry policies across much of the global north afford the wealthy separate and privileged access through easier visa processing, special immigration treatment for certain highly educated professionals with desirable skills, facilitated processing for tourists, and far less scrutiny and suspicion at border checkpoints than the controls to which everyone else is subject. Border control policies work to enable the mobility of those vetted as members of the global cosmopolitan elite whose mobility is desirable for capitalism. And yet even some members of the global elite get targeted by racist surveillance: the anthropologist Shahram Khosravi and other notable academics have written about how their travel is interrupted by extreme delays caused by border scrutiny of their documents and bodies when they have attempted to travel to EU states or the U.S. for professional conferences.[52] And the U.S. travel ban against people from Libya, Venezuela, Somalia, North Korea, Iran, Syria, and Yemen makes no exceptions for class or professional status.

HERITAGE CITIZENSHIP

Heritage citizenship often uses a logic of racial purity and clear ancestral connections to confer membership in the national body. Obviously, heritage conceived through whiteness is a fundamental component of the American, European, and other white settler nation-states, even as those states define themselves as multicultural and open to limited numbers of carefully selected immigrants. But many countries in the global north strictly reserve citizenship status for those who fit the culturally and racially constructed national self-image carefully crafted out of the tumult of colonialism and the two world wars. Claims about racial/ethnic/ancestral purity ground these policies, which enable strikingly stark divides between citizens and large imported labor forces, even when the latter dramatically outnumber the former. These countries vary in their approach to refugees—Israel and Hong Kong have allowed in more temporary residents than have other countries—but none offers a pathway to citizenship for refugees, asylum seekers, or migrant workers. Because citizenship status in these countries is reserved only for those who fit the national profile of race/ethnicity/ancestry, refugees and migrant workers who will never become members of society are easily racialized as outsiders and foreigners with no claims on the nation and no rights of belonging. The literature on this subject is large: what follows offers a short synopsis of the basis for membership in Israel; the East Asian countries of Hong Kong, Japan, Singapore, Taiwan, China, and South Korea; and the GCC countries. This overview necessarily omits many historic details of interest.

Immigration law in Israel since its founding in 1948 has been based on a definition of Israel as a Jewish state devoted to maintaining and protecting a Jewish character—a definition specifically intended to limit the rights and claims of Palestinians. The extension of citizenship to immigrants is based on the Law of Return, which offers virtually automatic citizenship to anyone in the world of Jewish descent, and the Citizenship Law, which offers virtually no means other than through the Right of Return for anyone to gain Israeli citizenship.[53] As a result of agreements made in 1948, one-fifth of Israeli citizens are Palestinians who, nevertheless, face a variety of forms of discrimination based on unequal distribution of resources as well as racial profiling that subject them to various forms of violence and exclusion. And, unlike Jews, relatives of Arab Israeli citizens are barred from Israeli citizenship or residence, a policy that makes clear who holds fully legitimate rights of citizenship in the eyes of the state and who does not.[54] The second-class citizenship and abuses from racial profiling enacted on Arab Israelis are even more extreme for Palestinians in the Occupied Territories, who are denied any citizenship rights within Israel.[55] In short, Palestinians within the Israeli state are identified as racialized others who hold inferior rights, and Israel's immigration and naturalization policies are specifically intended to ensure their ongoing political and social marginalization. Israel's management of citizenship and belonging is entirely predicated on promoting an Israeli identity specifically and exclusively reserved for Jews. Like Palestinians, the large number of migrant workers drawn to Israel by the demand for labor since the 1990s, as well as African asylum seekers who made their way there in the past decade, have no pathway to citizenship and are subject to periodic deportation campaigns.

Other countries in the global north that utilize a heritage-based definition of citizenship, such as Japan, China, and South Korea, do offer pathways to citizenship to foreigners, who must renounce previous citizenship and demonstrate cultural and linguistic competency in the national language, long-term residence, good moral character, and economic independence. These countries' immigration preferences are oriented toward immigrants with historic ethnic connections, such as, for Japan, Brazilians of Japanese descent, or, for China, people whose parents are Chinese nationals.[56] Manifesting these countries' reputation for nationalist insularity—a relatively new invention, as we will see below—the numbers of naturalized new citizens are quite small, drawn mostly from other Asian countries.

Japan, South Korea, Hong Kong, Taiwan, Singapore, and China all import hundreds of thousands of foreign migrant workers every year, mostly from the Philippines and Indonesia, whose presence has provoked national concerns about the maintenance of cultural and racial integrity. By one estimate, China hosts 2 million foreigners, 300,000 of whom are working illegally.[57] Even though several of these East Asian countries have histories of ethnic diversity and mobility, projects of nationalist consolidation by political elites emerged after World War II, provoked by the experiences of the war, foreign occupation such as the postwar imposition of U.S. military bases in Japan and South Korea, and the expansion of the middle classes. For example, prior to World War II, Japan's self-identity was multiethnic, due to its acquisition of Taiwan and annexation of Korea, which produced population movements and ethnic diversity. But following its defeat in World War II, the previously expansionist Japan turned inward toward the cultivation of an ethnically homogeneous, insular, self-protective self-image as a political project, only recently challenged by the enormous influx of migrant workers.[58] Although citizenship in Japan, as elsewhere in East Asia, is conferred through jus sanguinis (inherited through parents who are Japanese citizens), Filipina hostesses and maids who bear children by Japanese lovers find it extremely difficult to gain Japanese citizenship for their children. A major lawsuit in 2008 challenged this practice, but even when such children gain citizenship, anthropologist Nobue Suzuki reports that they remain culturally and linguistically outsiders who experience social rejection in Japan.[59] Only 2 percent of Japan's population is considered "foreign," a composition that Japan maintains with strict immigration controls.

South Korea's treatment of foreign migrant workers is similarly tied to the impulse toward insularity as a result of war, but here the consolidation of a nationalist Korean identity is rooted in the history of colonial occupation by invading foreigners (Japan and the U.S., and even further back, Mongols and Manchus). "The Korean race is thus tied together by common sufferings because of foreign belligerence," writes anthropologist Sealing Chen, which, combined with the effects of globalization and the arrival of large numbers of migrant workers since the 1990s, has prompted Korean politicians to promote a rhetoric of "national oneness" and a concern with racial purity.[60] South Korea is one of the most ethnically homogeneous countries in the world, with only 1 percent of its permanent population categorized as belonging to an ethnic minority (either Chinese, Japanese, or children born to a South Korean parent and a parent from the U.S. or another Asian country).[61] Many Filipina women work as hostesses in the clubs that service the constant force of 28,000 U.S. service members stationed in South Korea since World War II. Because of their associations with U.S. military bases, these women are in the crosshairs of debates about Korean nationalism, writes Chen, because the clubs symbolize U.S. occupation, intervention, aggression, and a challenge to Korean sovereignty. The women's sexual engagements with the occupiers place them firmly outside the nation proper. Journalist Se-Woong Koo suggests the racist exclusion of and periodic xenophobic uprisings against immigrants is unsurprising considering South

Korea's history of public education in which children were taught that South Korea is a "single-blooded nation—dubbed *danil minjok* in Korean," a "myth of racial purity . . . promoted to foster national unity."[62]

In Hong Kong and Singapore, employing a foreign maid has become a mark of upwardly mobile middle-class status for their ethnically Chinese employers. Anthropologist Aihwa Ong locates their treatment as racialized others in their employers' desire to maintain an ethno-racial social distance in order to protect their self-image as affluent Asians, explaining that "in postcolonial nations built upon founding or dominant races, questions of who is considered human or subhuman are still inscribed by ethnic biases or hostilities."[63] The racialization of Filipina maids in Hong Kong is rooted in its particular postcolonial logic: Hong Kong became a British colony in 1941, inhabited by Europeans, Chinese fishermen, and immigrants from mainland China who came to work. After China relinquished Hong Kong to the British after the Second Opium War, the population expanded and the demand for live-in full-time domestic labor rose as local women moved into the labor market in professional and service economy jobs. Chinese women, who had provided domestic labor for middle-class and wealthy households, were increasingly reluctant to do this work, and by the late 1990s the workforce of live-in domestic workers had become predominantly Filipina. In fact, according to Nicole Constable, "Filipina" had come to mean "domestic worker," used interchangeably with "maid." The Filipina maid doll, "with black hair, wearing a domestic worker's uniform, holding a miniature Philippine passport and a 'lifetime' employment contract," had become a popular children's toy. Constable argues that the convergence of "Filipina" and "maid" signaled the emergence of a racialized category of people viewed as naturally suited to domestic labor in Hong Kong and naturally unsuited to political and cultural membership in the Hong Kong polity.[64]

The policies governing the labor contracts of migrant workers in these East Asian countries will be addressed in chapter 4, but none offers domestic workers any pathway to citizenship, any claim to belonging in their host country, or automatic rights of citizenship for children they may bear to citizen lovers. Their racialization as foreigners consigned to do the domestic work of the nation but without any claims to membership in the nation reflects a logic of belonging that makes it perfectly clear whose status grants them the right to have rights.

China's management of the relationship between migration and heritage citizenship as the basis of membership in the nation is particularly fascinating simply because of the numbers involved. As noted above, China hosts an estimated 2 million foreigners while also having one of the largest diasporas in the world, estimated at 50–60 million, 32 million of whom reside regionally in East and Southeast Asia. The role of emigrants and their transnational lives has long played a role in Chinese nationalism, dating from the efforts of the Qing dynasty beginning in the 1880s to more tightly tie emigrants with their homeland through unbanning emigration, establishing consulates in Southeast Asia and the United States, building commercial connections and investments, and contributing toward efforts by Chinese emigrants to build a "Confucian nationalism" among diasporic Chinese. Simultaneously, revolutionaries and reformers promoting a "virulent Han racism . . . embedded within the idea of a global hierarchy of races" adopted the ideas of social Darwinism in their desire to build a homogeneous national identity free of foreign domination. The revolutionaries turned this vision of racialized nationalist Chinese Han identity against Western imperialists and the Manchu Qing rulers who had colluded with them, sentiments that continued to grow following the 1911 revolution.[65] The Chinese Communist Party took control in 1949 and expelled almost all of the 200,000 foreigners then living in China.[66] Cultivating insularity, the new foreign affairs system put in place to manage the very few foreigners who remained maintained "meticulous differences between foreigners and Chinese . . . in all spheres of life and politics."[67] Foreign visitors to China began to increase after Mao's death in 1976, growing so rapidly over the subsequent decades that Frank Pieke calls contemporary China "an immigration country."[68] They include students, professionals, businesspeople, traders, migrants fleeing North Korea, women from neighboring countries migrating as brides, and a "foreign floating population" of unskilled people searching for work opportunities.[69]

Concerned in particular about the latter category, the Chinese government began constraining its entry policies in 2013, giving priority to skilled professionals, ethnic Chinese, and children of Chinese nationals, while severely limiting the legal entry of unskilled people and those lacking a heritage connection to China. Citizenship is conferred through jus sanguinis, and the road to permanent residency for migrants who lack a Chinese national parent is extremely narrow. As laws for entry and for gaining permanent residency have become narrower, crackdowns on unauthorized migrants and Muslim Chinese citizens have grown, manifest most severely in the "reeducation centers" that currently incarcerate about a million people in Xinjiang Autonomous Region. Racist nationalism is on the rise since the reforms, promoted through social media, despite the commercial promotion of ethnic minority cultures for tourism and the growing cosmopolitanism of returning young Chinese emigrants.[70] As the world's most populous country, with one of the largest diasporic populations, China's new efforts to cohere citizenship, belonging, and racial identity through extremely restrictive entry policies, nationalist appeals to emigrants, and brutal crackdowns on internal minorities, including mass surveillance and mass incarceration, will undoubtedly carry enormous global influence. We will return to this question in chapter 5.

Turning to the Gulf states, most of the GCC countries—Bahrain, Kuwait, Oman, Qatar, Saudi Arabia, and the United Arab Emirates—are relatively recent creations shaped out of complex histories of global trade relations; British imperial support for particular royal families and territorial delineations; and local emirates, sultanates, kingdoms, and tribal groups. Contemporary citizenship is determined primarily by ancestral residence and ethnicity, managed by royal ruling families who employ a calculation of social units (tribe, ethnicity, sect, and so forth) to distribute access to various rights and rewards to those considered citizens.

GCC states are diverse, despite the popular perception of homogeneity, including people who trace their ancestry to pastoralist nomads as well as those who trace their ancestry to merchants and seafarers. There are Shi'a and Sunni, recent and historic Persian immigrants who may or may not identify as Arab, and people who trace their ancestry to African slaves. "Amidst this diversity," writes anthropologist Andrew Gardner, "one of the central features of society and state in Arabia is the ongoing construction and maintenance of nationalisms and, simultaneously, the legitimacy of the ruling families and tribes."[71] GCC governments invest in spectacular cities and in the heritage industry in an attempt to consolidate and promote particularist national identities. A "combination of factors—new nationalisms, small indigenous populations, hydrocarbon wealth, a tribally conceptualized authoritarian leadership, and rapid infrastructural and social development over the past four decades—characterize the shared experience of the GCC states," Gardner explains.[72]

Although several Gulf states automatically confer citizenship on the child of any male citizen living anywhere in the world, it is virtually impossible for foreign migrant workers, who represent up to 90 percent of the population in some Gulf states, where they may have lived for decades or even generations, to obtain citizenship.[73] Citizens, who receive substantial economic benefits and access to secure public jobs, are empowered to police the presence of migrant workers through the *kefala* system, through which migrant workers, mostly from the global south (India, the Philippines, and

Nepal), are allowed entry on visas controlled by citizens. In addition to putting migrants to work for a country whose welfare benefits they cannot access, the kefala system also enables rulers to push back against pan-Arab or pan-Muslim movements that might lessen their authority if laborers were drawn primarily from other Arab countries.[74] The kefala system enables a strict hierarchy between those whose ancestry grants them rights of belonging through citizenship/genealogy and those who lack such rights despite their economic contribution to the nation. It is a form of supremacy (with roots in the relationships between ruling families and British colonialism) that follows the same logic of identity and racialized belonging used to shape Canada, Australia, the U.S., and European countries as white states, Israel as a Jewish state, and East Asian states as countries of racial purity.

CONCLUSION

Rights to legal membership in the modern nation-state have taken shape through the delineation of territorial borders, the extension of rights of membership based on logics of belonging defined by settler colonialism (U.S., Canada, Australia, New Zealand, Israel), ethnicity/tribalism, heritage and the particular population dynamics in play under and following colonialism and/or foreign occupation (Europe, GCC states, East Asia), the management of documentation to identify who belongs and holds citizenship rights (passports and visas), and the identification and management of internal others who are temporary or permanent residents but who are denied full citizenship rights while also being racialized as foreigners. The chorus of scholars cited here has carefully charted how these processes took shape over centuries of what Cedric Robinson called "racial capitalism": the systemic processes of exploitation and profit that characterized settler colonialism, i.e., plantation slavery, the displacement of indigenous people, and the creation of racialized mobile populations of immigrant indentured labor and workers.[75] Concurrently, official policy and populist rhetoric in countries across the global north cohered an understanding of belonging that enabled the delineation, containment, and exclusion of those defined as foreign others—those who do not really belong to the nation. Policing the mobility of those who do not really belong has become a primary preoccupation of states in the global north, which, as we shall see, utilize a growing and astounding array of surveillance technologies to turn racialized bodies into borders to be monitored and interrupted.

CHAPTER TWO

PLUNDER

Economic dominance is very much racialized.—JEMIMA
PIERRE, *THE PREDICAMENT OF BLACKNESS: POSTCOLONIAL
GHANA AND THE POLITICS OF RACE*

Think what could have happened if Britain and other countries were not able to send excess population to the colonies? Read Cecil Rhodes' speech. If Europe exported itself
out of depression, on our backs, why can't we do the same?
—ALI JIMALE AHMED, "AFRICAN SOLUTIONS FOR AFRICAN
PROBLEMS: LIMNING THE CONTOURS OF A NEW FORM OF
CONNECTIVITY"

The second element of apartheid is the rendering of
ordinary life as unsustainable in areas designated
for the racialized underclass while also ensuring
that apartheid's authorities maintain a hand in monitoring
and managing such areas. The global south is not a creation of the global north in the same way in which South
Africa created arid and resource-starved homelands and
impoverished townships, but the global north has engaged in a variety of practices that have made life in the

global south insecure and, in some places, unsustainable, whether through political/military interventions, austerity regimes, or resource extraction.[1] We might thus question the extent to which the spread of insecurity in the global south is an intentional creation of the global north, and we might argue that the global north is not making life unsustainable solely in order to ensure a steady supply of exploitable labor. Rather, some of the powerful drivers of insecurity are less direct, such as austerity policies and the inability and unwillingness of those professionals in the global north who created austerity as a theoretical model for economic reform to recognize how it has stimulated displacement, resource grabs, and inequality. Similarly, militarized interventions by the global north into the global south are usually not about producing exploitable workers, but rather about ensuring capitalist penetration and extraction, political alliances, and performing spectacular feats of statecraft. And the global north bears the brunt of the blame for the extravagant consumption of fossil fuels that is contributing to displacements caused by global warming (due to droughts, desertification, and rising and warming ocean waters). But we can also argue that such interventions reflect a set of assumptions about which part of the world has the right to determine the conditions of life in another part of the world, and that these assumptions carry racist biases inherited from imperialist and colonial histories.

Scholars have recorded the devastating impact since the end of colonialism on local lives in the global south of a wide variety of interventions by governments and corporations based in the global north, sometimes working in collaboration with elites in the global south—actions that followed and sometimes continued the decades of plunder by colonial extraction. The list, which takes us from the Cold War to the rise of neoliberal globalization to the global war on terror, is, unfortunately, long. It includes military interventions, political alliances with oligarchs and dictators, austerity regimes, corporate plunder, unfair trade agreements, and land, resource, and capital expropriation. Such actions were often aided by or carried out in collaboration with local governments forced to respond to the mandates of structural adjustment policies requiring privatization and foreign investment and with local elites who stood to gain from militarization and economic neoliberalism. I again remind the reader that while I am building my argument using the terminology of global south and global north, I am not overlooking the existence of shared class interests across these geographical divides, nor do I mean to minimize the interests of local elites in the global south who benefit from privatization imposed by austerity policies, military and security mandates promoted through the global war on terror, and access to global capitalist markets.

We will take a look at the most overt and destabilizing forms of plunder, restraining ourselves to just a few examples in each category. Anthropological literature in each of these categories is voluminous, detailing with devastating clarity the ravages of plunder on people and places in the global south.

MILITARY INTERVENTIONS

The postcolonial era has been marked by Cold War–era proxy wars, alliances between powerful governments in the global north and dictatorships in the global south, support by powerful governments in the global north for insurgencies in the global south, and the global war on terror. Central America offers a revealing place to start because of the history of U.S. support for dictatorships in El Salvador and Guatemala, despite their appalling human rights records and mass atrocities, to safeguard American corporate interests and to guard against the threat of communism. El Salvador received $6 billion in support and the assistance of military advisers from the U.S. during the twelve years of its civil war (1980–92), in addition to loans from multilateral institutions, while the war pushed over a quarter of the population of El Salvador into exile. Guatemala suffered four decades of military dictatorship and genocidal practices against rural communities after the CIA helped to overthrow the democratically elected progressive government in 1954 and installed a military dictatorship. Violence in Guatemala during the ensuing civil war (1960–96) killed an estimated 200,000 people and displaced over a million more.[2]

As in Guatemala and El Salvador, covert CIA involvement and substantial U.S. aid and/or military support characterized relationships with many anticommunist dictators in the global south whose policies produced massive population displacement and out-migration. After deposing the democratically elected socialist president of Chile, Salvador Allende, the United States supported Augusto Pinochet's anticommunist reign of terror in Chile, which sent 200,000 people into exile. Another U.S. beneficiary, the dictator Suharto in Indonesia, purged up to a million people under suspicion of communist affiliations in the mid-1960s. After his government collapsed, Indonesia turned to an official policy of labor emigration to buoy its economy. Mobutu Sese Seko in Zaire/Democratic Republic of the Congo, installed after the CIA assisted in the assassination of the popular anticolonial politician Patrice Lumumba, amassed an estimated personal fortune of $5 billion while his country's debt grew to $13 billion, its infrastructure crumbled, and its economy collapsed, leaving it one of the poorest countries in the world. With the end of the Cold War, Mobutu—often held up as the iconic example of corruption, nepotism, and despotism—lost Western support and abandoned the country in 1997, leaving a disastrously violent patchwork of contestations over resources and power that have plagued the DRC ever since. During his years of U.S. support, Ferdinand Marcos in the Philippines enacted martial law, approved the use of torture and other human rights abuses, and amassed a personal fortune of $5–10 billion while creating government agencies to engineer massive labor out-migration from which his government would benefit. Somalia's dictatorship received $1 billion in support from the U.S. and other allies during the 1980s before falling apart following the post–Cold War withdrawal of U.S. support, precipitating one of the largest refugee flows in the world at the time. As is the case with Guatemalans and El Salvadorans, it is no surprise that millions of Indonesians and Filipinos now live abroad as migrant workers, and that millions of Congolese and Somalis continue to seek refuge outside their countries of origin.[3]

In some countries with either communist-leaning governments or direct Soviet intervention, proxy wars took the form of U.S. and allied aid and support for insurgencies—such as the Contras in Nicaragua, Renamo in Mozambique, UNITA in Angola, and the mujahideen in Afghanistan—or direct military intervention, as in Vietnam, Laos, and Cambodia. Laos, the most bombed country on earth, was pummeled by 2 million tons of bombs from the U.S.[4] Each of these wars left devastation and vast population displacement in its wake.[5]

Of course, militarized interventions by the global north into the global south did not end with fall of the Berlin Wall. The U.S. recently increased its investment in training and funding the Honduran military and police forces by offering at least $114 million in the wake of the 2009 coup against the popularly elected leftist president, support that has continued even after the faulty 2017 elections that consolidated oligarchic control.[6] According to the nonprofit research organization NACLA (the North American Congress on Latin America), "The remilitarization of Honduras has accompanied a free-for-all for Honduras's wealthiest families and for international investors, under the slogan 'Honduras is Open for Business.' State security forces have been deployed in areas with 'social conflicts' linked to mining, agro-industrial, hydroelectric, and tourism enterprises that displace or negatively impact communities, and which are often illegally carried out without prior consultation of local indigenous groups, as required under Honduran law."[7]

In fact, U.S. economic oligarchs had an important hand in reshaping the post-coup Honduran economy to their interests. In 2013 Honduras adopted a proposal to create Zones for Economic Development and Employment (ZEDES), promoted by a U.S.-based think tank called the Seasteading Institute that was founded by Milton Friedman's grandson. (The Seasteading Institute also promotes the creation of autonomous libertarian cities on platforms in the ocean.) Export Processing Zones have long existed in Honduras, but ZEDES introduce a novel twist: they are under the control of a team of Honduran and foreign investors and developers who establish their own laws, currency, police force, and judiciary. Four-fifths of the members of the committee that oversees ZEDES for the country are foreign, most of whom have long been aligned with market fundamentalist economic views. By embracing the model of ZEDES, the Honduran government "established the legal and institutional framework for conceding control of fragments of its sovereign national territory for the creation of pockets of corporate autonomy."[8] ZEDES concessions can expropriate land and displace residents, and the only entity with the authority to intervene is the Honduran military. China is now pursuing a similar model in Central America, having recently negotiated a plan to create a special economic zone in El Salvador through obtaining a hundred-year lease of coastal land, totaling 13 percent of El Salvador's land base, as part of its strategy to create an alternative trade route to the Panama Canal. The deal is currently on hold pending the outcome of protests by the families who would be evicted.[9]

Meanwhile, U.S. aid and military support for the Colombian government's war against rebels and drug traffickers over the past two decades produced the largest internally displaced population in the world during that time.[10] Joint U.S.-Colombian military interventions shifted Colombian drug trafficking routes toward Central America, where, as noted above, the U.S. has long been entangled with local oligarchs to protect U.S. business interests. As Honduras became a transit state for cocaine trafficking, narco-gangs operating with impunity added another level of violence as they commandeered rural areas as transit zones and demanded local complicity. The headline-catching migrant caravans of displaced people moving north from Honduras in 2018 are one outcome of an economic and political system firmly caught in the grip of narco-gangs, a narco-linked oligarchy, climate change displacement, and heightened militarization backed by the United States.

And, of course, there is the global war on terror. As of the end of 2017, the post-9/11 U.S.-led wars in Afghanistan, Pakistan, Iraq, and Syria had displaced almost 21 million people.[11] The 2003 U.S. invasion of Iraq, with support from Britain and Australia, precipitated disaster: an estimated half million dead (as of 2013), 3.25 million displaced, and destabilization that enabled the creation of ISIS. ISIS fighters joined the fight for control of Syria, where what began as a pro-democracy rebellion by Syrian citizens morphed into a complex battleground of bombing campaigns by the Syrian government, the U.S., Russia, Saudi Arabia, and, most recently, Turkey, which has displaced at least 12 million people. Of the almost 5 million people displaced from Afghanistan, about 1.3 million are currently staying in Pakistan and nearly a million more are in Iran, in addition to another 900,000 displaced from Syria and Iraq.[12] Hundreds of thousands of others have attempted to make their way north to find refuge.

The global war on terror has spread to Africa as well. The 2006 Ethiopian invasion of Somalia, aided and abetted by the U.S., displaced a million people and instigated the emergence of Al-Shabaab in reaction against the foreign military presence in Somalia. Since the 2008 creation of the U.S. Africa Command, or AFRICOM, as another arm in the war on terror, violence in Africa has expanded rather than receded. As U.S. intervention in Africa has grown to include 7,000 military personnel, 3,500 military missions, thirty-six named military operations, and hundreds of drone strikes, "key indicators of security and stability have plummeted according to the Defense Department's Africa Center for Strategic Studies, a Pentagon research institution." Since the creation of AFRICOM, the number of violent Islamist groups has risen from five to twenty-four and the number of violent events rose from 288 to 3,050. Analysts argue there is a direct correlation between the militarization of the continent by expanding U.S. military intervention and the violence that is displacing millions.[13]

While engendering destruction and displacement on an enormous scale in Iraq, Afghanistan, Pakistan, Somalia, and elsewhere, the global war on terror has nevertheless brought benefits to some state leaders who have used the post-9/11 anti-terrorism bellicosity promoted by the U.S. to enhance their authority and enact further measures to subjugate dissidents or minorities in their home countries. In his disturbing account of the trumped-up trials of people accused of terrorism in India and the U.S., Amitava Kumar recounts how anti-terror rhetoric has been a useful tool by Hindus against Muslims in India, by Charles Taylor in Liberia, by Robert Mugabe in Zimbabwe, and by the dictatorial Eritrean government.[14] Similar accounts from Uganda, Kenya, Niger, China, and Russia abound. Political persecution in the name of fighting terror pushes people into exile.

The point here is simply that postcolonial wars and insurgencies in the global south have never been just local wars: they are influenced, instigated, or financed by world superpowers in the global north (for whom local wars enact their geopolitical struggles over power and resources) and/or are enmeshed in criminal or business networks in the global north (for whom wars mean profit).[15] That some of those displaced by such wars would seek refuge in the global north seems both obvious and an ethical responsibility.

AUSTERITY REGIMES

During the neoliberalizing 1980s and 1990s, the World Bank and the International Monetary Fund (IMF) subjected many indebted governments in the global south to structural adjustment programs (SAPs), which were supposed to enable debt repayment through austerity policies and regulatory reforms that reduced government spending, required privatization of government holdings and industries (everything from railroads to gold mines), devalued local currencies, and reduced barriers to trade and direct foreign investment. The plan was to bring government spending under control while enabling foreign capitalist investment to globalize local economies and generate cash to be used for debt repayment. The IMF and World Bank offered loans to indebted countries on the condition that they accept SAP requirements of austerity, privatization, deregulation, and trade liberalization. Within a decade, SAPs had been imposed on seventy-five poor countries, including thirty in Africa and eighteen in Latin America. Somalia was the first country to accept an IMF-mandated structural adjustment program.

Some of the debt in the global south had been incurred by dictatorships that received loans in return for political alliances with the U.S. and European countries. For some, the rising cost of oil in the 1970s caused oil-importing countries in the global south to borrow to meet their energy costs from commercial banks flush with petrodollars. But the economic downturn of the 1970s precipitated a debt crisis because of increased interest rates and reduced revenues from the sale of raw materials, which were still the basis for many postcolonial economies in the global south. To address the crisis, SAPs effected a switch from a philosophy of economic development based on government-managed economies (through subsidies, protectionism, employment, and so forth) to a free-market philosophy sometimes called market fundamentalism or the Washington consensus.

Contrary to their stated purpose, SAPs negatively impacted or devastated every country where they were enacted: they destroyed the ability of governments to provide social services like public education, health care, subsidies, pensions, and infrastructure; they produced widespread unemployment through the shedding of government jobs and the transfer of resources into the hands of foreign corporations that often mechanized production and employed foreign professionals; the privatization of industries led to unemployment and infrastructural abandonment as investors laid off workforces and cannibalized factories and railroads for parts; they enabled the creation of enclave economies, in the form of either resource extraction (such as offshore oil drilling) or Export Processing Zones that contributed little to national economies because of tax benefits, deregulated labor and environmental practices, and paltry investment in local communities; they redefined national resources, such as forests, into marketable commodities, leading to deforestation and environmental destruction; currency deregulation caused price spikes in food and utilities, sparking riots in many countries; they produced a crisis of legitimacy for many governments because of high unemployment, high prices, and the collapse of social services; and they fomented indigenous and populist revolutions by those who felt unprotected or abandoned by governments that instituted neoliberal reforms.[16]

While accounts of the effect of SAPS are bleak everywhere they were implemented, reports from Africa are particularly dire.[17] Between 1970 and 2003, African countries repaid more than they had borrowed, and money flowing out of Africa for debt servicing and repayment was more than the aid flowing in. During this period, African countries received $540 billion in loans, repaid $580 billion in debt service, and still owed $330 billion in external debt. Many African countries paid more on debt service than on health care, and several, such as Zambia and Angola, spent more on interest payments than on health care and education combined.[18] The consequences of SAPS—rising unemployment, economic privation, hopelessness, and a crisis in political legitimacy—contributed to political violence in several African countries, most notably Liberia, Sierra Leone, and Rwanda, prompting large-scale population displacement.[19]

While SAPS did little to grow domestic economies, enhance economic opportunity, or improve the quality of life for the majority of citizens in affected countries, they were successful at opening economies in the global south for corporate profit in the global north, discussed in the next section, while displacing people through eradicating or severely restricting their livelihoods. Millions of those displaced from their jobs or their land by austerity programs left home to look for work, becoming excess workers within the new neoliberal world economic order. In an article arguing that U.S. foreign policy, and SAPs in particular, perpetrate white supremacy and global apartheid, anthropologist Faye Harrison minces no words: "In many respects, U.S. policy promotes the recolonization of markets and labor and, hence, helps to create a vast pool of men and women desperate for jobs and forced to work at below-subsistence wages. Women, disproportionately women of color concentrated in the Southern Hemisphere, have been designated as a 'new colonial frontier' for flexible capital accumulation."[20]

CORPORATE CAPITALIST PLUNDER

Capitalist plunder includes what Michael Watts has called "military neo-liberalism" throughout the global south by agents of the global north seeking to extract profitable natural and other resources, either directly or through agreements with militias or local political elites that bypass and exploit local residents.[21] In addition to the firm grip on Central American resources by U.S. corporations, Africa has perhaps been the most affected by capitalist plunder because almost all of Africa's tiny direct foreign investment is in extractive industries—oil, gold, diamonds, minerals, platinum, and timber—where investors usually pay little or no taxes, engage in corrupt business practices, contribute no long-term infrastructural investments, negotiate and profit from minimal regulatory oversight of labor and environmental practices, and sometimes utilize militarized force to ensure their access to resources. Scholars and journalists have reported on the devastating local effects of oil extraction in Nigeria, Angola, and Sudan, and of mining for tantalum, gold, and diamonds in the Democratic Republic of the Congo and West Africa, in addition to the impact in West Africa of overfishing by companies from the global north.[22] Such forms of capitalist plunder exist throughout the global south, producing what journalists Chris Hedges and Joe Sacco have called "sacrifice zones"—areas "that have been offered up for exploitation in the name of profit, progress, and technological advancement."[23]

Looking beyond Africa, another example is Indonesia, where corporate and political elites colluded on a militarized takeover of vast hardwood forests to enable corporate plunder that dispossessed locals.[24] Some areas in Colombia from which rural peasants were forced to flee because of violent conflict are now the sites of foreign-funded extractive industries, mono-crop agribusiness, and free trade zones. Those dispossessed by war in a country with the largest internally displaced population in the world now find themselves dispossessed by extractive businesses that are bringing record foreign investment to Colombia, creating zones that the government celebrates as bringing peace and social order.[25] Also in South America, widespread deforestation in the Amazon due to a massive expansion of soybean farming by agribusinesses connected to U.S.-based agribusiness firms is once again in the news.[26] The pervasive conversion of small farms and forests into large-scale, mono-cropped, commercial plantations has led some to suggest that the era of the Anthropocene is also the era of the Plantationocene, characterized by land dispossession, environmental degradation, and extreme inequality between those who own the plantations and those who work on them.

Elsewhere, violent conquest has forced open local economies for foreign capitalist profit, as in occupied Iraq where the U.S. installed an interim government that was charged with ratifying a series of orders reflecting SAP priorities to open Iraq to foreign business interests. According to Wendy Brown, "These [orders] mandated selling off several hundred state-run enterprises, permitting full ownership rights of Iraqi businesses by foreign firms and full repatriation of profits to foreign firms, opening Iraq's banks to foreign ownership and control, and eliminating tariffs. . . . [They] restricted labor and throttled back public goods and services. They outlawed strikes and eliminated the right to unionize in most sectors, mandated a regressive flat tax on income, lowered the corporate rate to a flat 15 percent, and eliminated taxes on profits repatriated to foreign-owned businesses."[27]

Some forms of capitalist plunder are based in the transformation of land tenure and agricultural practices to reorient economic production in terms profitable to foreign corporate interests. Banana plantations in Central America owned by agribusiness giants like Chiquita, Dole, and Del Monte are the classic example. In occupied Iraq, new laws prohibited Iraqi farmers from using heirloom seeds saved from previous seasons, forcing them instead to purchase seeds and inputs produced by giant agribusiness firms like Monsanto and Dow Chemical, permanently transforming Iraqi agriculture—previously based on self-sufficient practices utilized over millennia—into a source of profit for U.S.-based agribusinesses that can now control agricultural inputs and practices.

Finally, also worth noting is the recent transformation of extractive practices under Latin America's new progressive governments, many of which came to power because of anti-IMF, anti-SAP populism. Even where progressive governments have taken over managing resources and extractions previously controlled by private corporations, they are still required to conform and act within a world order that subordinates the interests of Latin

American countries in commercial agreements and trade treaties. "Neo-extraction" continues to disempower local populations and render local landscapes unsustainable for healthy life, even when progressive governments return some of the profit to local communities in the form of social services.[28]

These are but a few examples of the impact of capitalist plunder in displacing populations through militarized takeovers, the creation of free trade economic zones and zones of extractive industry, the spread of plantations into areas that had supported small farmers and forest dwellers, and the overharvesting of natural resources by entities created through alliances of foreign capital with national business and political elites. The state's role in such enterprises is usually to clear spaces of people whose presence might interrupt capital accumulation. Far from being an exception in moments of localized "crisis," displacement in the interests of capital is a defining characteristic of our era.[29]

UNFAIR TRADE AGREEMENTS

Trade agreements set the terms of things like taxes, tariffs, subsidies, and possibilities for investment, and can be negotiated bilaterally, regionally, and globally. They are complex instruments for managing commerce that carry the potential for uneven benefits, such as the effect of the North American Free Trade Agreement (NAFTA), which devastated Mexican farmers and cost Mexico an estimated 1.5 million agricultural jobs. Lower barriers to trade allowed highly subsidized American crops, especially corn, to flood Mexican markets, putting local farmers out of business. As Mexican journalist Alejandro Páez Varela says, NAFTA "created fifty-three million very poor people for whom the only solution is to emigrate, en masse, to the United States and send remittances home."[30] Another example of a trade agreement that benefited the global north at the expense of the global south is the successful effort by the U.S., responding to demands by Chiquita, to file a complaint with the World Trade Organization in order to weaken the Lomé Convention that gave former colonies in Africa, the Pacific, and the Caribbean preferential trade status with the EU, thus enabling the major U.S.-based banana oligarchies a near monopoly in the banana trade. Because these corporate banana producers can produce cheaper bananas by paying low wages and no benefits to an insecure, temporary labor force, changes to the Lomé Convention especially threatened small- and medium-scale banana producers in the Windward Islands, Jamaica, Guadeloupe, and Martinique.[31] Trade agreements like these contribute to displacement, as primary producers find they can no longer compete in a market stacked against them and lose their land to debt holders or large plantations.

LAND EXPROPRIATION

Another form of plunder is large-scale land acquisition for the production of biofuels, timber, and food crops in the global south by actors based in the global north. In a book tracking these takeovers, Saskia Sassen argues that a new logic of expulsion has been taking shape since the 1980s, through which large firms and governments in China, Saudi Arabia, South Korea, Japan, Europe, and the U.S. are displacing vast numbers of people through land expropriation in Sudan, Mali, Madagascar, Ethiopia, Tanzania, Mozambique, and elsewhere, enabled by regulatory reforms and structural adjustment policies that open indebted economies in the global south to direct foreign investment.[32] Economies weakened by structural adjustment policies have been unable to absorb the displaced, producing impoverishment and exodus. The 2008 food price hike resulted in huge land enclosures in Myanmar, Laos, the Philippines, Indonesia, and Cambodia by corporations and governments purchasing or leasing land for food crops to provision Chinese consumers and migrant workers in the Gulf countries. "The largest of these new enclosures, 1.6 million hectares in West Papua, was acquired by Saudi Arabia to grow rice, the preferred food of the Asian migrant workers on whom the Saudi economy depends," reports anthropologist Tania Li.[33] In a series of publications, Li documents the effects on rural Indonesians of massive land grabs that have displaced smallholders in order to expand palm oil plantations. Describing the infrastructural violence, mafia logics, environmental devastation, and abandonment of the displaced in plantation zones, Li concludes, "I fear for the well-being of millions of Indonesians condemned to live in plantation zones now and in the future."[34]

Even conservation efforts by NGOs from the global north have contributed to displacement. In a searing critique, journalist Mark Dowie offers over a dozen case studies documenting how major conservation organizations based in the global north convinced local governments across the global south to enclose land in order to meet the desires of northern conservationists for pure, uninhabited nature, while simultaneously evicting local residents from that land, with no recourse and little opportunity afforded for alternative life-sustaining opportunities. Such evictions have a racialized component, as those most often evicted are indigenous and/or racialized communities with little political power, despite their histories of local land and resource stewardship. In an ironic twist, Dowie reports that some of these forcibly uninhabited "paradises" are then made available to big conservation organizations for organized adventure tourism for their wealthy patrons.[35]

Another form of expropriation is emerging with China's efforts to finance major infrastructure and mining projects through lending huge sums to poor countries. To meet its energy needs, China has been buying up mines all over the world, including in Peru, Papua New Guinea, Australia, and, most of all, in Africa.[36] In 2016 alone, China committed $60 billion to a fund for infrastructure projects in Africa, but the fund stipulates that projects built with loans from the fund must be led by a Chinese-owned company, ensuring that much of the expenditure benefits China. China claims its involvement in such projects is economic and not a bid for political control, but some wonder if a new form of colonialism might be emerging. For example, the Sri Lankan government used Chinese financing to build, among other projects, an enormous airport at a cost of $209 million, saddling itself with an annual debt of $23.6 million for the subsequent eight years. The airport, a pet project of Sri Lanka's former president, currently sits empty. Combined with other projects financed by China, Sri Lanka's debt to China is currently estimated at $3–5 billion. China offered $1.1 billion in debt relief in exchange for a 70 percent equity claim over Sri Lanka's deep-water port for ninety-nine years.[37] Control over major infrastructure is hard to separate from political engagement, especially if new policies or resistances emerge that are unfriendly to China's aspirations.[38]

Similarly, in Ecuador, China stepped in to provide loans after Ecuador defaulted on its foreign debt in 2008 and the leftist government denounced the economic and political grip that the IMF and the U.S. had long held on the country. By 2018 Ecuador had received $19 billion in Chinese loans for infrastructure projects, including a massive dam built by Chinese companies at a cost of $1.7 billion. The dam failed immediately, plagued by cracks, silting, debris, and instability caused by a nearby volcano, and its poor construction limited its ability to generate even small amounts of electricity. In return for the loans, Ecuador must service its debt at 7 percent interest and give China 80 percent of its oil production at a discount as repayment. In order to meet its obligations, the government has been forced to impose austerity policies.[39] Ecuador is far from alone: from 2005 to 2018, Chinese banks provided over $140 billion in loans to Latin American governments, becoming the region's primary lender.[40]

Of particular interest is China's Belt and Road Initiative (BRI), launched in 2013, a massive development initiative linking Europe to western China and eastern China to Africa via Southeast and South Asia through developing infrastructural projects financed by Chinese banks and built by Chinese firms. Observers commenting with great interest and divergent opinions suggest that BRI goals include connecting China's poorer regions to neighboring regions, growing national and international connectivity through developing transport and communications infrastructure, supporting China's economy by producing the materials needed to develop BRI goals around the world, enhancing regional security through economic relationships, ensuring China's access to ports, and consolidating China's military presence in contested areas (such as the South China Sea). Observers note that the plan could make China the dominant global power, even as the government is becoming more authoritarian internally, and some suggest that China may be attempting to forge a new, alternative international order to the one led by the United States. Even though China's aspirations have faced resistance from local communities regarding land turned over by their governments to Chinese companies, and despite concerns in Southeast Asia about Chinese belligerence in the South China Sea and the role of 32 million diasporic Chinese in the region, regional governments have lined up for BRI projects: President Duterte in the Philippines is relying on Chinese investment to fulfill his "Build-Build-Build Infrastructure Plan"; Indonesian President Widodo will need Chinese investment to meet his desire to make Indonesia the center point of maritime activity linking the Indian and Pacific Oceans, and BRI investments have been embraced by the authoritarian governments of Cambodia and Laos.[41]

Just as SAPS used debt repayment as an excuse for forcing open economies in the global south to direct foreign investment and ownership, so China has been using debt to gain control over key ports and resources. Displacement inevitably accompanies major infrastructure projects, as well as the appropriation of land and coastal areas and austerity regimes imposed in order to service debt.

Turning to the Middle East, the dispossession of Palestinians in the Occupied Territories by the Israeli state and Israeli settlements has left hundreds of thousands of Palestinians landless. Dispossession has taken place through a complex web of laws and policies to control Palestinian mobility, backed up by militarized invasion and an army of settlers claiming Palestinian land, including rich farmland, for new Israeli settlements. Invasions, interventions, bans, closures, checkpoints, and dispossessions fracture, fragment, disconnect, and disarticulate Palestinian space, creating an entire nation of people "placed under erasure," alienated from places that were once theirs. As the economies in the Occupied Territories wither under the occupation, Palestinians have few options other than to leave or to remain and sell their labor to Israeli employers, under oppressive conditions we will address in chapter 4.[42]

In addition to these examples of land and capital expropriation by governments or government-linked entities, illicit economies that feed appetites for drugs in the global north leave their mark. Drug traffickers in Central America lay claim to land outside the purview of local governments for transit operations to meet the massive U.S. demand for cocaine. For example, drug traffickers took over huge swaths of territory in places like Moskitia in eastern Honduras after cocaine transit routes shifted from Colombia into Honduras, where the post-coup political environment favored the flagrant takeover of rural resources by elites. Because the narco-economy is so thoroughly integrated with the licit economy, the narco-capitalist land grab facilitated the appropriation of other resources by elites as well, a pattern repeated every time transit routes shift in response to anti–drug trafficking interventions (usually planned and carried out by the U.S. with local military partners). So long as cocaine remains illegal and the demand in the U.S. remains the highest in the world, Central American transit countries will bear the brunt of the impact of both narco-capitalism and militarized interventions against drug trafficking.[43]

The logic that structures life in areas controlled by criminal gangs, narco-traffickers, and militias who are empowered by the ways in which global neoliberalism has enabled the oligarchic takeover of the state and its military apparatus, often with U.S. support, is aptly described in this passage by Achille Mbembe:

> In the regions of the world situated on the margins of major contemporary technological transformations, the material deconstruction of existing territorial frameworks goes hand in hand with the establishment of an economy of coercion whose objective is to destroy "superfluous" populations and to exploit raw materials. The profitability of this kind of exploitation requires the exit of the state, its emasculation, and its replacement by fragmented forms of sovereignty. The functioning and viability of such an economy are subordinated to the manner in which the law of the distribution of weapons functions in the societies involved. Under such conditions, war as a general economy no longer

necessarily implies that those who have weapons oppose each other. It is more likely to imply a conflict between those who have weapons and those who have none.[44]

And those who have none are those displaced by the interconnected machinations of militarization and neoliberal globalization.

THE CASE OF JAKELIN CAAL MAQUÍN

On December 8, 2018, a seven-year-old girl from Guatemala died while in the custody of the U.S. Border Patrol. She had traveled to the U.S. with her father in one of the large migrant caravans of Central Americans heading north that formed in the final months of 2018. Her death brought widespread publicity and criticism of the U.S. Border Patrol's treatment of migrants, which provoked then–Secretary of the Department of Homeland Security Kirstjen Nielsen to blame Jakelin's father for joining the caravan with his young daughter, putting her at legal and physical risk as an undocumented migrant undertaking a long and dangerous journey. Writing in *The Nation*, historian Greg Grandin and geographer Elizabeth Oglesby challenge Nielsen's allegation with a succinct overview of the history of U.S. intervention in Guatemala, which they argue left Jakelin's father with little choice but to migrate. Their account is worth reproducing at length, because it shows how the interventions described above work in tandem to create instability and unsustainability, delivering a series of blows from which communities cannot recover. While being unique to her, the story of how Jakelin's short life ended horribly at the U.S. border nevertheless captures the dynamics of plunder and intervention that have left so many communities in the global south struggling, bereft of options, and on the move.

> Jakelin was Q'eqchi'-Maya, from the Guatemalan town of Raxruhá, in northern Alta Verapaz. Here, as in much of rural Guatemala, Maya communities have struggled for over a century to remain on their lands. For much of that time, US governments intervened on the wrong side of those struggles. The result was a vortex of violent displacement that continues to this day.
>
> At the beginning of the 1900s, Q'eqchi'-Mayas lived mostly in Guatemala's lush, fertile northern highlands. But during the 20th century, many were pushed out. First, coffee planters, who were members of Guatemala's colonial and military elite, as well as new European and North American investors, dispossessed them of their lands through violence

and legal chicanery. When Q'eqchi' villagers tried to fight back, they were killed or exiled.

The CIA-orchestrated 1954 coup against a democratically elected president, Jacobo Arbenz, was a turning point in the Q'eqchi' region. An ambitious land reform, which had widespread beneficial effects in Alta Verapaz, was reversed, and poor Q'eqchi's began a great migration—fleeing political repression and hunger—to the lowlands, either east toward the Caribbean or north into the Petén rainforest. Raxruhá, Jakelin's home town, was founded in the 1970s by these internal migrants. . . .

The end of the Cold War in the 1990s brought no peace to the Q'eqchi.' Policies pushed by Washington brought new afflictions: The promotion of mining, African palm plantations for "clean" biofuels, hydroelectric production, and hardwood timbering destroyed their subsistence economy and poisoned their water and corn land.

Meanwhile, Q'eqchi' communities were caught in the crosshairs of an escalating international drug war. As Washington spent billions of dollars shutting down South American trafficking routes, Q'eqchi' communities were turned into a transshipment corridor for cocaine moving into the United States. Throughout the 2010s, drug-related crime and violence that had previously been concentrated in Colombia engulfed Central America, including Jakelin's birthplace, accelerating migration north. In 2010, narcotics-related violence grew so bad, with the Mexican Zetas cartel effectively controlling large parts of Alta Verapaz, that the government placed the department under an extended state of siege.

Q'eqchi' men and women fought back, organizing social movements to defend their communities. But the repression continued. In 2011, soldiers working with private paramilitary forces evicted hundreds of Q'eqchi' families, turning their land over to an agribusiness financed by international development loans. One study estimates that between 2003 and 2012, 11 percent of Q'eqchi' families lost their land to sugar and African palm plantations. By 2018, the situation was even more dire, with a wave of murders of Q'eqchi' peasant activists.

And, so, growing numbers of Q'eqchi' refugees are forced to leave communities founded by their parents and grandparents, taking their chances on migration to the United States. Why would a father bring his young daughter on a perilous trek to reach the United States? CNN Español interviewed Jakelin's relatives in her hometown in Guatemala, who said that her father, Nery Gilberto Caal, 29, did all he could to "stay in his land, but necessity made him try to get to the US."[45]

CLIMATE CHANGE DISLOCATIONS

Honduras is the epicenter for climate change in the Americas, pushing farmers out of agriculture as their land dries up and crops wither.[46] The link between the impact of global warming in Honduras, U.S.-backed oligarchic control, narco-related gangs, and the swelling numbers of Hondurans arriving at the U.S. border in recent years is direct. There is no official status for climate change refugees, so those displaced by climate change cannot claim any rights to mobility or asylum. And yet climate change will undoubtedly instigate future mobility on a scale not yet seen. Journalist Todd Miller estimates that at least 700 million people living in coastal areas alone risk displacement due to climate change in the near future. The International Organization for Migration (IOM) notes that nearly 18.8 million people were newly displaced by environmental disasters in 2017, and the special rapporteur on extreme poverty to the UN Human Rights Council warns of a "climate apartheid" future where the rich can afford to protect themselves from the effects of climate change while abandoning the poor, against whom they are fortifying their borders.[47]

The countries most at risk for climate change–related disasters and displacements are all in the global south: in addition to Honduras they include Nicaragua, Guatemala, Haiti, Myanmar, the Philippines, Bangladesh, Vietnam, Pakistan, and Thailand, as well as many island nations, a list that Todd Miller notes "often overlaps with the roster of border enforcement flashpoints."[48] As just one example, the island of Tuvalu in the South Pacific is in immediate danger of being submerged by the ocean, and a fifth of the population has fled. Although Tuvalu's neighbor Australia is one of the largest carbon dioxide emitters in the world, Australia has refused entry to Tuvalan climate refugees.[49]

The risk of dying from a climate-related disaster is five times greater for people who live in the forty-eight least developed countries than in the rest of the world, even though these countries contribute "less than 1 percent of the emissions that contribute to global warming."[50] The world's biggest polluters—the U.S., EU, China, and Russia—are all in the global north and are among the countries most invested in erecting strict border regimes. The U.S. Department of Defense, which is pioneering models for how to intercept climate change refugees trying to make their way north, is the largest greenhouse gas emitter in the world, spewing 1,212 million metric tons since the onset of the global war on terror.[51]

Climate change accentuates and deepens preexisting inequalities and vulnerabilities. The world's biggest global polluters—those most responsible for contributing to global warming—are literally destroying the homelands of everyone else while blocking their ability to relocate to new homes of their choice. Instead of developing an international legal/administrative/humanitarian regime to assist, support, and coordinate those displaced by climate change, the global north is hardening its borders and investing in military operations to blockade disaster refugees. As climate change realities become clear, "militarization will intrude ever more deeply into our everyday lives, our schools, our transportation, our communication, and our sense of citizenship, community and humanity itself," warns Todd Miller. "Border enforcement is not only growing, but is increasingly connected to the displacement caused by a world of fire, wind, rain, and drought."[52] We will return to these maneuvers in chapter 5.

PLUNDERING LOVE

All these factors intersect to structure a global economy that concentrates wealth and influence in the global north and exerts pressure on the global south to conform to political and economic mandates and militarized barriers defined by the global north. Governments of indebted countries in the global south in need of foreign currency may adopt policies that encourage their citizens to work abroad, such as the "labor export policy" of the Philippines and Indonesia, or El Salvador's efforts to promote emigration while ensuring its migrants retain an ongoing connection to their home country.[53] And the incomes that professionals can earn in the global north, even in service jobs, often exceed what is possible at home, contributing to a brain drain that pulls teachers, nurses, technology professionals, and others with skills toward emigration.

While this chapter has focused on the sorts of militarized, capitalist, and environmental interventions that make life unsustainable across many places in the global south, not all migrants are motivated solely by economic, political, or environmental imperatives. Affect and desire also influence their decisions. Ethnographic reports from West Africa, Mexico, Southeast Asia, and elsewhere document modernity's attractions for young people in the global south who long to participate in arenas they view as cosmopolitan and exciting or who are eager for greater autonomy from their families or confining social mores. The domination of global popular youth culture by American and European media exerts a cultural pull on young people frustrated by feeling excluded from globalization circuits, rotting away in some village, as one of Hans Lucht's interlocutors put it.[54] Lucht coined the phrase *existential reciprocity* to capture this desire—the attempt by the young migrant men he has worked with to reconcile their desires with the ability of the world to accommodate those desires. The journeys of his interlocutors from Ghana to Italy are part of their attempt to fashion a life in and of the world, to make a life of their choosing. "Indeed, the power to take charge of one's life and direct it toward desired goals—in time building one's own house, driving one's own car, sending one's children to better schools—seemed a matter of the greatest importance to the Guan informants—possibly more than could be explained by the acquisition of material rewards alone."[55] This passage is heartbreaking in its simplicity. Who does not want this? Why should it take a perilous journey to seek this? "Having connectedness to the powers that sustain life, however fragile those connections may be (and however 'dirty' the forms they take), not only supports material and social needs but also reduces the devastating feeling of insignificance, of being the plaything of external constraints, that so many of the world's immigrants are consigned to 'by accident of birth.'"[56] A yearning for emotional connection to significance—to being significant—may also take the form of plunder, however. Barbara Ehrenreich and Arlie Hochschild suggest that the global north's dependence on care work performed by migrant women (as nannies, domestics, elder care providers, sex workers) is plundering the emotional and sexual resources of the global south, who through their mobility are taking part "in a global heart transplant."[57] The global north is extracting love from the global south, they argue, with a substantial emotional cost to the children left behind in the care of relatives and to families separated for years or decades. We will return to this issue in chapter 4.

CONCLUSION

Elizabeth Povinelli has argued that late liberalism is about making any form of life that does not create market value dispensable, and, if such non–market productive life forms are defined as threatening to the market, then the state strangles them as a potential security risk. When applied to a theory of global apartheid, it becomes clear that the aggressive penetration of neoliberal capitalism and capitalist plunder in the global south have created "excess populations" that are to be either captured for the market as cheap producers, exploitable workers, or temporary guest workers or made expendable through forced removals and displacements, incarceration in refugee camps, or being allowed to sicken and die.[58]

CHAPTER THREE

CONTAINMENT

Shahram: Why are there refugees?
Amir: It is simple. The rich world plunders the poor world. . . . This is our situation. As long as there are plunderers, the plundered ones will want to come and see where their wealth has ended up. —ANTHROPOLOGIST SHAHRAM KHOSRAVI INTERVIEWING AMIR HEIDARI, A KURDISH MAN FROM IRAN INCARCERATED IN SWEDEN FOR HUMAN SMUGGLING. *"ILLEGAL" TRAVELER: AN AUTO-ETHNOGRAPHY OF BORDERS*

As the number of people crossing borders grows, countries across the global north are emplacing various forms of containment to interrupt and refuse the mobility of people from the global south—people from their former colonies, displaced by their military interventions, or separated from sustainable livelihoods by their corporate takeovers, mandated trade policies, or climate change impacts—who are now seeking safety and/or employment. In addition to the millions of people who move across borders every year after receiving authorization—

the focus of the next chapter—a far greater number of people displaced from their homes face a battery of barriers to their ability to enter the global north. Such "unauthorized" or "irregular" people in the global north who lack appropriate entry documents because they managed to enter without documents or overstayed their visas are targeted by contemporary immigration panics that conflate undocumented status with criminality or terrorism, drawing out racialized fears of immigrants and producing a surge of policing and surveillance to identify, incarcerate, and remove the unauthorized.

"Crimmigration"—new policies that criminalize migrants—has accompanied the racialization of immigrants in the global north. Such policies grew in the United States after the shift from mostly white to mostly brown immigrants since 1965; in the EU's border management regime inaugurated in the 1990s to hold back migrants from African and Arab countries; in Australia's "fanatical attempts to quarantine itself" against Kurdish, Afghani, Timorese, and other migrants through the imposition of mandatory detention in 1992 and offshore processing centers in 2004; in Israel's construction of a wall across the Sinai in 2012 to keep out African migrants; in China's 2012 law cracking down on unauthorized migrants through mandatory detention, fines, and possible deportation; and in Russia's move in 2013 to target for detention and deportation unauthorized migrants, especially those from Tajikistan, Kyrgyzstan, Uzbekistan, and Vietnam, derogatorily called "Blacks" to distinguish them from Russia's Slavic nationalist identity.[1] The racial logics motivating and guiding these practices mirror the management of pass law violations in apartheid South Africa that filled jails with Black people. In the global north of today, just as in apartheid South Africa of the last century, states have embarked on programs of intensive border management, mass refusal, mass incarceration, and deportation to discipline, punish, and remove unauthorized foreigners. Such policies and practices both betray and augment how migrants are simultaneously racialized and criminalized as foreign criminal aliens who can be targeted for incarceration and expulsion in response to prevailing political moods. This chapter turns our attention to the containment and refusal practices that the global north wields against the mobile from the global south whose mobility has not been authorized by officials in the global north.

SOVEREIGNTY AND EXCLUSION

We begin with refugees. The creation of the international refugee regime since 1950 is a paramount example of the link between nationalist associations of race and place, identity documentation, and border control. The international apparatus initially built to manage the millions of displaced people in post–World War II Europe has since become a formal global process of refugee identity documentation and management that makes extensive use of refugee camps—what Khosravi calls "the most significant characteristic of the modern nation-state"—as holding facilities to restrict the mobility of refugees.[2] Gaining official refugee status from the United Nations High Commissioner for Refugees (UNHCR) is contingent upon a strict reading of political persecution that gives people the right to have crossed an international border without the threat of being forcibly returned to the places from which they fled, but then strips them of all meaningful political and civil rights in countries where they do not "belong." While international refugee law protects those seeking asylum on the basis of a claim to persecution from being returned to the places from which they have fled, it does not guarantee them entry to another state and it does not require other states to accept them. Refugee camps exist to manage the tens of millions of people who have fled persecution and catastrophe but who lack the right to settle in another country.

The international system of such camps, many of which are administered by UNHCR, provides minimal care while protecting state sovereignty. The contemporary international refugee regime (containment camps, the decision-making process for granting official refugee status, the regulated and policed mobility of documented refugees) is designed to protect the wealthier countries in the global north, which fund the agencies that manage refugees, from the movement of people in the global south, where the majority of refugees originate and the majority of refugee camps are located.[3] It is thus no surprise that 85 percent of the world's refugees are housed in the global south, led by Turkey, Lebanon, Pakistan, Jordan, Uganda, and Iran. Even during the height of the exodus from Syria in 2015, a minority of the total number of those displaced went to Europe, sparking hyperbolic language about Europe's refugee "crisis," while the vast majority went to Turkey (2 million), Jordan (1.4 million), and Lebanon (1.2 million). The U.S., Gulf states, and Russia took in hardly any.[4] By the end of 2017 European countries had granted asylum to about 675,000 Syrian refugees, while the number of Syrian refugees held in Turkey alone had soared to 3.5 million.[5] Meanwhile, some of the world's least developed countries (according to the UNHCR definition), such as Cameroon, Chad, the Democratic Republic of the Congo, Ethiopia, Kenya, Uganda, and Sudan, together housed 28 percent of the world's refugee population.[6]

Locating refugee camps in the global south is a strategy to keep refugees close to the borders of the countries in the global south from which they have fled and far from the borders of nations in the north where they might wish to apply for asylum.[7] As Albahari has observed, the "overarching aspiration" of Frontex, the EU agency responsible for border control policy, created in 2004, is to ensure that "potential asylum seekers and persons needing protection do not reach the territory of EU countries in the first place" because of the legal obligation to consider the asylum applications of those who manage to cross the EU border.[8] The same desire governs asylum policy in the U.S., where President Trump has introduced measures to force migrants from Central America to remain in Mexico while attempting to apply for asylum, and in Australia, whose brutal militarized efforts to bar ships carrying refugees from docking corroborates the charge of "'White Australia' exclusionism."[9]

Israel's version of this theme includes building one of the largest detention centers in the world, as well as investing half a billion dollars to fortify a wall at the border with Egypt in 2012, in an attempt to thwart African refugees who arrived by the thousands after 2007, and then flatly denying almost all asylum claims and blocking any right to legal employment or state benefits for African immigrants.[10] Although the flow of immigrants from Africa into Israel slowed with the construction of the wall, perhaps 45,000 remained in the country with no right of residence, work, or public benefits other than in the detention centers. Elsewhere in the global north, Japan and South Korea accept only a few refugees each year, citing concerns about maintaining cultural and racial integrity as a justification for their closed-door policy. China accepted just nine Syrian refugees.[11] The GCC states have allowed some refugees to enter, but as temporary guests and not as refugees with a path to citizenship, and Russia's asylum process prioritizes Ukrainians while denying almost everyone else, including Syrian refugees, despite Russia's involvement in the Syrian conflict.

The international refugee regime's management of refugees is thus based on a fundamental inequality that grants power to the global north (and the staff employed by humanitarian agencies funded by a few countries in the global north) over people in the global south who are fleeing persecution, war, or disaster, often for reasons, as enumerated in the previous chapter, in which countries in the global north are deeply implicated or directly involved.[12] The UNHCR recommends less than 1 percent of the people housed in its refugee camps for third-country resettlement, and its critics argue that its practices follow racist logics, such as the employment of a very constrained definition of basic material needs because of a racist assumption that presumes poor people from the global south have less need of rights than other people. Furthermore, critical ethnographies describe refugee camps as places of neocolonial totalitarian control, where refugee residents are denied the rights of mobility, self-determination, and democratic participation, and where refugee camp administrators operate with impunity.[13] Refugees living in camps in the global south are essentially incarcerated while bureaucrats in the global north figure out where they will be allowed to go. Meanwhile, people who carry passports from the global north can usually go wherever they want.

BORDER-THICKENING AND EXTERNALIZING

Most people on the move in the global south are not categorized as UNHCR-recognized refugees and, as we saw in the previous chapter, are moving for a variety of reasons that do not fit neatly into the official requirement for refugee status. Most migrants and displaced persons do not live in refugee camps, but rather seek work and security in cities and towns, traveling to new destinations when migratory routes open or their living conditions deteriorate. Over the past several decades, the global north has been thickening and externalizing borders by investing in forms of containment, such as detention centers and offshore holding facilities, and outsourcing containment to the global south, in order to arrest and repel the movement of those who lack official entry visas. As fears about immigrants from the global south overtake the global north, countries in the global north have expanded laws that illegalize migrants, against whom they wield the tools of racial profiling, augmented policing and surveillance, mass incarceration, and mass deportation. Such policies rest on a logic of using the criminalization of mobility to return people to where they "belong," through deportations, border crossing refusals, and the use of migrant camps to detain people.

Borders are not simply territorial lines on the map: they are also processes, events, ideas, assemblages, and symbols. Border regimes are made up of "many little lines of force that run in multiple directions, constituting the border regime as a complex and dynamic multiplicity."[14] Borders are imagined, experienced, militarized, moved, disappeared, broadened, made lethal, made irrelevant, and used in different ways by different actors. Borders can be hardened and thickened to keep people out, and they can be disseminated internally to target enemies within.[15] As a tool of sovereignty, borders can be materialized and idealized in response to shifting political desires and economic imperatives, utilized to create categories of criminality, and enacted across space to incarcerate and contain. Sovereign borders animated as criminalizing mechanisms in turn iterate new bordering mechanisms: racial profiling, targeted raids, detention centers, offshore holding facilities, jails, and prisons. As Didier Fassin has noted, "borders as external territorial frontiers and boundaries as internal social categorizations are tightly related in a process in which immigrants are racialized and ethnic minorities are reminded of their foreign origin."[16] Even bodies can become borders, both through the use of biometric screening and tracking technologies and through racial profiling.[17]

Bordering practices are thus sweeping and iterative—a decision to criminalize visa overstayers, for example, translates into factory raids, the deputizing of police officers and social workers as immigration enforcement operatives, the sharing of biometric information across various branches of government and the private sector to identify the unauthorized, the surveillance of transport hubs and hospitals by immigration patrols, the enlistment of citizens to be vigilant. A routine police stop for a traffic violation can become a life-changing moment of arrest, detention, and deportation.

Israel's labyrinth of borders in the Occupied Territories offers an instructive primer on border-thickening and externalizing practices, serving "as a laboratory for politics and technologies restricting mobility, particularly to police social inequalities."[18] Israel claims that security concerns justify its need to hold tight control over Palestinian mobility. Because "managing 'dangerous' populations is a central concern for most governments in an age when terrorism, crime, immigration, and labor have been compounded into a broad range of security threats to states," Israel's management of the West Bank offers an example that other parts of the world have drawn upon in the global war on terror. "The knowledge, technologies, and institutional logics of the population management apparatus in the West Bank have proliferated throughout Europe, the United States, and South Asia in the last decade," argues Israeli lawyer Yael Berda.[19] Israel depends on the labor of Palestinians, and, citing security concerns, also wants total control over their mobility, and so has developed an elaborate, complex, opaque, multilayered bureaucracy of permits, checkpoints, blockades, closures, and walls that completely penetrate Palestinian space in the West Bank. Because Palestinians are a racialized population and those living in the Occupied Territories lack citizenship rights, Israel treats their right to mobility as a privilege for which they are required to hold a permit. But Israel retains the right to persistently interrupt the mobility of Palestinians in the West Bank, including those with permits, through closures, checkpoints, and security restrictions, all managed on an ad hoc basis through an accretion of policies and decisions that change by the day and that are not collected into any sort of published guidelines, thus allowing the state and its agents enormous day-to-day flexibility and no accountability. The permitting regime relies on "space, race, and documents": containment, closures, blockades, exclusion from citizenship, and identification requirements used to maintain a racial hierarchy. It makes prolific use of profiling, biometrics, and other kinds of data collection, making every Palestinian "an individual target of surveillance and monitoring," whose mobility is determined and monitored by the Israeli state.[20] In Israel, Palestinian bodies are borders to be policed, interrupted, monitored, and contained.

ILLEGALIZING IMMIGRATION AND OFFSHORING BORDERS

Rivaling Israel, the United States has led the world in instituting a cascading set of laws and technologies since the 1980s to externalize and internalize its border, dramatically militarizing the southern border, criminalizing migrants, and handing ever greater authority to surveil and incarcerate to local officials throughout the country. Political discourse during the 1980s harped on the dangers posed at the southern border by immigrants and drug traffickers. Racism threaded through this discourse, blatantly visible in the differential treatment of Haitian and Cuban asylum seekers. While Cuban arrivals were processed as "entrants," Haitians were first incarcerated on a missile base before being sent to various military bases and, later, jails. In response to court challenges about the disparate treatment of Cubans and Haitians, the Reagan administration opted to extend immigrant detention in general and to direct Coast Guard ships to intercept refugee boats from Haiti before they reached the U.S. coastline. Policies for managing Haitian refugees who arrived in later years turned toward using prisons and jails and constructing immigration detention facilities. Recounting this history, geographer Jenna Lloyd points to the link between the antiblack racism that governed the U.S. treatment of Haitian asylum seekers, mass incarceration, and immigrant detention. "The reliance on imprisonment explicitly to deter Haitian asylum seekers built on the existing national racial formation and chain of association linking Blackness, poverty, and criminality to a carceral solution."[21]

Another strand of this discourse conflated the war on drugs with border security, allowing political leaders to direct high-tech military technologies to border control and expand criminal sentencing for undocumented migrants. Rhetoric criminalizing migrants grew during the Clinton presidency, prompting Operation Gatekeeper in 1994 and the 1996 Illegal Immigration Reform and Immigrant Responsibility Act (IIRIRA). Operation Gatekeeper enhanced border control securitization and instituted the Prevention Through Deterrence policy that intentionally pushed undocumented border crossers into the most life-threatening desert environments in an effort to use the desert as a deterrent, which produced a rising death toll rather than a depressed migrant flow. The 1996 IIRIRA increased funding, personnel, and technology for the Border Patrol, expanded the reasons for inadmissibility and deportation, made it much harder for unauthorized migrants to legalize their status, expanded the actions that could define migrants as felons, depressed judicial review of immigration cases, raised the bar for asylum claims, imposed an annual cap on the number of people whose removal proceedings could be waived by judicial review, introduced an expedited removal process, expanded mandatory detention for people being processed for removal, mandated new monitoring systems for tracking migrants, and appropriated funding for antimigrant security enhancements at Mexico's southern border.[22] As legal anthropologist Susan Coutin explains, "Acts that, under criminal law, were neither aggravated nor felonies became 'aggravated felonies' for immigration purposes—and thus offenses that made noncitizens deportable. Such acts included driving under the influence (Texas), simple battery, shoplifting, and selling small amounts of drugs."[23] The expanded list of crimes for which a person could be deported was applied retroactively, which meant people could be deported for things they had done years previously, even if they subsequently held clean records. As a consequence of the law, new detention centers filled with newly criminalized people in removal proceedings proliferated, deportations soared, and deportability became weaponized as the most significant distinction between those with and those without citizenship status.

The U.S. Patriot Act of 2001 and the Homeland Security Act of 2002 introduced many more security measures and reasons for deportation, reorganized the policing and management of migrants, and directed vastly more funding to securing borders, instigating an upsurge in raids by Immigration and Customs Enforcement (ICE) in the form of military-style assaults that utilize racial profiling to target suspected undocumented migrants. Even more shockingly, the Patriot Act created a "Constitution-free zone" stretching one hundred miles from any U.S. border, within which border patrol agents can surveil, stop, interrogate, and search anyone they suspect might lack official entry or citizenship documents. Border agents can set up roadblocks, board public transportation, or pull over anyone to ask them about their citizenship status or to ask to see their papers if they claim that they have reason to suspect their citizenship status.[24] The Constitution-free zone encompasses roughly two-thirds of the population of the United States.

In an effort to manage the massive numbers of people swept up by immigration raids and enhanced border management, Operation Streamline, introduced in 2005, expanded and streamlined the criminal prosecution of virtually all unauthorized migrants and allowed recently apprehended border crossers to be sentenced en masse.[25] Operation Streamline made illegal entry a criminal rather than a civil offense, and illegal reentry a felony offense, "both with mandatory prison sentences prior to deportation. . . . Between 1992 and 2012, criminal prosecutions for unlawful reentry increased twenty-eight-fold, and by 2012, people with convictions for unlawful reentry made up a quarter of all sentenced federal offenders, spending an average of two years in prison before being deported."[26] Migrants brought into court under Operation Streamline are shackled as if they were violent offenders, an unnecessary performance weighty with emotional and psychological implications.

Deportations grew under the policy initiative called Secure Communities, first introduced in 2008 but suspended in 2014 because of its harsh and terrorizing impact on Latinx communities, only to be reauthorized by President Trump in 2017. The Secure Communities initiative deputized local police forces to act in conjunction with the FBI and the Department of Homeland Security as deportation agents, by, among other things, requiring local police departments to send fingerprints of anyone arrested for any reason (but not yet convicted) to the Department of Homeland Security to assess citizenship status.[27] Communities of color in the U.S., already under hypersurveillance by the police, thus received yet another layer of criminalization. Secure Communities enabled the police to detain anyone suspected of immigration violations even if they had committed no crime, thus contributing to "newly disproportionate risks for communities of color" because their "criminalization is based on the active presumption that immigrant communities are criminal enclaves and as such somehow legitimate objects of disproportionate policing."[28] The UK inaugurated a similar program in 2012 called Operation Nexus, which required police to check the citizenship status not only of those arrested, but also of witnesses and victims. In a particularly disturbing move, Operation Nexus also allows hearsay, suspicions, and allegations contained within someone's police file to stand as sufficient evidence for deportation.[29] Canada followed suit with border panics of its own in 2018–19, resulting in mandatory detention for all unauthorized migrants, heightened xenophobic rhetoric, and more deportations.[30]

In short, new policies and initiatives emplaced in the U.S. since the 1980s—and echoed in the EU, Canada, and Australia—dramatically expanded the number of criminal offenses for which migrants can be detained and deported and directed particular scrutiny and surveillance at racialized communities, most especially Latinx and Muslim communities.[31] Federal prosecutions for immigration offenses grew from 5.4 percent of all federal prosecutions in 1993 to 54 percent in 2015, when twice as many people were removed to detention because of immigration violations as were incarcerated by the Federal Bureau of Prisons. While the extraordinary number of migrants behind bars implies a high level of criminality, in fact the vast majority either have never been convicted of any crime or have as the only blot on their record a minor infraction such as a traffic violation or minor drug offense.[32]

Because much of the focus of criminalizing policies has been directed to the southern U.S. border region, the percentage of federally sentenced offenders who are Latinx has skyrocketed to 48 percent, making the criminalization of migrants seem like a war against the presence of Latinx people in the U.S.[33] Yolanda Vasquez calls crimmigration "a mechanism for continued racial subordination" because immigrants of color are so disproportionately targeted for surveillance, detention, and deportation. Latinx people make up 90 percent or more of those in detention, prosecuted for immigration violations, and deported. The overrepresentation of Latinx people in the criminal justice system because of federal "racialized mass removal" policies has effectively branded Latinx people as a criminal population, Vasquez argues, with resounding implications in all domains of American society, from housing to the workplace to the political arena.[34] The set of policies that have criminalized undocumented migrants since the 1980s is a form of "systemic legal violence" that has profoundly impacted the emotional and psychological health of immigrant communities of color who live under constant, unrelenting scrutiny and suspicion.[35]

The number of people employed to carry out this work is staggering. The U.S. Customs and Border Protection (CBP) is the single largest federal law enforcement agency in the U.S., with 60,000 employees. Immigration and Customs Enforcement (ICE) employs another 20,000. When added to the 240,000 people employed by the Department of Homeland Security and the 650,000 police officers affiliated with border security, the total number of personnel assigned to work on border security has become "the equivalent of a small army."[36]

From 2003 to 2018 the number of U.S. Border Patrol agents nearly doubled and the number of ICE agents dedicated to Enforcement and Removal Operations nearly tripled.[37] More money is dedicated to federal immigration enforcement than "'all other principal federal criminal law enforcement agencies combined,' including the FBI, the CIA, the U.S. Marshals Service and a few other agencies."[38] The American Immigration Council offers these astonishing tallies, as of May 2019:

> Since 1993, when the current strategy of concentrated border enforcement was first rolled out along the U.S.-Mexico border, the annual budget of the U.S. Border Patrol [a division of U.S. Customs and Border Protection] has increased more than ten-fold, from $363 million to more than $4.7 billion.
>
> Since the creation of DHS in 2003, ICE spending has grown 103 percent, from $3.3 billion to $6.7 billion today [May 2019]. Much of this funding has gone to increasing the agency's ability to hold immigrants in detention in locations around the country.
>
> Since 2003, the budget of CBP, which includes both the Border Patrol and operations at ports of entry, has more than doubled, rising from $5.9 billion in FY 2003 to $14.7 billion in FY 2019.
>
> Since 1993, the number of U.S. Border Patrol agents has skyrocketed from 4,139 agents to a congressionally authorized 23,645 agents in FY 2018, although due to hiring issues Border Patrol only had 19,555 agents in FY 2018. Of those agents, 16,608 are deployed to the U.S.-Mexico border, more than four times the 3,555 agents deployed to the U.S.-Mexico border in FY 1992. An additional 2,097 agents are deployed to the U.S.-Canada border, more than seven times the amount deployed in FY 1992. A further 248 agents are deployed to the Coastal Border Sectors.
>
> The number of CBP officers staffing ports of entry (POEs) grew from 17,279 in FY 2003 to 23,002 as of February 2018.
>
> The number of ICE agents devoted to Enforcement and Removal Operations increased from 2,710 in FY 2003 to nearly 8,000 in FY 2018.[39]

Combining the CBP budget of almost $15 billion and ICE's budget of $6 billion makes a total devoted to border and immigration enforcement that is over twelve times greater than the INS budget in the 1990s.[40] In addition, in 2019 President Trump appropriated over $9.5 billion for his desired border wall.[41]

The EU has followed suit: the explosive rise in funds allocated by the EU and EU border states for border management during the early 2000s evidenced a "seismic shift" in the treatment of borders.[42] With rising numbers of migrants trying to make their way north in 2015, panic spread across the EU about a refugee "crisis," although migration scholars argue that 2015 was less a departure from previous years than a continuation of prior patterns. New antimigrant patrols and the Dublin Regulation augmented these patterns, producing overcrowding in places like Lampedusa in Italy and Lesbos in Greece because of the requirement that refugees request asylum at their first point of entry. As noted previously, the Schengen Agreement and visa regime—which Scheel calls "a vast machine of illegalization"—allows for the free movement of people within the twenty-eight countries that make up the Schengen region, but makes the country of first entry responsible for vetting and authorizing entry to the region.[43] Those people from the countries from which a visa is required to enter the Schengen region who are caught within the region without authorized documents are returned to their ports of first entry, placing the burden for processing migrants who arrived by sea on Spain, Italy, and Greece. The ability to maintain tight border security has become a requirement for countries seeking to join the Schengen area: Italy, Greece, Portugal, Spain, Hungary, Slovakia, Poland, Estonia, Latvia, Lithuania, Malta, Slovenia, Bulgaria, Romania, Croatia, and Serbia have all been either required to demonstrate their ability to meet rigorous border control standards or received funding and support from the Schengen Facility to strengthen their border controls in order to participate.[44]

The active interruption of migrant routes from the south into Europe first began with Spain's imposition of visa requirements for entry on people from African and Arab countries in the early 1990s, followed by Spanish and joint Spanish-African marine patrols in the early 2000s.[45] Spain's rapid securitization offers a remarkable case study in the EU's compulsion toward "Europeanization" for its member states. In the 1980s Spain had basically no immigration policy, but

> legislated its first Aliens Law in 1986 in preparation for joining the European Union (EU). At that point, Spain had no detention centers for illegalized migrants. Since 1991, however, when the first boats carrying migrants and refugees from Africa arrived on Spanish territory, the country has seen a massive public investment in fencing its borders, establishing numerous detention centers throughout the country, setting up special police units for fighting illegalized migration, and running an elaborate deportation apparatus that includes both "voluntary" return programs and forced removals. . . . This violent response to unauthorized mobility

in Spain is the norm in the EU, where the European Commission's report on progress towards accession of new members states has recommended, for example, that Bulgaria constructs adequate detention centers for illegal aliens in order to meet criteria necessary to enter the area of "security, freedom and justice."[46] In other words, striving for security, freedom and justice as envisioned by the EU is predicated on the ability to detain and deport illegalized aliens, who clearly pose a threat to this noble goal.[47]

As migratory routes shifted eastward in response to Spanish patrols, Italy negotiated with Libya to capture and return migrants attempting the sea crossing, and even began paying Libya to return thousands of migrants to their home countries in 2004.[48] The EU created Frontex in 2004 to coordinate this work across the Mediterranean and the Maghreb, which was augmented a few years later by EUROSUR, Europe's External Border Surveillance System. Frontex operations replaced Italy's Mediterranean rescue operation, Mare Nostrum, after its first year, but shifted the focus of patrols from rescue to the policing and repulsion of migrants (largely leaving the job of rescue to humanitarian volunteers and activists).[49] The start-up funding was enormous: €2 billion invested in fences, surveillance systems, and personnel during 2007–13, and a Frontex budget that expanded from €6.2 million in 2005 to €98 million by 2014.[50] The 2014 Frontex budget dwarfed the €14.5 million allocated by the EU to the European Asylum Support Office that year.[51] By 2016, in the wake of the refugee "crisis," the Frontex budget soared to €176 million, reaching €302 million by 2017.[52] The "bewitching" language of crisis justified the further expansion of Frontex powers with the European Border and Coast Guard in 2016.[53] Kalir reports that between 2008 and 2016, "more than 6.8 million people were apprehended for 'illegal presence' in the EU, more than 4.6 million were ordered to leave EU territories, and about 3.5 million non-EU citizens were refused entry at the borders of EU member states."[54]

The criminalization of those who assist migrants and the blockading of safer routes forced migrants toward more perilous crossings, and as patrol and repel operations replaced rescue, the death toll soared. Between 2014 and mid-2018, the central Mediterranean was "the deadliest crossing in the world," with over fifteen thousand deaths, and by late 2018 the sea journey had become deadlier than ever, even as the number of migrants attempting to cross by sea dropped to its lowest level since 2015.[55] The rising number of deaths by drowning is the unsurprising result of a militarized curtain intended to push people into the most dangerous sea routes. Because militarizing the borders is legal, migrant deaths in the sea (or in the desert at the U.S.-Mexico border) cannot be legally attributed to the border security policies of the global north, making deaths on the border battlefield unacknowledged as a casualty of war.[56]

At the same time, the EU has enhanced its funding to Libya to intercept migrant boats, even outside of Libyan waters. The *New York Times* reported that Libyan ships intercepted about twenty thousand people in 2017, returning them to conditions of extreme human rights abuses in Libyan detention centers, and Doctors Without Borders claims that during the first half of 2018 more than 130,000 migrants were captured and returned to Libya, where they were put in detention.[57]

"Fortress Europe" is thus not simply a gated fortress, but rather is created through iterative layers of bordering practices that extend from patrols on the Mediterranean to police monitoring of transportation networks within the EU (train, bus, and metro stations) to containment camps in Turkey and North Africa. "A vast amount of financial resources, military hardware and sophisticated surveillance equipment has indeed been dedicated to prosecuting an asymmetric 'war' by the world's largest economy (its member states include 15 of the 20 wealthiest countries) against a relatively small number of migrants from the world's poorest, most violent regions," writes Fran Cetti about Fortress Europe. She continues:

> This vastly disproportionate response rarely fulfils its stated purpose—desperation forces many migrants to continue to attempt to cross the border no matter what the cost, and the smugglers oblige by changing their itineraries to increasingly hazardous routes. It was the EU's "success" in disrupting the routes from Morocco to the Spanish enclaves of Ceuta and Melilla, and then to the Canary Isles, that forced migrants' boats into the treacherous crossing from Libya to Malta, and then from Libya to the former Italian prison island of Lampedusa.
>
> Meanwhile, increased surveillance and joint naval patrols in the Aegean have forced many migrants travelling through Turkey to attempt to cross the Evros River at the country's remote, heavily militarised land border with Greece, a journey also fraught with danger. But it is the Mediterranean—now one of the most militarised oceans in the world—that continues to be "the world's most lethal graveyard." Even Fabrice Leggeri, director of Frontex, the European agency at the heart of the attempts to "secure" the external border, admits that closing one route simply leads to the opening of another, noting that migration routes "are extremely

flexible and can change rapidly." However, any official recognition of the systemic contradictions of this border regime is silenced by the huge financial profits to be made within the security-asylum industrial juggernaut, its articulation with other aspects of the EU's neoliberal order, and the ideological benefits it appears to offer national politicians.[58]

The pattern in the EU has thus seen migrant routes shift over the past two decades in response to the imposition of patrols and fences: from Spain toward Italy, then toward Greece, and then into Bulgaria and toward the overland so-called Balkan route. As sea arrivals in Greece dropped from 856,000 in 2015 to 29,718 in 2017, the countries along the overland Balkan route implemented new border control strategies in response to their own internal politics and EU desires to contain migrants. In addition to imposing expectations on EU member states, the EU also began a more expansive practice to externalize its borders by finalizing a deal in 2016 that gave Turkey €6 billion to stop migrants crossing toward Greece and by promising €1 billion to Niger for 2018–20 and €100 million to Sudan in return for their assistance in interrupting migrants.[59] The new Emergency Trust Fund for Africa has committed €3.4 billion for twenty-six partner states in Africa to implement migration management strategies. In all, the EU has agreements with more than forty countries from Central Asia to North Africa that "let the security forces of third countries do the dirty work of interception, detention, and expulsion of people on the move, far from European citizens' eyes."[60] One of the latest moves to interrupt migrants making their way toward Europe is the i-Map created by the International Center for Migration Policy Development, which tracks migratory routes across the Sahara, Mediterranean, and Eastern Europe toward the EU in order to mark and plan apprehensions. Sebastian Cobarrubias argues that the mapping project aligns the EU and its partner countries in a common vision to identify migrants as already illegal at the very start of their journey.[61] The racist logics driving border security penetrate into North African countries charged with detaining Black Africans, which periodically round up Black people to display for official visits from their European funders.[62] Morocco and Niger have each recently perpetrated brutal crackdowns on migrants and those who assist them, in response to generous EU funding.

The U.S. has similarly been turning to its southern neighbor to do the work of migrant interruption and containment, externalizing its border far to the south, directing nearly $3 billion between 2008 and 2015 to Mexico to enhance the ability of Mexican security forces to capture and deport migrants from Central America and combat drug trafficking.[63] In the first seven months of Plan Frontera Sur, the U.S.-backed anti-immigrant program in Mexico, Mexican authorities apprehended more than ninety thousand Central Americans, twenty thousand more than were caught in the U.S. during that same time period.[64] The U.S. was already using offshore detention centers to incarcerate Haitians and Cubans intercepted at sea in the 1990s, a practice expanded with the Coast Guard's "Operation Global Reach" to interdict migrants at sea after 1997. Learning from this model, Australia developed its "Pacific Solution" in 2001 to interdict migrants at sea and detain them indefinitely on Nauru and Papua New Guinea in detention centers staffed by contractors—sending more than three thousand into these offshore detention centers during 2013–18—while also financing detention in Indonesia of migrants from Afghanistan, Iraq, Sri Lanka, and Burma. In a particularly crafty move, the Australian Parliament retroactively declared several hundred islands off the coast of Australia no longer part of Australia as part of their antimigrant curtain.[65] The appalling treatment of migrants held in Australia's secretive facilities and the very high rates of suicide among children held in offshore detention centers has been the subject of international outrage. Nevertheless, New Zealand established a policy in 2013 to use Australia's offshore holding centers as a model in the event of mass arrivals.[66] It is worth noting that such border outsourcing operates outside of American, European, and Australian regulatory control, is subject to little oversight or transparency, and offers countries on whose behalf migrants are detained and deported deniability about human rights abuses conducted by the countries and contractors they fund.

DETENTION AND DEPORTATION

People caught without documents at the border of the EU, the U.S., Canada, or Australia, like those swept up in raids, are usually sent to detention centers while authorities determine their fate. Detention centers originated in South Africa when the English colonists created internment camps for Boers and Black Africans during the 1899–1902 Second Boer War and have since become a favored model for countries across the global north for managing unwanted immigrants.[67] Whereas some countries such as Canada, the UK, France, and some Gulf states incarcerate detained immigrants in the general prison population, the U.S. and Australia utilize private contractors to run some (U.S.) or all (Australia) of their detention centers, and others have constructed dedicated immigrant detention centers, such as Israel's enormous complex in the Negev desert and in Russia's plan to expand its total number of detention centers to 104.[68]

In the U.S., after the 1986 and 1996 immigration reform acts expanded the criteria for detaining and deporting immigrants, the number of detainees ballooned to over 400,000 per year since 2012, held across a shadowy and secretive network of public and private facilities, with a budget for their detention of over $3 billion in 2018. Between thirty and fifty thousand immigrants, the vast majority from Mexico and Central America, are imprisoned in detention centers in the U.S. on any given day, meeting a quota set by Congress (in response to powerful lobbying efforts by private prison corporations) and fulfilled by ICE. A great majority are held in private prison facilities, and consequently the business of detention has become hugely profitable. Taxpayer dollars in 2017 to pay for immigrant incarceration totaled $184 million to the GEO Group and $135 million to CoreCivic, formerly Corrections Corporation of America.[69] One recent study of the connection between the criminalization of immigrants, mandatory detention, and lobbying by private prison companies (CoreCivic and GEO Group spent $10 million to lobby for Department of Homeland Security appropriations between 2006 and 2015) offers this understated denunciation: "corporate interests have helped to fuel the growth of immigrant detention and to convert the criminalization of immigrants into a profitable industry."[70] Because of the outsize impact of corporate lobbying by private prison companies on immigration policy, the authors conclude that mandatory detention and the mandatory bed requirement should be repealed.

Detention removes from society those considered undesirable while authorities decide where they should go. "Detention thus becomes an effort to contain and fix the identities of migrants," who can then be deported to the locations where they are told they belong.[71] By all accounts, detention is experienced by the incarcerated as inhumane, humiliating, traumatizing, and terrifying. Patchy oversight, restrictions on visits by outsiders, refusal to provide information to family members about the location of their incarcerated loved ones, poor medical attention, inadequate food, harmful living conditions, racist treatment of prisoners, and little accountability are just some of the persistent allegations about the detention industry. One has only to remember the images in 2019 of people apprehended at the U.S.-Mexico border and held behind barbed wire under a freeway overpass in Texas, or the appalling reports of children removed from their parents after apprehension and then "lost" in the system, to grasp the extent of abuse.

The confluence of immigration law and criminal law in the creation of "crimmigration" means that unauthorized people are treated differently from others who are charged with crimes: they are typically treated as a mass rather than as individuals in court proceedings, they are encouraged to accept plea agreements that result in deportation or face longer periods of incarceration, their punishment is more severe, they are in effect doubly punished because they serve time and then are also deported and slapped with a lengthy restriction on reentry, and the entire process through which they are put is itself a form of punishment. Detainees are typically shackled during court appearances, denied legal representation, and humiliated in a courtroom in a carceral performance of justice that is intended to show them how little value they hold. Ben Bowling prefers the term *immcarceration* to describe the convergence of immigration and criminal law, arguing that "there is no pretence that the purpose of immcarceration is rehabilitation or reform; its manifest goals are incapacitation, deportation, and deterrence," to which I would add humiliation, degradation, and symbolic violence.[72] Ethnographic studies of the treatment of immigrants in detention centers and prisons reveal the contours of such forms of double punishment. For example, in England detainees awaiting a determination of their cases or deportation for unauthorized entry are subject to the individualized power of detention center officers, who treat their charges with suspicion as abstract bodies to be constantly monitored and degraded.[73] In Norway, where foreign nationals comprise a third of the prison population, the rehabilitative goals of the welfare state no longer extend to them. Foreign nationals are housed in separate prisons or separate wings, denied the rehabilitative and reentry support programs for which Norway is well known, and often deported back to their countries of origin to serve out their sentences. Their marked exclusion as unredeemable noncitizens clarifies their disposability.[74]

Detention is the final step before deportation. The spectacular rise in deportations in the U.S. over the past decade has led scholars to call this the Age of Removal and to label the U.S. as a Deportation Regime. Indeed, former President Obama was hailed as the "Deporter-in-Chief" because deportations during his presidency, thanks in part to the Secure Communities initiative, reached an astounding number of over 3 million people, a figure that does not include those turned away at the border, whose numbers totaled about 27 million between 1993 and 2016.[75] Due to streamlined deportation policies, by 2013 a record number of immigrants were deported without ever appearing before a judge (83 percent of deportations).[76] Immigration courts are woefully underfunded relative to the funding available to catch and detain the undocumented, resulting in massive backlogs in immigration courts (1.2 million cases in 2020). For those who do appear in court, speed trials are the norm in many courts in border states, where detainees have about twenty-five seconds before a judge, who hands down a lighter sentence in return for guilty pleas, after which the incarcerated are deported and permanently barred from reentry.[77]

During 2008–16, the EU "returned" about 1.75 million people to non-EU member states.[78] Kalir estimates that by 2016 EU member states were deporting about 200,000 people a year and detaining an equal number in detention centers, figures that do not include the hundreds of thousands of people living in camps awaiting processing of their asylum applications. Assisted Voluntary Return is another strategy employed by EU member states to get people to "self-deport" by targeting the most marginalized, impoverished, and vulnerable immigrants and convincing them to leave rather than offering them support to adjust to their new context.[79] The portion of the Frontex budget devoted to deportation expanded from €80,000 in 2005 to €53 million in 2017.[80]

Since deportations require authorities to figure out where they think deportees belong based on the logic that ties people to place, people are deported to countries they may have left as infants and/or perhaps never even visited, such as refugees born in Kenyan refugee camps, raised in Canada, and deported to Somalia, or people born in Mexico to El Salvadoran parents, raised in the U.S., and deported to El Salvador. The resonances with apartheid South Africa's insistence that Black South Africans "belong" to homelands where they may never even have visited is obvious. Research on the fate of deportees reveals the stigma, dislocation, and alienation they experience after being sent to countries where they lack social networks, language skills, and political rights. They are "de facto aliens in their country of citizenship."[81]

DEATH

The disregard for human life, dignity, and basic rights evinced by refugee camps, detention centers, offshore holding facilities, and deportation is made even more brutally clear with the murderous effects of border management regimes whereby Mediterranean maritime patrols for Frontex push migrants into more dangerous sea routes, the Prevention Through Deterrence strategy along the U.S.-Mexico border funnels migrants into ever more hostile desert environments, and Australia's maritime patrols push boats overloaded with migrants back out to sea. Because of these strategies an estimated twenty thousand people drowned in the Mediterranean during 1994–2014, in addition to the fifteen thousand drowned since 2014, trying to reach Europe. Thousands have died in the Sonoran Desert, most disappearing by the desert's desiccating power before their remains can be discovered. An estimated two thousand people have died, most by drowning, at the Australian frontier during 2000–2016.[82] The now-normalized practices of abandoning people in refugee camps, incarcerating people in secretive detention centers, and interrupting migrant routes in order to push people into life-threatening environments show the centrality of racism for creating categories of the disposable and killable and the lengths to which countries in the global north will go to restrict the entry of brown people from the global south because they lack entry documents.

Such outcomes will likely only increase with the emergence of smart borders that use a combination of biometric and other data sets to manage mobility. For example, the biometric border utilized by the US-VISIT (U.S. Visitor and Immigrant Status Indicator Technology) program relies on a strategy of defining the mobile according to a hierarchy of "risk" characteristics. An algorithmic analysis of a broad array of data sets, including biometric, health, financial, educational, travel, communications, and other information produces a risk assessment of each traveler and identifies risky categories of people, long before a traveler reaches the U.S. border. As Louise Amoore argues, the application of biometric borders and the push to clearly and unambiguously define illegitimate travelers will mean that the undocumented can be profiled as terrorists and thus made subject to violent interventions, including detention, imprisonment, and death.[83] Since racial profiling is allowed by the U.S. Department of Homeland Security and by border security operations in the EU and Canada, there is no doubt that smart borders will continue to utilize racial criteria to target immigrants, most especially the undocumented, for scrutiny and disposability.[84] We will return to this newest iteration of border security in chapter 5.

Countries across the global north not only are sharing technologies and techniques for patrolling and managing their borders, but are also sharing politicized rhetorical strategies that connect immigrants with criminals and terrorists, a strategy initially honed in the U.S. but increasingly adopted elsewhere. Such shared technologies and rhetorics are producing, in the words of Ruben Andersson, "the partial reinvention of race." He argues:

At the southern U.S. border, sadistic sheriffs or vigilantes loudly proclaim they are not racist but merely act against "illegals" and criminals; in Europe, similar arrangements are made by xenophobic politicians calling for military interventions against migrant boats. In such all too frequent examples, racism is intimately related to mobility—that is, selectively applied to the poor who dare to move. This mirrors the deepening world divide between rich and poor . . . and illegality serves as a gloss for this divide, hiding the new configuration of race on display among shuffling and clinking feet in a U.S. courtroom, in European or Moroccan round-ups, and in the images of border and boat crises broadcast from the Canaries, Australia, and Arizona.[85]

CONCLUSION

Bordering regimes produce an industry of illegalization that fetishizes the border and racializes criminalized migrants, who are subjected to legitimized forms of violence—arrest, detention, deportation, abandonment in third-country jails and holding facilities—where there is no accountability for their treatment.[86] The treatment of migrants and the death toll at sea is, according to migration scholar Nicholas de Genova, "an historic moment of racial crisis" for Europe, whose "borders represent a racist division: open for the free movement of capital and citizens of the West, closed for formerly colonized people or those who are simply not rich enough to get a legal visa."[87] The same is true for every other country in the global north.

In arguing that the phrase *militarized global apartheid* best captures the emergent world order of structures of control that securitize the north and foster violence in the south, the argument signals the normalized specter of boats filled with migrants from Africa and the Middle East that sink in the Mediterranean while ships bearing European national flags stand by watching but not assisting, of boats filled with refugees from Myanmar and Afghanistan turned away by Australian government authorities when they request help, of U.S. Border Patrol policies that channel Mexicans and Central Americans into the most extreme parts of the Sonoran Desert to starve or die of dehydration, of women from South and Southeast Asia forced to give up their officially stateless babies to orphanages in the Gulf countries when they are deported for having become pregnant in violation of their work contracts, and of U.S. presidential candidates who gain popularity by calling for policies to deport all Muslims and build border walls against Latinx migrants.

The security apparatus described above, like apartheid, dehumanizes racialized others through blocking their routes of mobility, channeling them into the most dangerous regions of the sea and the desert, incarcerating them in refugee camps in remote and inhospitable regions for indeterminate periods, and subjecting them to removals from white space over and over and over again. The United States, Europe, Australia, Israel, and other countries in the global north are claiming to maximize their own self-protection through gating, policing, removing, and drowning people. These are state-sanctioned investments in forms of structural violence that cause people to die. Border controls, deportations, and deaths in the desert and at sea reveal state sovereignty at its points of enactment and clarify how the state uses law, territorial boundaries, and militarized security structures to promote and ensure a particular hegemonic racial identity. In the U.S., the extensive removal of minorities into prisons and immigrants into detention centers affirms, in case there was any doubt, the hegemony of whiteness as an ongoing state project. States shape populations by policing who gains entry and by removing the undesirables. Removals are acts of racism—they are racist projects of cultural consolidation, and they are often hidden within self-serving discourses of security.

CHAPTER FOUR

LABOR

Encoded in the notions of immigrant and refugee are meanings of ethnic absolutism that invent or renew racial identities on reconfigured landscapes of national inclusion and
exclusion. Paradoxically, although certain categories of immigrants are viewed as troublesome parasites whose cultures
threaten the purity of European nations, their economic participation in ethnically and sexually segmented labor keeps
their host economies thriving and enriches their employers.
—FAYE HARRISON, "GLOBAL APARTHEID, FOREIGN POLICY,
AND HUMAN RIGHTS"

While engineering the most highly elaborated border controls ever, the global north remains dependent on the labor of border crossers for everything from agriculture to domestic service, restaurant and
hotel work, elder and childcare, amusement parks, food
processing, landscaping, logging, construction, sex work,
military work, and more. Because the demand for cheap
labor confronts the fortress mentality, many countries

in the global north have created complex, layered forms of "hierarchical integration"—policies that allow the entry of temporary migrants to perform certain economic functions while denying them basic rights of self-determination, democratic participation, and civil protections, just like South Africa's pass law system.[1] In fact, guest worker programs in the global north are modeled on South Africa's program inaugurated a century ago that imported Mozambican men to work on temporary limited contracts in white-owned mines, a model that by 1910 had become the basis of the pass system to regulate Black labor for the benefit of white employers.[2]

Temporary migrants are allowed to cross borders into countries in the global north through a dizzying array of work visa categories that carry different rights and protections and apply to different sectors of the economy and different countries of origin. Work visas for temporary workers, which are intended to ensure control over them, share a set of similar characteristics across the global north: most do not offer a pathway to citizenship but rather are short-term, controlled by employers (and sometimes by governments) but not workers, cancelable at any time, and designed to create a flexible, replaceable, disempowered, and disposable workforce that cannot make demands on the host country and will not challenge the cultural integrity of the host culture. The International Organization for Migration offers an admittedly conservative estimate that in 2013—the last year for which statistics are available—about two-thirds of the world's immigrants, or 150 million people, were international migrant workers, about 50 percent of whom worked in North America and Europe.[3] In many countries in the global north, the contained and controlled workforce of authorized guest workers is augmented by a much larger workforce of undocumented people who endure exploitation, racism, insecurity, and the persistent threat of deportation in order to perform jobs that citizens refuse to do for low pay.[4] This chapter sketches the basic outlines of temporary guest worker programs throughout the world, with a specific focus on those on the lower rungs of the labor market, from agricultural workers in North America to construction workers in the Gulf states to maids in Hong Kong. Their precarity and exploitation is exceeded only by the situation of undocumented workers, whose labor and taxes benefit host societies that, as with temporary guest workers, refuse to acknowledge their equality as workers or their rights to claim residence and belonging in the countries where they live and labor.

After emerging a century ago in South Africa (and in Prussia, which imported Poles), temporary foreign worker programs grew in popularity across the global north after the First and especially the Second World War as a way to balance employers' demands for seasonal labor with racist and xenophobic fears of immigrants in the context of emergent nationalist identities. As we have seen, governments across the global north introduced immigration restrictions in the late nineteenth and early twentieth centuries in order to orchestrate particular kinds of national identities, but the wartime and postwar demand for labor encouraged governments in the global north to creatively manage cross-border mobility in ways that benefited employers. During World War I France imported nonwhite workers to carry out the least desirable jobs, but, in contrast to their white immigrant colleagues, they were underpaid, required to carry passes, and expelled following the end of the war.[5] After World War II, Germany imported hundreds of thousands of guest workers, mostly from Turkey, with the mistaken idea that they would eventually return "home." Many Western European countries utilized guest worker programs from the end of the Second World War until the 1973–74 oil crisis and recession, when Germany, along with France, the UK, the Netherlands, and Switzerland, suspended their guest worker programs. Castles argues that the real reason for the suspension of temporary guest worker programs in 1973 was that guest workers were overstaying their visas, having families, fighting for democratic rights, joining unions, and creating alarmingly permanent communities of ethnic minorities.[6] For the next three decades these countries tried various measures, unsuccessfully, to encourage foreign immigrants to return to their countries of birth. Public rhetoric flourished about the dangers posed by internal foreigners, especially Muslims, to European cultural integrity and heritage—coded language embraced by politicians who wished to avoid speaking in the language of race because of associations with the Holocaust.[7]

Despite such concerns about the threats that brown and Muslim foreigners posed to European cultural integrity, by the early 2000s a renewed need for low-skilled labor for hotels, restaurants, and construction resuscitated interest in guest worker programs in Europe. These competing concerns led to new plans to fortify borders while building a highly monitored cyclical labor migration stream of deportable workers from the global south. Neo-nationalists who favored policies to protect the white working class and European cultural integrity came to an agreement with neoliberals who advocated the economic benefits of globalization on a strategy to once again allow cyclical migration into Europe of temporary foreign workers.[8] This compromise approach, utilized as well in the U.S., Canada, Australia, Russia, Malaysia, Japan, South Korea, Hong Kong, Taiwan, Singapore, Israel, and the Gulf states, satisfies almost everyone except the migrants themselves.[9] We will briefly review these different parts of the world to see why.

In the U.S., the agricultural labor shortage caused by World War II and the immigration exclusions applied to Chinese, Japanese, and Filipinos resulted in the creation of the country's first guest worker program, targeting Mexicans, in 1942. Since Mexican workers had just been subjected to a mass deportation of half a million people during the Great Depression, the Bracero program was designed to meet new short-term labor needs while still ensuring deportability. The program brought in almost 5 million Mexicans from 1942 to 1964 on visas controlled by their employers, but concerns about the large number of additional workers who came without documents and a recession in the early 1950s resulted in Operation Wetback, a second mass deportation of over 800,000 undocumented Mexican workers, in 1954 (which also included some people with U.S. citizenship).[10]

As the most ambitious guest worker program in U.S. history, the Bracero program reflected the desire of the U.S. government to import and deport workers at will, while subjecting workers to controls and regulations to limit their autonomy and ability to demand protections and rights. A form of "imported colonialism," the program offered no pathway to citizenship and denied workers New Deal protections and benefits while subjecting them to segregation, ensuring "that agribusiness would continue to have free rein over its workforce and that the South and Southwest would remain racialized, colonial-type backwaters of the nation."[11]

The H-2 guest worker visa inaugurated in the 1950s utilized the same strategy to bring workers from the Caribbean for short-term work on Florida sugar plantations. Created through bitter struggles over the exclusion of domestic workers, the design and implementation of the guest worker program specifically sought to break "African-American militancy" about worker rights and protections in the brutal conditions of Florida's sugar plantations.[12] The model—so desirable for employers—was expanded in later decades to include workers from other countries, as well as nonagricultural work, such as in hotels, restaurants, landscaping, seafood processing plants, and more.[13] H-2 visas are good for one year and are renewable for up to three years, drawing people primarily from Mexico, Jamaica, and Guatemala.

Temporary foreign worker programs have been lauded by multilateral organizations such as the IOM, World Bank, and UN as offering a win-win situation for countries in the global north facing labor shortages, and for countries in the global south in need of economic support, even though such programs ensure employer demand by limiting the rights of workers.[14] Canada's Seasonal Agricultural Worker Program (SAWP), in particular, was held up by the World Bank in 2006 as a desirable model for other countries because it includes more protections—although still quite limited—for temporary workers. The Canadian government contracts directly with governments in English-speaking Caribbean countries and Mexico to bring in over 25,000 workers to work all over Canada. Canada inaugurated its first SAWP after changing its race-based immigration law in 1962, which had excluded Black immigrants from Commonwealth Caribbean countries because of racism and fears about racial difference. Under pressure from growers who advocated for Caribbean workers after the success of the U.S. program, Jamaicans became the first to arrive. In an effort to reduce wages, the program was later expanded to include Mexico as well, ensuring that Mexico and Caribbean countries compete with each other to send workers, keeping wages low and putting a damper on the willingness of sending governments to complain about abuses or exploitation.

Home country governments select workers for the program, who are offered contracts to work for a minimum of forty hours a week at just above minimum wage for time periods that range from a minimum of six weeks to a maximum of eight months. They receive some support for their transport costs, rent-free employer-provided housing, health insurance, and the opportunity to pay into a pension plan from which they can draw funds at the end of their working life. Workers must pay employment insurance, which they are not eligible to collect, and they are forbidden from engaging in collective bargaining, switching employers during their contract, or requesting a different employer until after they have returned to Canada for three seasons with same employer. They can be fired at any time, following which they are immediately deported. End-of-season employer reports determine whether or not a worker will be accepted back into the program the following year, which means "extensive and relatively unchecked employer power undermines many contractual rights and guarantees, including the worker's right to refuse dangerous work or employer requests to labor overtime or on the weekend."[15]

Although the worker return rate of 70 percent might imply a high rate of worker satisfaction, anthropologist Leigh Binford, who followed workers from their homes in Tlaxcala, Mexico, to their short-term contracts in Ontario, suggests a far less rosy story. The men who leave Mexico to work in Canada have been pushed out of the Mexican economy by neoliberal restructurings that have entrenched poverty and limited opportunities at home, forcing men to search for temporary positions abroad. They endure racism, structural violence, and exploitation in Canada in order to ensure their ability to return because alternative economic options are so limited. While their remittances are critical for their families left behind, Binford defines their earnings as a "poverty regulation program, not a development program" for Mexico because remittances provide for subsistence needs but are not enough to stimulate economic development in Tlaxcala.[16]

This is an important observation, echoed by many other ethnographers who have followed migrant workers from their homes to their jobs abroad and back. Migrant workers from low- and middle-income countries remitted an estimated $529 billion in 2018, a figure three times the amount of official development assistance to those countries.[17] Remittances constitute a significant portion of the GDP of many low- and middle-income migrant-sending countries in the global south but are not sufficient to stimulate economic development or even to ensure life-enhancing sustainability in places ravaged by austerity policies, violence, climate change, or resource dispossession. Rather, migrant earnings are a new basic subsistence strategy for those squeezed by these forces, and indebted countries rely on migrant remittances to avoid social unrest over austerity and neoliberal reforms and to help service their debts, rather than to invest in development.

As "nations of emigrants," to borrow Susan Coutin's descriptive phrase, governments of the world's major sending countries operate as labor brokers for the global north.[18] The top sending country in Asia, the Philippines, has sent almost a million people abroad to work annually since 2000. Filipinos working abroad sent a collective total of $32.21 billion in remittances home in 2018, most of which came from migrants in the U.S., the Gulf countries, Japan, Canada, Germany, the UK, Singapore, and Hong Kong.[19] Other major sending countries, such as China and Indonesia, have established an interlocking array of regulatory policies, bureaucratic requirements, and private recruitment companies to manage the selection, training, and travel of migrant workers on guest worker contracts. This "migration infrastructure has turned migration into an object of intensive regulation, commodification and intervention, but has not necessarily enhanced people's migratory capability in terms of making independent decisions, exploring new paths, and cultivating transnational social relations," write Biao Xiang and Johan

Lindquist. Rather, their research shows how migrants from China and Indonesia are "escorted and encapsulated from the beginning until the end of the migration circuit" by the bureaucrats and labor brokers who manage their contracts.[20] By enacting a regulatory and commercial infrastructure to manage and control temporary migration under terms set by receiving countries, major sending government like the Philippines, Indonesia, China, Nepal, and El Salvador agree to take responsibility for reproducing a mobile labor force of workers in return for the benefits brought by their remittances. Migrant workers agree to a cyclical working life away from their families, in which they are offered limited agency, choice, or opportunities in their places of employment. Scholars call these arrangements a form of debt bondage, a neocolonial form of indentured labor.[21]

The toll on migrant workers of this global arrangement is unquestionably high. Dire reports by ethnographers and labor activists about the consequences for workers of the temporary visa programs in the U.S. and Canada's SAWP decry their injustices: workers have no pathway to citizenship, and because they are bound to the employers who control their visas, it is nearly impossible to challenge widespread wage theft, derelict housing, demands for overtime, abuse, confiscation of documents, retaliation, debt bondage, blacklisting, and denial of access to medical care.[22] Tracking the frustrating and humiliating attempts by his indigenous Triqui migrant farmworker interlocutors from Mexico to access health care in California and Washington for their work-related injuries, medical anthropologist Seth Holmes observes that "migrant and seasonal farmworkers suffer the poorest health status in the agriculture industry" and receive the fewest labor protections, due in part to the fact that migrant foreign farmworkers are prohibited from unionizing or collective bargaining. The Southern Poverty Law Center indicts guest worker programs as "a modern-day system of indentured servitude."[23] To add insult to injury, in many parts of the global north migrant workers are managed by independent labor brokers whose practices are left largely unregulated. Because labor brokers' fees can be exorbitant, many workers arrive so deeply indebted that they do not earn enough to repay their loans by the conclusion of their contract.[24]

Although some countries, such as the U.S., allow temporary guest workers to bring their spouses under a separate visa category, spouses are forbidden from working. The economics of working as a migrant laborer thus mean that most guest workers must live apart from their families during the duration of their contracts. Many countries do not allow guest workers to bring spouses, and no major immigrant-receiving countries have ratified the

United Nations' International Convention on the Protection of the Rights of All Migrant Workers and Members of Their Families, which requires recognition that migrant workers have a right to be with their families.[25] Separation from their families, and especially their children, leaves long-term scars. Research on the impact on the children left behind to be cared for by relatives of migrant workers reveals unquantifiable costs: emotional distress, resentments, feelings of abandonment, behavioral problems, and more.[26] Temporary guest worker programs harm families.

While the U.S., Germany, and Russia are the largest host countries for migrants, the countries most dependent on guest workers are the six states that make up the Gulf Cooperation Council countries—Bahrain, Kuwait, Oman, Qatar, Saudi Arabia, and the United Arab Emirates—where guest workers, primarily from India, Pakistan, Bangladesh, the Philippines, and Indonesia, make up between 50 percent and 90 percent of the population in each country. Guest workers arrive through the kefala (or kafala) system, which is an agreement between the state and employers to admit migrants, each of whom must be sponsored by a citizen. These petrostates ensure public-sector employment for all male citizens and then delegate to them control over migrants. Kefala visas are controlled by employers, do not grant workers protection by labor laws, forbid their involvement in labor unions, deny them a path toward citizenship, require celibacy of women guest workers, impose stringent rules about family reunification, and make it nearly impossible to protest abuse. The citizen controls the location, temporality, and status of the work permit and thus the worker's mobility, all within the laws set by the state.[27] Because of poor economies in their home countries and debt peonage to predatory labor recruiters, many workers move from contract to contract, cycling through different jobs and different countries over the course of their working lives.

While men migrate to the Gulf primarily for construction work, women migrate to the Gulf to perform domestic and care labor, earning them condemnation as bad mothers in their home countries and ensnaring them in stringent laws regulating their sexual lives in their countries of employment. Sociologist Rhacel Parreñas minces no words about the gendered, racialized work undertaken throughout the global north, most particularly in the Gulf countries, by Filipina and Indonesian women, who make up 70 percent of the emigrants from those two countries: "In various industrialized countries, a disproportionate number of women of color and immigrants staff hospitals, nursing homes, child-care centers, and private homes of affluent families as the rich increasingly rely on the poor to care for their families" while denying them the right to care for their own families, who are not allowed to join them.[28]

Women who break their contracts, either intentionally or through out-of-wedlock pregnancy, are levied high fines, criminalized, and deported. Anthropologist Pardis Mahdavi describes the painful plight of those who become pregnant, which brings a charge of unlawful conduct (the crime of *zina*), imprisonment, deportation, and blacklisting for reentry. Their children become stateless if the father fails to register paternity, if the mother holds citizenship in a country that recognizes citizenship only through the male line, or if the state where she is a temporary worker designates her as an unfit mother. In the latter cases, the babies are sent to local orphanages while the mothers are forcibly deported. The irony is stunning—women brought to the Gulf countries to work as caregivers are denied the right to their own children as unfit mothers.[29]

Because of the humiliation, abuse, and even death suffered by so many women from South and Southeast Asia in the Gulf states, Nepal, Bangladesh, India, and the Philippines have periodically enacted partial or full bans against their female citizens accepting guest worker jobs in the Gulf states. Rather than stemming their migration, however, such prohibitions seem to have simply shifted migration strategies from traveling on legal contracts as exploitable guest workers to illicit journeys as even more exploitable undocumented migrants.

The newest countries to join the global migratory networks are Hong Kong, Taiwan, Singapore, South Korea, and Malaysia, which began importing foreign domestic and entertainment workers on a significant scale between the 1970s and the 1990s, mostly from the Philippines and Indonesia. Their numbers continue to grow.[30] Migrant care workers in these countries face a set of constraints similar to those listed above. Although specifics vary across countries, they generally work on employer-controlled contracts with no pathway to citizenship; are prohibited from bringing their families, forming unions, or receiving government benefits like retirement or other forms of welfare support; have no vacation time, no protection against overtime, and no guaranteed days off (except in Hong Kong, which mandates one day off a week); are excluded from minimum wage laws that protect citizens; can be deported at any time; undergo mandatory HIV and STD tests for sex workers (who, if they test positive for HIV in South Korea, are not treated but immediately deported); and are prohibited from becoming pregnant (domestic workers in Singapore, Taiwan, and Malaysia must submit to regular pregnancy tests). Most domestic servants are required to live in their employer's home and work six or seven days a week for less than minimum wage on two- or three-year contracts, at the conclusion of which they must repatriate immediately before beginning a new contract. Many Filipina and Indonesian women take out huge loans to gain a contract overseas, paying enormous fees to the recruitment agencies mandated by their home governments for managing foreign domestic worker migration. As is the case elsewhere in the world, workers who overstay their contracts become illegal, although in Hong Kong a worker can apply for asylum on the basis of a torture claim, which allows her to stay in Hong Kong—although she is forbidden to work—until her claim is adjudicated.

Nicole Constable, who has studied the experiences of Filipina and Indonesian domestic workers in Hong Kong for decades, describes the training programs to which such workers are subjected, which teach them to be docile, obedient, hygienic, not too beautiful or too dark, and expressively grateful for the opportunity to live and work in Hong Kong. The opportunity to work as a maid in Hong Kong is promoted almost as a form of charity, she explains, which positions migrant workers not as professionals but as charity cases who should feel grateful to be given jobs, even low-paid, low-status, grueling jobs.[31] Calling the "logic of incarceration" that structures the working and personal lives of domestic servants in Singapore, Hong Kong, and Malaysia a form of "neo-slavery," Aiwha Ong argues that their treatment directly reflects the particular convergence of neoliberalism and ethnonationalism in East Asia: "The neo-slavery of migrant women emerges out of a postcolonial intersection of racialized nationalism, neoliberal strategies, and disjunctive moral economies based on kinship and ethnicity."[32]

Filipina and Indonesian maids fill a racialized role that visibly marks the upward mobility of the middle classes in these countries, and even countries with greater hostility to immigrants such as Japan are joining the trend. Japan's number of foreign workers swelled to nearly 1.3 million in 2018, and Parliament approved an additional quarter million visas for unskilled guest workers for 2019 who will be subject to rules very similar to those outlined above.[33]

In all countries where they are used, guest worker programs enable the importation and expulsion of people in response to economic fluctuations, political currents, and security panics. Just as with the periodic deportation frenzies of Mexican workers in the U.S., Malaysia, Singapore, and Hong Kong deported nearly 900,000 migrant workers during the 1997–98 economic downturn.[34] Gulf states expelled Yemeni, Jordanian, and Palestinian workers after their home countries supported Iraq in the 1991 Gulf War, and after the First Intifada Israel replaced Palestinian workers who commuted from the Occupied Territories with imported workers from Thailand, Turkey, China, and the Philippines. Israel's importation of 200,000 workers during the 1990s became 10–12 percent of the labor force, although the new wave of migrant workers lacked access to benefits and protections and were targeted by mass deportations in 2002–4 and again in 2012 in response to an economic downturn and a political campaign that promoted the deportations as a security measure to protect Israel's Jewish character.[35] Legal protections for migrant workers developed slowly in Israel, related to cases fought in court by NGOs advocating for health care access and due process during deportation, protections against police brutality, and anti-trafficking laws. When a domestic migrant worker sued for the right to access medical care in Israel for a serious medical condition after seven years of employment, the government instituted a new law stating that migrant workers can never be considered residents for purposes of social security benefits.[36] Additional limitations were enacted to curtail the ability of migrant workers to establish themselves in Israel, such as the requirement that migrant workers permanently remove their babies from Israel when a mother's visa expires; the requirement that if guest workers marry, one member of the couple must leave Israel; and the prohibition against two family members receiving simultaneous guest worker visas. The "exclusionary and oppressive effects" of the legal regime governing migrant workers is multiplied by abusive racial profiling practices during the periodic deportation campaigns, ensuring that migrant workers are persistently and only recognized as temporary and expendable foreigners.[37]

In addition to the legal vulnerability of foreign migrant workers in Israel, the work permits required of Palestinians living in the West Bank create vulnerability of a different sort. Because the forms of containment enacted across the West Bank by Israel have so damaged the economy, many Palestinians depend on receiving permits to work in Israel. But the permitting regime is used by the Israeli security agency Shin Bet as a bargaining chip to force their security priorities on Palestinians. Shin Bet identified almost a quarter million Palestinians in 2006 as security threats, which prohibits them from receiving work permits. Israeli lawyer Yael Berda, who worked through hundreds of cases to try to figure out how security threats are assessed, realized that "security threat" is a flexible category created through a secretive process from a compilation of different kinds of information that become relevant in different ways in different contexts and at different times, depending on who is doing the assessing. To get a permit or to have a security restriction lifted, Shin Bet often demands Palestinians become informants, using the permit system to grow its security apparatus.[38] Work permit regimes not only open workers to state surveillance, but through demands for loyalty and information make them vulnerable to exploitation by state authorities as well as employers.

OUTSOURCING WAR

Temporary foreign worker programs also offer a new opportunity for wealthy countries in the global north to pursue international geopolitical desires through violence but without overly endangering their own citizens. Countries such as the United States and Saudi Arabia are outsourcing their wars by employing temporary migrant workers for everything from frontline battle to provisioning in regions where they are pursuing military interventions. The U.S. occupation of Iraq depends on the daily labor of thousands of migrant workers brought from the Philippines, Pakistan, India, Nigeria, Kenya, and Sierra Leone—a dependence on private military contractors and temporary guest workers in a war zone on a scale never before seen. In fact, the employment of third-country nationals (TCNS) at CENTCOM bases is far greater than that of U.S. citizens, and they often outnumber U.S. citizen and local contractors combined.[39] In high-risk security jobs in the U.S. military occupation in Iraq, they have at times outnumbered U.S. citizens by a ratio of ten to one.[40]

Recruited by private military contractors hired by the U.S. to staff the military occupations in Iraq, Afghanistan, and other CENTCOM bases, TCN migrant workers from the global south receive contracts with substantially different benefits and rewards than their American counterparts, who earn vastly greater salaries for doing the exact same jobs. Lawyer-anthropologist Darryl Li reports that "a 2012 study by the ACLU estimated that TCN janitors make around $275 per month; waiters $300 per month; cooks $500 per month; and chefs $1,000 per month. Armed security guards from Uganda made around $400–$500 per month in 2011. In contrast, the monthly basic wage for the lowest enlisted rank in the U.S. military is $1,531.50 per month."[41] Contract workers from the global south are denied the right to organize or protest abusive treatment, are excluded from most protections in U.S. labor law, and often receive less pay than promised and no overtime pay, limited support for work-related injuries, and no benefits other than low family benefits if they are killed, while enduring extremely harsh and dangerous work conditions. Sociologist Kevin Thomas, who conducted fieldwork with contract workers from Sierra Leone who worked in Iraq for the U.S. occupation, joins Li in highlighting the questionable ethics of outsourcing risk to migrant workers in a situation where private military contractors can successfully exploit wage inequalities to recruit migrants from poor countries for life-threatening jobs in military occupations perpetrated by wealthy countries.[42]

Another disturbing story is emerging from Yemen, where Saudi Arabia is pursuing a vicious war financed by its vast oil wealth but fought by mercenaries, including tens of thousands of survivors of the wars in Darfur, Sudan. An estimated 20–40 percent of the Sudanese mercenaries employed by Saudi Arabia in Yemen are under the age of seventeen. According to a *New York Times* report, they face great pressure from their families to enlist; a mercenary's monthly salary is greater than that of a Sudanese doctor working multiple jobs and overtime in Sudan.[43]

These reports conjure images of a world in which the young men of societies in the global south emerging from civil wars are targeted as war workers for wealthy countries in the global north—as mobile military labor whose value to the world is their willingness to risk their lives in the wars of others for a minimal wage. Whereas countries like the Philippines and Indonesia understand that their comparative advantage in the world economy might be their export of female domestic workers, other cash-strapped governments might be encouraged to see the marketing potential of their former child soldiers as war mercenaries. This new reality brings an even more chilling dimension to the language of disposability that analysts use to talk about the treatment of the poor in the global south by power brokers in the global north.

THE UNDOCUMENTED

The cyclical migration of temporary guest workers who travel on contracts is augmented by workers who lack authorization documents, either because they overstayed their visas or because they crossed a border without detection. Nondemocratic states, like in those in the Gulf, can import huge numbers of guest workers on visas while enforcing restrictions on their rights and making "draconian use of deportation," but democratic countries such as the U.S. and Japan prefer to tolerate high levels of undocumented workers instead because of the possibility that documented workers will use democratic ideologies and institutions to fight for expanded rights and pathways to citizenship.[44]

The numbers are very high, indeed. One in four foreign-born persons in the U.S. is unauthorized, totaling over 11 million people in recent years.[45] Mexicans make up 58 percent of those undocumented in the U.S., many of whom work in agriculture, where Mexicans constitute 94 percent of the workforce, half of whom are unauthorized.[46] Gomberg-Muñoz puts the labor force participation of undocumented men in the U.S. at 94 percent.[47] Visas for nonagricultural short-term jobs are capped far below demand, and, while visas for agricultural workers are not capped, many employers choose to hire undocumented workers rather than confront the bureaucracy required to apply for legal papers for the workers they seek to import.[48] Undocumented people earn less and pay taxes, but are barred from accessing any public services except public education and emergency medical care, have less job security and more dangerous jobs, have greater financial insecurities, cannot complain about poor work conditions or abuses in the workplace, and have no opportunities for upward mobility. As the penalties for being undocumented continue to expand and become more punitive, the opportunities to legalize their status are increasingly narrowed. As a result, undocumented workers in the U.S. are in effect imprisoned because the barriers to their ability to cross borders have become so great. Gomberg-Muñoz, who has conducted several extensive studies of undocumented Mexican migrants in the U.S., writes: "The current employment visa system does not seem to prevent the migration of low-paid workers so much as it keeps workers in low-paying positions by foreclosing their possibilities for legal immigration and any opportunities for upward mobility that legality affords." Their situation is "precarity as policy."[49]

The implications of such a large undocumented workforce extend throughout society, as an estimated 16.6 million people in the U.S. live in mixed-status families, where undocumented workers are dependent on their documented spouses for things like driving and bank accounts, and where families face the daily fear of being torn apart by discovery and deportation.[50] Anthropologist Deborah Boehm uses the phrase "contingent citizenship" to describe those who hold U.S. citizenship but whose families include documented and undocumented members, U.S. citizen children forced to return to Mexico with deported parents, and U.S. citizen children sent to live with relatives in Mexico by their undocumented parents in the U.S. who fear deportation. For Boehm, this category is shared by those who are U.S. citizens marginalized through racism and those who lack legal papers but work and pay taxes.[51]

As with South Africa's periodic efforts to erase squatter settlements formed by Black people whose presence in white cities was illegal, deportation raids in American communities ensure that the undocumented and their families feel constantly under threat. And in a Machiavellian irony, across the U.S. immigrants held in detention centers awaiting trial and possible deportation are used as cheap labor. Through the deportation regime, their underpaid labor as undocumented workers can be devalued even further when they become prisoners. Some people who work while jailed receive only credits toward toiletries and food in return, while others earn about thirteen cents an hour, a pay rate put in place for prisoners in 1950 and unchanged since then for immigrant detainees. During 2013, according to the *New York Times*, somewhere between 60,000 and 135,000 immigrants "worked in the federal government's nationwide patchwork of detention centers—more than worked for any other single employer in the country." The irony is not lost on incarcerated workers, one of whom told the *New York Times*, "I went from making $15 an hour as a chef to $1 a day in the kitchen in lockup." These are not people convicted of a crime—they are civil detainees awaiting a judge's determination of their legal status.[52] And the incarceration industry profits from their labor.

China is often figured as one of the world's largest exporters of unauthorized migrants, and yet there are parallel practices within China to those described above. In China, the mobility of rural people is tightly controlled through a guest worker system that allows people to move outside their area of residence for certain kinds of jobs under certain kinds of circumstances. Agreeing to insecure labor contracts, about 40 million rural Chinese laborers migrate to Chinese cities each year, where they are not allowed to gain legal residency rights.[53] Because of China's restrictive *hukou* system, which distinguishes rural from urban zones and requires people to work where they are registered to live, labor contractors usually broker employment opportunities in urban areas for rural workers, and abuse of workers is rampant: Alexander and Chan call the Chinese guest worker system a "quasi-apartheid pass system."[54] Guest workers kept in isolated and exploited conditions work on urban construction projects, but they and other workers also labor in factories where they produce goods for the global north, embodying a sort of local containment that may represent the far extreme of global apartheid. The corollary in the U.S. may be the private for-profit prison industry described above, which utilizes an overabundance of incarcerated minorities as exploitable workers, or the use of prisoners in detention centers to produce goods very cheaply. In these situations, workers are literally incarcerated profit-producers for those who control the terms of their incarceration and the commodities they produce.

The resonance with South Africa's apartheid-era pass laws is evident. Neoliberal restructurings, plunder, and wars across the global south perpetrated through global geopolitical agendas pursued by powerful countries in the global north force people to migrate to make a living. In addition to hardening, thickening, and externalizing borders, the global north is profiting from these displacements by creating a system of labor control that depends on importing people from regions that have been made unsustainable for human life and ensuring their exploitability in the global north, whether as temporary contract workers, undocumented workers, or detained and imprisoned workers. Exploitability has been easily enacted by criminalizing the presence of those who lack documents, ensuring the deportability of imported workers, giving employers sole control of temporary migrant worker contracts, and refusing to extend the same protections and rights to guest workers that citizens enjoy. Migrant workers come from a huge cross-section of the global south, ranging from poor, landless former peasants in Guatemala and Honduras to college-educated teachers and nurses in the Philippines who can earn more as a maid in Hong Kong than in their profession at home. The poorest migrants may go deeply into debt in order to make the journey, while others may be accepted into government-to-government programs that cover most of their costs, but across the board the labor structure simultaneously ensures that temporary foreign workers submit to racialized hierarchies that put them on the bottom and deny them rights and recognition as members of the national body in the country where they work, often for their entire working lives.

In short, the current approach to migrant labor in the global north intentionally creates an exploitable racialized underclass. Ethnographers writing about the experiences of those in the global north who hold guest worker and undocumented status document the racialized hierarchies of belonging, rights, and human value created and reinforced by the migration apparatus. Holmes writes of the symbolic violence inherent in the normalization of racism and discrimination directed at Mexican immigrant farmworkers in the U.S. and the structural violence of a system of profound inequality through which people are forced to leave their homes to become exploitable workers whose bodies are broken down by grueling work while their families bear the emotional burden of separation and the economic burden of reproduction. A strict "ethnicity–citizenship hierarchy" operates on farms that employ migrant workers in the U.S. West, where Mexicans of Indian descent occupy the lowest status and most poorly paid positions, subservient even to unskilled local white high school students. In the U.S. Southeast, the dilapidated housing of racialized immigrant farmworkers is used to justify their low-status jobs and the humiliating and degrading treatment directed toward them by farm administrators.[55] Gomberg-Muñoz writes of the rigid restaurant hierarchies in the U.S. that consign Mexicans to the back of the house as busboys and dishwashers while white employees work the front of the house. Likening the current treatment of Mexican migrants to the Jim Crow era, Brennan observes, "This widespread abuse of migrants—both documented and undocumented—often in communities with long histories of racial discrimination, has prompted labor organizers and civil rights leaders to refer to life in certain counties and states [in the U.S.] as life under 'Juan Crow.'"[56] Researchers working in Europe, East Asia, Canada, Israel, and the Gulf states similarly reveal the racialized hierarchies that define and subjugate guest and undocumented immigrant workers, as described here and in previous chapters. Employers throughout the global north racialize jobs through stereotypes that naturalize the connection between certain racial/national groups and certain jobs: fruit trees and workers from the Caribbean in Canada, Mexicans and ground crops in the U.S. and Canada, Filipinas and domestic service in Hong Kong, and so forth. Writing about domestic servants who are migrant workers in the UK, Bridget Anderson finds resonances with Aristotle's discussion of slavery: "Conquest in global economic terms makes contemporary legal slaves of the poor of the Third World, giving the middle class of the First World materialistic forms of power over them. Racism also continues to make of certain people 'natural slaves,' however, regarding them as suited by nature to subjugation and labor. This is particularly true of domestic work."[57]

This chapter has deliberately focused on the hierarchies, structures, regimes, infrastructures, bureaucracies, and regulations that create and maintain a disposable labor force from the global south for the benefit of the global north. In closing, it is perhaps important to emphasize, again, that guest workers and undocumented workers are not simply passive victims of a grand global apartheid scheme to control their labor. Migrant workers exercise agency in making choices about whether or not to accept guest worker contracts, to overstay their visas, or to cross a border without authorization. And they do so for all sorts of reasons, which can vary from pressing economic needs and family pressures to a personal search for adventure, travel, greater freedoms, or greater access to material comforts. But agency is not the same as freedom, and migrant workers are not free in the same ways that citizens are free. The point of this chapter has been to argue that the policies that differentiate guest workers and undocumented workers from citizens intentionally create hierarchies of differentiated rights, protections, and benefits that serve the interests of those in the global north at the expense of those in the global south, that this hierarchy is intentionally racialized, that it harms people and their families, and that it is wrong.

CHAPTER FIVE

MILITARIZATION

We are bringing the battlefield to the border. —AN ENTHU-
SIASTIC SECURITY TECHNOLOGY PURVEYOR TO JOURNAL-
IST TODD MILLER AT THE 2012 BORDER SECURITY EXPO IN
PHOENIX, "FORTRESS USA: THE WILD WORLD OF BORDER
SECURITY AND BOUNDARY BUILDING IN ARIZONA"

The previous chapters have charted the processes
through which the global north has racialized the
world; contributed to dispossession in the global
south through plunder and military incursions; created mechanisms to contain the dispossessed, displaced,
and undesirable mobile such as refugee camps, offshore
holding facilities, detention centers, and prisons; criminalized mobility unauthorized by state permitting regimes; and developed programs and policies to manage
the controlled mobility of people for the purpose of ex-
ploiting their labor. Here, we turn our attention to the final
pillar of apartheid: the militarized security apparatus built
to maintain racialized hierarchies of labor and mobility.

Cathy Lutz offers a particularly useful definition of militarization:

This process involves an intensification of the labor and resources allocated to military purposes, including the shaping of other institutions in synchrony with military goals. Militarization is simultaneously a discursive process, involving a shift in general societal beliefs and values in ways necessary to legitimate the use of force, the organization of large standing armies and their leaders, and the higher taxes or tribute used to pay for them. Militarization is intimately connected not only to the obvious increase in the size of armies and resurgence of militant nationalisms and militant fundamentalisms but also to the less visible deformation of human potentials into the hierarchies of race, class, gender, and sexuality, and to the shaping of national histories in ways that glorify and legitimate military action.[1]

Militarization in the interests of global apartheid manifests itself in various ways, including:

- the spectacularized performance and production of border security through walls and marine cordons;
- technologies of surveillance, identification, and risk assessment in the form of "smart borders" that track the mobile and link mobility, criminality, and terrorism into a trifecta security risk of such proportions that militarized responses against risky people both external to the state and within the state are normalized and valorized;
- the redirection of national spending toward military enhancements in the name of securitizing against mobility-criminality-terrorism, which feeds the growth of industries of militarization, from prisons to weapons to surveillance technologies;
- the transmogrification of sovereignty into a form of security imperialism.

The result, argued throughout this book, is a shape-shifting ethical register of necropolitics, or the acceptance, through the rhetoric of war, that the state can and should target people for death by drowning, desiccation in the desert, untreated illness in migrant camps and offshore holding facilities, and deportation to places where they are likely to be killed.

South Africa's apartheid system depended on the profound militarization of South African society, expressed through things such as a police force that doubled in size from 1985 to 1990, military and police cordons around and constant patrols and actions in urban Black communities, an expanding carceral industry to imprison people whose mobility was criminalized and whose anti-apartheid activities got them labeled as terrorists, a compulsory conscription policy that drew 600,000 white men into military service in apartheid's final year alone, and a budget that grew from 3.2 percent of total government expenditures in the 1960s to over 18 percent by the late 1970s.[2] South African police and defense forces worked together to combat internal opposition to the apartheid government while also engaging in military activity in Namibia, Botswana, Angola, and Mozambique in support of the apartheid government's pronounced anti-terrorism objectives in those countries. Characterizing challenges to apartheid rule by the African National Congress (ANC) and other groups as a "total onslaught," the apartheid government promoted the patriotic call to duty and the absolute necessity of extreme military measures as part of its "total strategy" to protect the state against the purported threats of communism and terrorism embodied by the ANC and its anti-apartheid collaborators and supporters. "Total strategy was, at one level, a program of counterinsurgency that sought to bring security concerns to bear on all aspects of life and entailed the heavy militarization of ever-increasing spheres of society and state."[3]

The militarization of borders and the use of incarceration and surveillance to control mobility and contain people defined as risky across the global north follows these apartheid logics, but I will also argue that the contemporary global securitization of space is expanding these logics into new forms of imperialism. Security imperialism is emerging from and shoring up global militarized apartheid—imperialism based in the identification and containment of "risky" bodies throughout the globe in concert with the expansion of securitized spaces produced through material, affective, and ontological expressions of militarism by security states of the global north. Whereas apartheid South Africa focused its militarized security goals against internal dissenters and their regional collaborators, these emergent imperial formations are spatial and technological rather than territorial, taking shape through global imperial projects that not only extract resources but also racialize and incarcerate people domestically and across borders. These projects engage carceral logics to secure cosmopolitan class privilege and capitalist extraction while tethering the concept of security to militarization.

We begin with walls.

"I will build a great, great wall on our southern border and I will have Mexico pay for that wall, mark my words." A rising global obsession with walls—marked here in Donald Trump's June 16, 2015, speech announcing his presidential campaign—is perhaps the most obvious and clunky expression of an upsurge in anti-immigrant militarization. Trump's obsession with building a wall along the U.S.-Mexico border brought the U.S. government to a historic thirty-five-day shutdown that ended when he retreated from his demand for congressional approval of $6 billion for the wall (although just a few months later the U.S. Supreme Court gave him the right to redirect billions of dollars from other military purposes for wall construction). President Trump admiringly acknowledged Israel as his model: "They were having a total disaster coming across and they had a wall. It's 99.9 percent stoppage," he claimed.[4] As the *New York Times* and other media outlets noted, no one seemed to know which wall in Israel Trump was referring to, but such details don't really matter. The specter of a wall offers such a potent symbolic icon of nationalism, security, and sovereignty that many governments around the world are turning to walls as a performative symbol of their sovereignty and determination to protect the nation from invading immigrants who are, as we have seen, increasingly prefigured as criminals. Israel's wall-building sets the technological and performative standard—snaking throughout and around the country to separate Palestinians and keep out Africans—but border walls built or under construction are stretching throughout the EU, at the borders of Turkey (against Syria and Iran), and elsewhere.

Post–Cold War border walls in the EU began with Spain's border walls in the North African enclaves of Ceuta and Melilla in the 1990s, and since then have grown in explicit reaction against immigration. Fourteen walls to stop immigrants, covering almost a thousand kilometers, have been built by EU countries, as well as Norway and Macedonia, since 2012.[5] Interrupting migration along the Balkan route motivated the first group of walls built by Greece, Bulgaria, Hungary, Macedonia, Austria, Slovenia, and Serbia in 2015, followed by Norway's wall in 2016 as migratory routes shifted north in response. As migratory routes continue to shift, Poland and the Baltic republics have indicated their intentions to fortify their borders with walls. Walls are extremely expensive and require dedicated militarized patrols and equipment, which means states must direct significant resources toward their construction, maintenance, and patrolling.

In addition to building walls, the EU has replaced humanitarian rescue operations in the Mediterranean and the Atlantic with militarized interventions to repel migrants in an effort to create marine walls across the sea, as we saw in chapter 3. The most recent maritime operation, the EU Naval Force's Operation Sophia, partners with NATO patrols to challenge and destroy migrant smuggling networks in the central Mediterranean. With a mission to capture and return migrants to non-EU countries, it is explicitly not a rescue operation but rather a military assault against those who assist migrants to cross the sea.[6] Maritime walls erected by militarized marine patrols complement land walls in an effort to ensure complete control over mobility into the EU and Schengen areas.[7]

In the United States, material repurposed from the Vietnam and Gulf Wars became early parts of a border wall with Mexico in the 1990s. Worried that the effects of NAFTA would prompt large-scale migration, the Clinton administration also invested in new border surveillance technologies, including "infrared night scopes, thermal-imaging devices, motion detectors, in-ground sensors, and software that allowed biometric scanning of all apprehended migrants," as well as stadium lights that shone into Tijuana.[8] In a first for the military, legislative reforms in the 1990s linked to the war on drugs allowed the military to join local police and the Border Patrol to provide training, equipment, technology, border surveillance, and intelligence, and even to deploy ground troops.[9] The mid-1990s marked the first time that unauthorized immigrants were defined as a national security threat by the Pentagon and the first time that the U.S. president (Clinton at the time) publicly announced that the U.S. military would be engaged in immigration control enforcement at the border.[10] Leading military contractors such as Raytheon, Lockheed Martin, and Northrop Grumman were invited to design border control technologies for the southern U.S. border based on military technologies they had developed for the U.S. military's invasions and occupations in Iraq and Afghanistan.[11] Additional augmentation arrived with the 2006 Secure Fence Act, which directed billions of dollars to buy "drones, a 'virtual wall,' aerostat blimps, radar, helicopters, watchtowers, surveillance balloons, razor ribbon, landfill to block canyons, border berms, adjustable barriers to compensate for shifting dunes, and a lab . . . to test fence prototypes."[12] In subsequent years, thousands of National Guard troops have been deployed to the border, along with military units that provide intelligence and training in military technologies.

As is the case in other border zones with militarized walls, the effect of border militarization on the U.S.-Mexico border, in concert with the

Constitution-free zone stretching inland a hundred miles from the border, is a de facto military occupation where policing has shifted from community-oriented to militaristic; where militarized language and behavior are now the norm for local police and Border Patrol agents; where military tactics like raids, interrogations, and extensive surveillance techniques are routinely employed; where military training to identify specific targets translates to racial profiling to catch those suspected of lacking documents; where militarized operations are conducted in secret without public review; and where civil rights do not need to be observed.[13] The Constitution-free zone has become "an intensely controlled border zone buzzing with armed authorities openly patrolling strip malls, flea markets, residential areas, train stations and bus depots—to the degree that many in the borderlands, from federal magistrates to grassroots activists, have compared what they experience to a military occupation."[14] The vision of the border as a war zone has also been promoted by Fox News, which for years used the title "America's Third War" in stories about the U.S.-Mexico border.[15]

The U.S. military is not only engaging with immigration enforcement at the southern U.S. land border; it also partners every other year with the Coast Guard, Homeland Security, and Customs and Border Protection to run mock exercises in the Caribbean on confronting and pushing back a hypothetical mass migration. Mindful of the impact of the Haitian earthquake on migration and the likely effects of climate change on Caribbean islands in the near future, Operation Vigilant Sentry is a "mass-migration contingency plan" to interrupt, detain, and return people attempting to migrate by sea.[16] The U.S. military's forward-thinking approach to climate change is preparedness for quickly enacting a militarized maritime cordon against mass migrations.

Calling Arizona ground zero for testing all kinds of new border enforcement technologies and policies, journalist Todd Miller writes, "As Arizona defines the line of scrimmage for U.S. border security strategy, it is also preparing the way to export its products of social control not only abroad, but also to your hometown, or to wherever a boundary needs to be built between the rich and the poor."[17] What is happening at the southern U.S. border suggests one direction in which the securitization of "the homeland" is going—one in which walls and militarized spaces become the new normal throughout the country, evidenced in everything from the proliferation of gated communities to military-style raids on workplaces suspected of employing undocumented migrants to armed ICE authorities patrolling highways, checkpoints, and public transport centers to interrogate passengers. Gated communities now make up 10 percent of new housing stock in the U.S., their designs copied around the world as their manufacturers market American-style ideas of domestic security.[18] The U.S. and Israel share designs, technology, and subcontractors, as well as mutually reinforcing justifications for their militarized border walls.[19] Israeli border security companies are developing remote-controlled weaponry— "robo-snipers"—a new technology to be used against Palestinian communities, soon to be followed by the arrival on technology markets of automated machine guns and grenade launchers. Elbit Systems, an Israeli security company, is developing an automated wall with surveillance towers that can "see" for up to seven miles and coordinate with each other and with drones and motion sensors.[20]

Other countries eager to join the turn toward militarized security invite industry leaders to show them the newest innovations in homeland security. U.S. Customs and Border Protection has carried out trainings on border management and control in over a hundred countries, and security companies hold huge expos where people from around the world can come to see the newest products.[21] The potential for accretive border militarization seems unlimited. India has been particularly busy, building a wall over three thousand kilometers long on its border with Bangladesh, to complement another along its border with Pakistan, a wall across Kashmir, and a planned new wall across its border with Myanmar. The wall on the border with Bangladesh, with which India has long had peaceful and cordial relations, is just one expression of India's enthusiastic embrace of Islamophobic anti-immigrant discourses and policies so ascendant in the global war on terror.[22] India is home to 15 million Bangladeshi migrants, and yet Indian border patrols have shoot-to-kill orders at the wall with Bangladesh, which has resulted in over a thousand deaths between 2000 and 2015, only one of which was ever prosecuted.[23] Anti-immigrant "counterterror" border walls have been erected by Saudi Arabia (against Yemen and Iraq), by the United Arab Emirates (against Oman), by Uzbekistan (against Kyrgyzstan and Afghanistan), and by Turkmenistan (against Uzbekistan).[24] Justified in language that tilts toward a concern with "criminality," anti-immigrant border walls are now under construction or discussion across Latin America: in Argentina (against Bolivians), Belize (against Guatemalans), Costa Rica (against Nicaraguans), Mexico (against Central Americans), and Chile (against Peruvians). The tools and technologies of the security empires built by the global north to control mobility spark iterations across the global south, and walls become a tool of difference-making and hierarchy.

And yet, despite their razor wire, bricks, concrete, metal, electrification, spotlights, fortification technologies, surveillance technologies, robo-snipers, automated weaponry, and ships, land and sea walls have not actually been all that effective at keeping out the mobile. Tunnels, ladders, boats, planes, holes in the fence, and sympathetic or corrupt guards still let people pass, and smugglers are fabulously creative at finding ways to move their products through, over, and under walls.[25] Until very recently, the vast majority of immigrants who attempted to cross the U.S. border without documents have been successful, leading some commentators to suggest that the militarized performance of border security is intended to appease white racism and discipline brown migrants, drawing a clearly demonstrated "line of exclusion, guaranteeing eternal inequality between those who have and those who do not," while also ensuring a steady supply of exploitable labor.[26] The militarized border has thus operated like a spectacularly costly form of hazing that makes visible a "merciless logic of disposability" that stops some and kills some while forcing those who get across successfully to endure painful, wrenching, humiliating journeys that demonstrate with utter clarity that the global north sees them as replaceable, exploitable, abusable, and forgettable.[27]

Because walls are only partially effective, and the appetite in the global north for ever-enhanced security measures seems only to be growing, security technology companies are creating all sorts of devices that will expand material boundaries into surveillance systems that not only track border crossers but also enable the identification and containment of risky bodies long before they have even reached the border. Such technologies of identification and risk assessment extend to those already living within the border walls as well, targeting internal populations for extra monitoring and control. The surveillance society is the new normal.

SMART BORDERS

Shortly after 9/11, the U.S. began requiring airlines to submit passenger lists in advance and include biometric information in the documents of foreign nationals seeking entry. The consultancy firm Accenture was hired to design a virtual border that could identify, track, and assess the riskiness of travelers and migrants using "smart" technology. Accenture and its consortium of security firms known as the Smart Border Alliance launched the US-VISIT (U.S. Visitor and Immigration Status Indicator Technology) program in 2004 to assess the risk of all travelers to the U.S. With these requirements emplaced by the U.S., smart border technologies quickly began proliferating across the global north, making the collection and analysis of biometric data the current global standard for securitizing mobility. Smart borders utilize biometrics, surveillance, data mining, and algorithms, much of which is collected and processed in secret, to create risk profiles for travelers. Such technology is eminently adaptable, shareable, and transferable, which means that security technologies designed in one location for one vision of securitization can be adopted in other locations in ways responsive to the particular imaginings of risk that are ascendant there.[28] Because such technologies collect and store biological and physiological information—everything from fingerprints to DNA to iris and retinal scans to facial and gait recognition—their deployment can be particularly attuned to social constructions of race that target certain characteristics to identify travelers subjected to extra surveillance. The U.S. allows border security technology and officials to employ racial profiling in assessments of risk, and, under President Obama, even expanded "the definition of racial profiling to include religion, national origin, gender, sexual orientation and gender identity."[29]

It is perhaps not surprising that state use of biometrics—"the identification of people by machines" through the automated collection of biological and physiological information—originated in the early twentieth century in South Africa by British colonial authorities eager to segregate and control the mobility of indentured Asian workers through creating an Asiatic registry of fingerprints.[30] South African colonial authorities saw biometric registries "as the lynchpin of a segregated state," useful for taxing, deporting, fining, and imprisoning subject populations whose movements and business practices defied state desires.[31] Gandhi, when launching his resistance movement against the mandatory fingerprinting of Indians in South Africa, saw it as tool of humiliation. South Africa's innovative use of biometrics gives it "a special place as a twentieth-century laboratory of empire, for the technologies of racial segregation and . . . the marriage of bureaucracy and despotism."[32]

The contemporary use of biometrics to segregate, control, and humiliate subject populations also hearkens back to the historic practices of surveillance of Black people in the U.S. through the "one-drop rule, quantitative plantation records that listed enslaved people alongside livestock and crops, slave passes, slave patrols, and runaway notices," as well as the branding of enslaved people, lantern laws in eighteenth-century New York City requiring Black people to carry candle lanterns after dark to ensure their identifiability, and the British colonial *Book of Negroes* that recorded data on Black people leaving the post-revolutionary U.S. for Canada on British vessels. Simone Browne calls the *Book of Negroes* "the first government-issued document for state-regulated migration between the United States and Canada that explicitly linked corporeal markers to the right to travel."[33]

The use of biometrics as a technology of identification for the purpose of segregation, surveillance, and containment is now practiced across the global north. Accenture's subcontractor Raytheon designed the UK's e-Border program. The EU's Smart Borders program continues to grow, currently including the Second Generation Schengen Information System (SIS II), which enables data sharing among police, national border control, and customs in the Schengen area; Eurodac, which is a fingerprint registry of all asylum seekers used to track and catch "asylum-shoppers"; the Visa Information System (VIS), which links EU countries and their consulates in non-EU countries to a centralized infotech processing center for sharing biometric data about travelers; and EUROSUR, which links these databases to Frontex. Similar logics power Australia's Advanced Passenger Processing programs, and inform the Smart Border Declaration between Canada and the U.S.[34] As soon as someone has purchased a ticket to travel, these programs assess how much risk they pose by combing through a huge range of databases, including police, health, financial, and travel records, to gather information that is subjected to an algorithmic assessment of risk. "Before a plane can land, a border crossed or a port entered, the most prosaic and apparently scattered data (from past travel bookings and credit card transactions to visa applications and in-flight meal choices) appear to hold out a new promise— that if only it can be integrated, the 'gauge set' and the algorithm 'refined,' the various programmes of UK e-Borders, EU PNR [Passenger Name Record], USVISIT and ATS [Automated Targeting System] might render preemptive security action possible."[35] Louise Amoore likens the security risk calculus used in smart borders to data derivatives, because the algorithms put together disparate pieces of information to make inferences and predict possibilities for behavior in order to produce a risk profile attached to every traveler.[36]

The UK, Canada, the U.S., Australia, and New Zealand created the "Five Country Conference" in 2009 to share biometric and other data, including "fingerprints, DNA, travel documents, and details of deported aliens."[37] Canada and the U.S. have an additional agreement to share data about travelers, without their knowledge or agreement, which means that U.S. conceptions of risk infiltrate Canada's security system as well. Because U.S. security profiles utilize racial profiling, the designation of certain racialized bodies as riskier influences Canadian conceptions of risky bodies, influencing in turn, suggests sociologist Karine Côté-Boucher, how people in Canada conceive of what it means to be Canadian.[38] Australia is exporting its security practices through trainings and grants to dozens of other countries throughout the Asia-Pacific region with the intent of ensuring wide regional collaboration in their goal of denying visas to people suspected of attempting to travel to Australia in order to apply for asylum. By prefiguring potential asylum seekers as criminals, the language contained in Australia's border security policy conflates asylum with criminality, creating a category of high-risk travelers whose mobility is to be contained.[39]

In effect, smart borders are thus mobile borders carried on and in the bodies of travelers, whose riskiness is assessed on the basis of data collected about them through surveillance and data mining and shared between countries as well as private carriers. Governments in the global north are creating hierarchies of citizenship through which they rate the desirability of migrants from elsewhere, defining citizens of countries that are rated as risky as themselves risky while offering to "desirable" travelers programs that facilitate their mobility. These intentionally differentiated mobility pathways reflect not only racialized rankings based on colonial hierarchies, but also Islamophobic paranoias nurtured through the global war on terror and the precoding of possible asylum seekers and other migrants from the global south as already suspiciously criminal simply because they are on the move.[40]

Louise Amoore calls these smart border systems "algorithmic war," a new front in the global war on terror-criminals-migrants that combines militarization, commercialization, securitization, surveillance, and public fear to reproduce "the war-like relations of power seen in the overtly militarized spaces of Afghanistan and Iraq."[41] Algorithmic war separates the world into safe and risky populations, enabling militarized interventions against the latter in the name of protecting the former. The latter might be a migrant worker, an asylum seeker, or a student from a "risky" country, whose risk score offers a seemingly neutral assessment that obscures the racist dimensions of profiling.

Smart borders thus move with travelers, are not territorially fixed, and can be deployed anywhere, including to surveil and police internal populations defined as risky. China leads the world in its coordinated surveillance capabilities oriented toward its own citizens, with an estimated 176 million surveillance cameras (and plans for 450 million by 2020), many of which contain facial recognition technologies connected to databases to track behavior and movements. This mammoth surveillance system was initially motivated in part by the government's desire to police rural peasants arriving in China's cities during the massive internal rural–urban migration of the 1990s, and is planned to expand by 2020 toward a complete surveillance system called Skynet, which will combine data mined from government records, private companies, and social networks with facial recognition software to track, monitor, and score everyone.[42] China is currently deploying its mass surveillance technology most extensively in the Xinjiang Autonomous Region to monitor Uighur and other Muslim populations, whose agitations for self-rule were recoded by the Chinese government after 9/11 as aligned with Islamic terrorism. China's adoption of the anti-Muslim war on terror rhetoric justifies an increasingly brutal crackdown that involves racial profiling, total surveillance, exclusion from citizenship rights, forced indoctrination, mass incarceration, violent repression, limitations on mobility, and demonization. Not surprisingly, such extreme repression instigates resistance, creating a violent cycle of retribution: as they are treated as terrorists, Uighurs have turned to acts of terror.[43]

A Chinese engineer for the company that designs the surveillance technology in Xinjiang explains that the surveillance systems treat the areas under surveillance like a battlefield where they can "apply the ideas of military cyber systems to civilian public security."[44] With a price tag of nearly $8.4 billion in 2017, internal security in Xinjiang includes data collected from cameras, mandatory smartphone apps, transit checkpoints, monitoring of public spaces, service centers, mosques, data mining, biometrics, purchasing records, and more, which are sent to command centers to be monitored and analyzed by a legion of analysts. The approach in Xinjiang is "segregated surveillance" because the technology explicitly targets minorities for data collection while ignoring the region's Han Chinese residents. The surveillance program identifies people to be sent to the government's "reeducation centers," which held over a million minorities by late 2019. Evidence suggests that China may be transferring people from the reeducation centers to prisons, the regional budget for which doubled in 2017.[45]

The only country that comes close to rivaling China's investment in supercomputers to crunch and store all this data is the U.S., which is subjecting not just foreigners but also citizens to increasingly pervasive surveillance and monitoring.[46] Proliferating surveillance and security technologies, the compulsion toward manufacturing hierarchies of risk to define people, and the turn toward militarization to contain those deemed risky offers a potent combination for managing internal populations. Mass incarceration is the most direct and obvious outcome, shape-shifting in form in response to growing calls to dismantle the prison-industrial complex. Surveillance has grown to include ankle monitors, monitoring of cell phone and internet use, and other tracking devices in place of or after incarceration to track those deemed risky, with the result that anyone in contact with those being monitored is also being monitored, thus targeting entire communities for surveillance. Algorithms that track movements and interactions use guilt by association to identify suspicious people. "Predictive policing" is one outcome—software programs developed in the U.S. and now used around the world that predict where future crimes are more likely to occur based on past criminal activity, leading to "hot spot" policing that, again, brings particular neighborhoods under extra surveillance.[47] Because of racial bias throughout the American policing and criminal justice system, neighborhoods where minorities live are being singled out for extensive surveillance and monitoring, most particularly through laws that allow extra surveillance to combat gang activity and identify people suspected of gang affiliation. The gang injunction heavily used in California, for example, allows the police to draw up a list of everyone in an area they suspect of being in a gang, including as many John Does as they like, and then subject those on the list to a sprawling variety of constraints against their ability to be together anywhere—at the dinner table, in public, in a car or carpooling, at a meeting or community event. Police have the right to stop and frisk anyone on the list at any time. Reports about the impact of gang injunctions in Los Angeles, as well as how the suspicion of gang affiliations is being used as a justification for mass deportation in Long Island, describe not only the extreme injustices being perpetrated against these communities but also the community devastation left behind.[48] Decarceration through the proliferation of electronic monitoring promises a huge boon to the private for-profit prison industry, whose provision of monitoring devices is profitable because those being monitored must pay for them. Electronic monitoring replaces structural prisons with digital prisons, and makes the imprisoned pay for their own e-incarceration.

Mass incarceration and counterterrorism are two sides of the same militarized securitization coin, both of which employ mass surveillance. Joe Masco shows how the U.S. national security state as a "counterterror" state emerged from the previous "countercommunist state," distinguished by its management of secrecy. Masco notes the effect of classifying knowledge—turning secrets into threats of the highest order should they be revealed to the public—in forging a new social contract that redefines all aspects of life as subject to surveillance and secrecy. The national security state initially prioritized nuclearism as an immediate and constant threat that demanded constant readiness, a condition now filled by the current war on terror.[49] The government uses the screen of secrecy to render those it targets as terrorists as unknowable and unintelligible to the American public, a logic that one can see repeated in the secretive management of immigrant detention centers and the insistence that secretive deportation efforts are security actions to remove dangerous criminals and potential terrorists from the country.

Watchful vigilance against risky bodies also extends far beyond the borders of the securitized state, through the universe of satellites currently orbiting the earth, of which 400 out of 950 are owned by the U.S. These observation satellites are maintained and managed in secret, "an imperial trick" that allows their owners to survey data from all over the world gleaned from internet traffic.[50] Such "sovereign visuality" is a tool of power used by security states to demand of citizens not only their complicity in allowing secretive security surveillance by their governments but also their participation in watchful practice through ubiquitous calls to "say something if you see something."[51] Watching for the abnormal is predicated on being able to see difference through visually classifying people as out of place or risky and reporting their presence and actions to authorities, a practice directed most acutely at Black people as well as Muslims. The ubiquitous border directed toward recognizing internal aliens who are to be watched aligns with state efforts to watch and identify risky bodies attempting to cross the border, allowing complicit citizens to feel participatory in guarding the American homeland from dangerous outsiders.[52] The use of such programs distributes responsibility for risk assessment throughout society, including to private transport carriers, making border patrol a responsibility of citizens as well as government agents and thus enlisting private citizens in the watchful politics of risk assessment. China, the Gulf states, and Israel employ similar logics by requiring landlords (in China) and employers (in the Gulf states and Israel) to surveil foreigners living in their apartments or working for them.

These world leaders in ubiquitous surveillance export to other governments models of how secret surveillance can be a tool of authoritarian control and used to target and punish undesirable populations, whether internal dissidents or aspiring immigrants. For example, Japan's Secrecy Act of 2013, which Edward Snowden claims was authored by the U.S., allows the government to punish anyone found guilty of reporting on state secrets. This Act was followed two years later by the Conspiracy Bill, which allows the government to secretly collect all communications and punish anyone it finds talking about criminal/terrorist activity. Snowden claims the U.S. National Security Agency played a major role in designing this legislation as well, which reflects the long-standing U.S. involvement in surveillance and intelligence-gathering activities in Japan. Midori Ogasawara reports,

> Snowden explained to me that this is a common strategy of the NSA when pressuring other countries to legalize hidden surveillance systems and covert activities. According to him, the NSA has a group of about 100 lawyers who research how the NSA can get around human rights restrictions written in constitutions and laws in different countries, which prevent the governments from spying on their own citizens. Removing these legal protections is an important task for the NSA to collect more data and classify it while keeping the process out of the public eye. The NSA first developed this scheme of creating judicial run-arounds with a group of countries called Five Eyes (U.S., Britain, Australia, New Zealand, and Canada), and then exported it to other countries. "You don't have to pass the law exactly as we say. But in our experience (we say), this is what you should aim for, you should do this, you should do this, you should do this. Those other countries go, 'Well, hey, we should do this,'" said Snowden.[53]

Countries around the world are taking notice. The ultra-right Polish government passed a new surveillance law in 2016 that allows it to collect telecommunications data as well as a new anti-terrorist act that allows "practically unrestricted invigilation" including "phone tapping, bugging the house (also with cameras), access to all forms of correspondence along with all the data aggregated or sorted electronically by the person" of all foreigners, including non-Polish EU citizens.[54] Beirut adopted CCTVs for continual surveillance with the aid of a World Bank loan in 2002, and many other Middle Eastern countries are adopting biometrics.[55] Argentina is tightening its immigration policies and is working with other Latin American countries on a shared database to track and monitor the mobile.

To date, critical studies on the security state have primarily focused on the global north, but as countries in the global south expand their security capabilities with funding and support from the global north, it will be important to understand the extent to which such capabilities are simply responsive to the security agendas of funders in the global north and in what ways security states in the global south are bending their security capabilities toward security agendas of their own. Pakistan, the largest known recipient of NSA funding from the U.S., offers to the U.S. logistical, intelligence, linguistic, and other data about Pakistani citizens and air travelers departing from

Pakistan.[56] Evidence suggests that Pakistani authorities also turn such technologies against internal "marginalized, racialized, and dissident peoples and communities" such as Pashtun and Baloch populations, who are much more likely to be surveilled, arrested, deported, abused by authorities, and imprisoned.[57] Similar accounts show how the counterterror state in Kenya targets Somali communities for particular abuse, and Kashmir's experience with the Indian counterterror state has recently been much in the news.[58] The Indian state has also been using military tactics against indigenous Adivasi communities, who the state charges with abetting revolutionary Maoist Naxalite guerrillas who move through their territories. The Indian state uses the presence of the guerrillas as a pretext for counterterrorist military incursions into Adivasi areas, which have the effect of clearing an area of indigenous communities in order to enable the penetration of big mining companies eager to gain unhindered access to the area's natural riches. "In the name of fighting the guerrillas, the government was covering the rich mining areas with military barracks to make life brutally unpleasant, accusing locals who did not comply with them of being Maoists so that eventually they would either be forced to leave or could simply be arrested or killed. It was a slow clearing of the ground, a slow purging of the people," writes anthropologist Alpa Shah, whose book *Nightmarch* recounts her ten-day sojourn across Adivasi territory with Naxalite rebels.[59] Similarly, counterterror surveillance, repression, and authoritarianism in Eurasia has pushed Tajiks, Uzbeks, and Chechens, as well as Uighurs, as described above, into militant action, bolstering Russia's and China's roles as authoritarian states pursuing important counterterror efforts on the global stage.[60]

THE BUSINESS OF SECURITY

"The state has shrunk to its security function," argues Cathy Lutz, who continues,

> and the notion of security has shrunk from that of human welfare and its partial achievement to that of protection from violent others and to the argument that security must always fail to be achieved. . . . Understanding how and why this is happening requires understanding the capture of the state not only by military industries/military corporations and contractors but its capture by those many other corporate sectors that benefit in the short term at least from an ineffectual regulatory regime. They can pose themselves as beyond regulation with the claim that they work in

emergency conditions and in required secrecy and in the interests of all. The militaries and other security activities associated with many states are in fact more private corporate entities than public ones, in any case, as when contractors outnumber uniformed soldiers in the interventions in Afghanistan and Iraq, and large private militias provide protection for elite landowners in the Philippines.[61]

Security in and of itself is not necessarily about militarization, but the story unfolding throughout this chapter is about the transformation of security from something that refers to the reduction of harm and the enhancement of safety to something that is imagined to exist only through the application of military engagement and military technologies. This shift has militarized the security of everyday life, bending the state's expression of security toward militarism within and without. And as security has been bent toward militarized forms, we see its expression in the increasing use of militarized technologies for all sorts of security purposes, propelled in no small part by the opportunities militarization provides for capitalist profit.

Security is touted by "capitalists, police and politicians to justify maintaining a crisis-ridden late capitalism" for its application to the containment of resistance, control of labor, and to secure class privilege.[62] As militarized security becomes the basis for organizing contemporary life, private security firms are proliferating and producing ever more technologies to securitize and militarize everything from the body to the home (smart surveillance technologies, security technologies) to the neighborhood (gated communities, private policing) to the city (closed circuit cameras, video surveillance, the securitization of spaces like shopping centers and schools) to the state (militarized borders and regions, secret surveillance and constant data collection, policing practices, carcerality, political discourse) to empire-building (military interventions, offshoring borders, reducing diplomacy to its security functions, prioritizing the global war on terror, exporting military/surveillance technologies, and so forth).[63]

While companies were developing security technology for the military and commercial markets well before 9/11, the post-9/11 reorganization of security in the U.S., combined with a neoliberal approach to governance, intensified the market to astonishing heights. In line with the Bush administration's policy of outsourcing most functions of statecraft and governance, the U.S. Department of Defense created a venture capitalist research division to locate start-up companies that could produce desired security technologies. Private contractors took over security research and design, surveillance, intelligence, and analytics as well as the grunt work of military occupation in Iraq and Afghanistan. As Naomi Klein puts it, "Whereas in the nineties the goal was to develop the killer application, the 'next new thing,' and sell it to Microsoft and Oracle, now it was to come up with a new 'search and nail' terrorist-catching technology and sell it to the Department of Homeland Security or the Pentagon."[64] Funding for militarism seems to have no limit. The post-9/11 wars in Afghanistan, Iraq, and Pakistan alone have cost the U.S. an estimated $5.9 trillion.[65] As journalist James Risen has noted, most of this has gone to "shadowy contractors," "secret intelligence contractors who perform secret counterterrorism work for the CIA, FBI, the Pentagon and other agencies. Because it is all classified there is no public debate about the massive amounts of money being poured into these contractors. . . . It is one of the largest transfers of wealth in American history, and yet it has gone largely unnoticed."[66]

Salaries for CEOs of the thirty-four top U.S. defense contractors doubled after 9/11.[67] A new lobbying presence represents the burgeoning new industry: in the five years after 9/11, the number of security-oriented lobbying firms on Capitol Hill grew from two to 543.[68] When government officials "conflate what is good for Lockheed, Halliburton, Carlyle and Gilead with what is good for the United States and indeed the world, it is a form of projection with uniquely dangerous consequences," because these companies rely on the militarization of everything to make their money.[69]

The U.S. is far from alone. The global homeland security market is now booming, reaching an estimated $558 billion by 2014.[70] Israeli security exports nearly quadrupled in the decade after 9/11, as Israel successfully marketed itself as a global leader uniquely practiced in counterterror militarized security.[71] *Forbes* lauds Israel's ability to achieve global dominance in the $82 billion cybersecurity industry because of the partnership between Israeli Defense Forces, which research, develop, and incubate cybersecurity technologies, and civilian engineers, including global firms with offices in Israel such as IBM and Oracle.[72] The European security industry has a combined turnover of about €96 billion and sells their products throughout the globe.[73] And most corporate players in the security technology world seem to be agnostic about human rights: although major security trade shows exclude representatives from authoritarian regimes accused of human rights abuses such as Sudan, Iran, North Korea, Syria, and Cuba at its annual events, through legal loopholes and work-arounds security companies still find ways to sell to regimes with questionable records on human rights.[74]

The argument of the previous sections begins to bring into view interlinked, iterative, mutually reinforcing imperial formations that I call security empires. These empires are emergent in the sense of being incomplete; they are not fully formed entities. Some security empires based in security states and regional state-based entities, like the U.S. security empire, the EU security empire, or the Israeli security empire, are more easily discernible; others, like the imperial initiatives of China, Saudi Arabia, and India, are not yet fully apparent.[75] Overarching, undergirding, and cross-cutting these empires are particular logics. One is the Islamophobia through which the U.S., EU, Australia, Israel, China, and India share rhetorics and technologies to pursue anti-Muslim initiatives. White supremacy, through which the U.S., EU, Australia, Canada, and New Zealand work together to police mobility and labor, is another. White supremacy racializes the globe, creating a hierarchy that is simultaneously global but also locally elaborated in the ways in which hegemonic white normativities associated with the U.S. and Europe infiltrate life around the world.[76] Thus the material cited here suggests the emergence of something we might call "Islamophobic imperialism," associated with the global war on terror, or "white supremacist imperialism," as (re)newed global formations. In addition to these imperial formations, another security logic is the protection of capitalist extraction that binds elites across the globe. Authoritarian tendencies that animate moves toward anti-Islamic, anti-immigrant securitization and militarization policies are reshaping political landscapes with particular implications for mobility and for mobile labor, as well as for the transformation of democratic governance by secrecy, surveillance, and mass carcerality. And the logics of militarization, as "the handmaiden of imperialism," and in particular carceral militarization, provide the ideological and technological weaponry to carry out the occupations, surveillance, and containment activities that security logics justify.[77]

Other scholars seeking to put a name to the political formations discussed here have offered concepts like "security assemblages" or "security landscapes" in an effort to capture the multiplex, multilayered, multidimensional ensemble of players, interests, materialities, and harms carried and perpetrated by security imperialism. I prefer the latter term because it suggests that power has a directionality in these imperial formations—that through them the powerful can exert their templates for security throughout the rest of the world. Security imperialism, based in surveillance practices, militarization, and a set of justifying logics, is oriented toward controlling and containing risky racialized bodies while ensuring capitalist opportunities. It brings the internal policing of suspect, undesirable, foreign, and minority others into the same security apparatus as the external identification and containment of risky migrant-terrorist-criminals, subjecting both to the profit logics of private security contractors. Thus, the concept of security imperialism offers a global perspective on how securitization practices transcend nation-state boundaries, linking domestic carcerality to extra-state forms of military intervention, counterinsurgency, and border control. Security imperialism spans borders; bends sovereignties toward its goals by imposing security requirements, interventions, laws, and practices; and prioritizes the extractive objectives of political and economic elites.

We have argued that militarized global apartheid upheld by security imperialism benefits the interests of capitalists and governments for a variety of reasons: (1) states use the specter of illegalized migrants to push an agenda of security threats/terrorism/challenges to cultural integrity in order to gain populist support for strengthening the state as well as the military; (2) illegalized migrants are beneficial to employers because they are outside regulatory control, so demonizing illegalized migrants keeps them in the shadows while ensuring employer control; and (3) illegalized migrants are useful for enacting legal regimes that can also be used to discipline internal others (minorities, racialized groups) because the wider society is often tolerant of efforts to curtail and constrain the civil rights of illegalized migrants, and those curtailments can then be turned against internal populations as well. Capital's interests intersect here with racism, and racism remains strategic as a way to police dissent. Racialized language about the criminal/terrorist/migrant links to the policing of internal dissent (politicized Uighurs, Kashmiris, African Americans, Palestinians), serving the interests of authoritarians. Thus, policing global mobility through racist assessments of risk and the management of labor works in the interests of capitalists and authoritarians, who can use the militarization of security to pacify the nation and the threats posed by the criminal/terrorist/migrant to redirect attention away from autocratic moves and yawning inequality.

Bringing security imperialism into focus allows us to track the securitization and militarization of particular spaces and how those processes are produced by and responsive to power brokers who may not themselves occupy those spaces and/or control them through sovereign claims. Unlike states, security imperialism is not territorially delimited, but rather is defined by the ways in which spaces, environments, and inhabitants are made subject to the security aspirations of powerful states and their extra-state and corporate alliances. The imperial projects that have occupied this book align, overlap, and compete; they borrow security language (the fight against terrorism, the threats of Islamic fundamentalism), techniques (concentration camps, detention centers, reeducation centers, mass incarceration, militarized border regimes and occupations), and technologies (biometrics, data mining, algorithmic risk analyses, surveillance systems, military hardware) from each other, and they reinforce each other's visions and goals.

Security imperialism is a mode of power that compels governments across the globe to accede to the security goals of the world's most powerful security states and their corporate and other nongovernmental allies. It works to structure, enable, maintain, and perpetrate militarized global apartheid through a set of iterative, mutually reinforcing security logics that: (1) racialize suspect populations across borders, with a particular interest in racializing, vilifying, and containing Muslims; (2) depend on ever-expanding forms of carcerality to contain people identified as risky; (3) secure cosmopolitan class privilege, in part through protecting capitalist extraction as well as the ease of mobility for cosmopolitan elites; (4) model authoritarianism as a legitimized governance model; and (5) tether the concept of security to militarization. Envisioning security imperialism in this way allows us to see how certain logics—white supremacy, Islamophobia, capitalist extraction, class privilege, labor control, racialized carcerality—work through security empires to create militarized global apartheid.

Let's pause for a moment to consider semantics. Critiquing efforts to define empires in clearly bounded terms linked to geopolitical stabilities, Ann Laura Stoler offers the concept of "imperial formations": "What if the notion of empire as a steady state (that may 'rise' or 'fall') is replaced with a notion of imperial formations as supremely mobile politics of dislocation, dependent not on stable populations so much as on highly moveable ones, on systemic recruitments and 'transfers' of colonial agents, on native military, on a redistribution of peoples and resources, on relocations and dispersions, on contiguous and overseas territories?"[78] Stoler is interested in finding new ways to see, understand, and articulate what she calls "imperial duress," the ways in which older colonial and imperial forms resurface, reemerge, haunt, and find new expressions and configurations in the present as well as in the imagined (subjunctive) future. Cautioning against the inclination to see contemporary forms of empire as either ongoing continuities of previous forms or entirely novel, she urges attention to how older imperial forms are threading through new contexts, recalibrating, reanimating, reconfiguring, and realigning political order and social life. For example, a fundamental characteristic of empire is the ability to claim the right to exception—to change laws and overlook founding principles in the name of security and self-protection. "'Security' has long been the conceptual and political nexus of the expulsions and containments in which imperial formations invest," she writes, but then clarifies that older security concerns of past colonial empires "are decidedly not the same as—but they are embedded in—the consolidated and honed technologies of security that thrive today."[79]

I use the terms *security empire*, *security imperialism*, and *imperial formations* with a similar intent, trying to bring into view an emergent global politics that draws on histories of racialization, conquest, slavery, exclusion, white supremacy, and authoritarianism to forge a global order fundamentally based on the ability to control mobility and to unilaterally assess the risk of racialized mobile subjects while imposing carceral regimes as the antidote to risk. This is a global politics of imperialism built through alliances between certain governments, corporations, and extra-state actors to manage migrant flows and enact risk protocols while still ensuring benefits to capital. As a result, sovereignty around the world is evolving from the control of territorial borders and the prevention of foreign incursion toward the management of mobility and security regimes in ways that reflect and promote the security logics and desires of the global north.

Security empires conceived as nonlinearly bound multidimensional sets of relations—a convergence of interests—characterized by unequal power thus can be spatially mapped in ways that can take account of how the U.S., for example, can interfere with Kenyan terrorism laws while directing the Kenyan military and police toward certain kinds of engagements in Somalia and with Somalis living inside Kenya. Kenya is a sovereign state, but aspects of its governance are forcibly reshaped to the contours of U.S. imperial interests in its region. The concept of security empire accounts for how the EU can enlist Niger in its desires to contain migrants in certain kinds of ways, such as through changing laws about how migrants are assisted, tracked, and contained in Niger, and how the EU can partner with extra-state militias in Libya to incarcerate migrants in camps.

Southern Somalia, one of the more insecure places on earth, is subject to a variety of security interventions directed by security entities external to the Somali state, and most especially the U.S. security empire: the designation by the U.S. of Al-Shabaab as terrorists, a rhetorical device with very real material and political effects; the role of the Kenyan army as partners responsible for securitizing the southern Somali space through military incursions; the training of Somali security forces by contractors paid for and trained by foreign militaries, including the U.S.; the imposition of an internationally funded African military force to contain Al-Shabaab violence and support the internationally backed Somali government; the constant presence of U.S. drones in the sky over southern Somalia, which people describe to me as the sound of terror; the persistent flight of refugees from southern Somalia to Kenya, which the international community insists must contain them; the dramatic rise in deportations by the U.S. of Somali refugees; and the bar against the entry into the U.S. of Somalis under the so-called Muslim ban. Southern Somalia is not home to U.S. troops on the ground, and its semi-autonomous government does not receive direct funding or have diplomatic relations with the U.S., and yet southern Somalia is entirely within the geometric frame of the U.S. security empire.[80]

Lawyer-anthropologist Darryl Li offers an illustrative account of how the U.S. security empire works through Bosnian sovereignty in his description of what he calls "circular carcerality." Two men, one from Algeria and one from Egypt, went to Bosnia to fight during the Bosnian war in the early 1990s, marrying locally and gaining citizenship before being stripped of their citizenship and deported at the behest of the U.S. after 9/11 during "the worldwide U.S.-driven hunt for 'out-of-place' Muslims—immigrants and travelers who arouse suspicion for moving across the Global South."[81] One was deported to Guantánamo, the other to Egypt. The man deported to Egypt was tortured and ultimately exonerated by a Bosnian court; the man incarcerated at Guantánamo was eventually set free through a judicial challenge to his and others' detentions.

After a court of law found that stripping one of the men of his citizenship in order to deport him was a violation of Bosnian law, the Bosnian government rewrote the law under the guidance of U.S. and British officials, and U.S. assistance, funding, and technology helped to build a new policing structure through which undesirable Muslims were to be identified, detained, and deported. "The United States and its allies crafted Bosnia legislation and enmeshed themselves in state institutions. . . . By acting as a buffer [in deporting Arabs identified as undesirable by the U.S.] the Bosnian state permitted the United States to avoid direct responsibility for the removal of the Arabs. And the Arabs lacked any ability to petition directly an authority that might truly determine their fate."[82]

This is a security empire in action. Li's account shows how U.S. imperial interests run through and shape sovereign decisions in ways that leave those targeted no avenues for redress or reconsideration. That Bosnia allows people of Arab origin to be stripped of their Bosnian citizenship and deported in accordance with U.S. desires is a "refraction" of U.S. sovereign power.[83] Li cites the global network of secret prisons used by the U.S. through which rendered Arabs are moved with the complicity and involvement of other sovereign states, their circulation worked out through sovereign relationships in which some of the rendered can be returned to their places of origin so as to allow those governments to take responsibility for their detention and, perhaps, disposal. Such "carceral circulation"—the circulation of out-of-place Muslims directed by the U.S. as part of the global war on terror—is an expression of a U.S.-led security empire.[84]

CONCLUSION

The security logics described here do not, of course, serve the interests of most people living in the global south, nor many living in the global north either. What security and securitization look like for people living in much of the world is often a mix of authoritarianism, extractive and deadly forms of capitalism, military interventions, state surveillance, and violence, all in the name of security for the global north, as well as, in certain locations, local governments that adopt for their own purposes the security logics of the global north. It is important to be clear about whose interests are most served by security imperialism. The evidence presented throughout this book suggests that corporate-military-authoritarian interests meet in the creation of spaces that have been cleared of dissent and resistance against the imposition of capitalist modes of extraction and militarized desires for hegemonic control, as well as populations defined by those interests as problematic on the basis of race and class. Military, corporate, and authoritarian interests combine in the system of global militarized apartheid to control mobility and labor in the name of security through using the tools of racialization and weaponry. In other words, security imperialism is what allows militarized global apartheid to take shape and find expression. Recall the new Zones for Economic Development and Employment (ZEDES) in Honduras, which are under the control of a team of Honduran and foreign investors who make their own laws, currency, police force, and judiciary; or the plantation zone in Indonesia where millions of smallholders are involuntarily dispossessed by massive palm oil plantations; or Xinjiang, China, where a million minorities are incarcerated for resisting the state; or the anti-Maoist campaigns of India that aim to clear away guerrillas and the communities that support them in order to open their land to extraction; or the Occupied Territories in Israel/Palestine, where the work-permitting regime for Palestinian workers gives Shin Bet extraordinary power to engage in mass profiling and mobility restrictions as a form of punishment; or the green zone in Iraq. These are apartheid spaces—spaces in which an authoritarian agenda, pursued by military methods and aided by corporate goals, hierarchize space and populations for governance, control, and extraction. The most immediate and pronounced goals may vary from space to space—corporate extraction in Honduras, Iraq, Indonesia, and India, authoritarian hegemony, military domination, and other forms of extraction in China and Israel—but all are pursued in the name of security and as part of militarized imperial projects of control.[85]

CHAPTER SIX

FUTURES

The system of militarized global apartheid is not sustainable. Just as South African apartheid failed because of its own contradictions, the debilitating financial cost of its security apparatus, its inherent evil, and powerful local and international multiracial opposition movements, so too will global militarized apartheid have to give way to an alternative future. The question is, what will follow?

Apartheid's trajectory in South Africa came to a close at the end of the twentieth century. Many factors contributed to its demise, from the moral and militant power of the anti-apartheid movement and the government's inability to squelch it to the collapse of communism as a "threat" that could be used to justify ongoing counterinsurgency. In addition to forming a militarized and internationally supported resistance movement, staging huge popular demonstrations against pass laws, and organizing local and nationwide strikes, Black people simply refused to adhere to influx control laws and regulations, insisting with their bodies on their right to mobility and to building (unauthorized) settlements all over the country in locations where they were not supposed to live. By the end of apartheid, between 15 and 20 million people had been arrested for pass law violations alone, and all major cities were ringed with informal communities.[1] The government's containment policy was failing.

Additionally, it was becoming clear that the apartheid system was headed for economic distress. Business leaders feared that the effort to maintain a high standard of living for white people at the expense of widespread Black poverty—an economy that sustained a few at the expense of the majority—would not grow. Understanding that economic stagnation, global condemnation, international sanctions, and the standoff between government forces and militant anti-apartheid resistance did not create a promising economic environment, white business leaders began brokering conversations in the late 1980s with the incarcerated Nelson Mandela about how to negotiate a transition to democracy and thus Black majority rule.

Furthermore, the security apparatus required to manage containment and sustain apartheid was hugely expensive and expansive, draining millions from government coffers and enabling a proliferation of inhumane and appalling police practices in the name of security that left terrible personal and social damage.[2] The South African security state implicated its neighbors as well: militarized anti-apartheid groups located training camps and military installations in neighboring countries, which the South African government used as a justification for launching violent attacks across its borders in the name of fighting a communist insurgency (in addition to its intervention against communist-aligned movements within those countries). When the fall of the Berlin Wall meant that the South African apartheid government could no longer tout communism as a realistic threat either internally or regionally, the entire security edifice was called into question. No small amount of effort had gone into vilifying Black people as criminals, terrorists, and undesirables, but antiblack National Party propaganda began losing its power as more white South Africans recognized the immorality of the system. Mahmood Mamdani argues that when the anti-apartheid opposition began defining the evil as white supremacy and not white people, this angle gave white people a reason to join the anti-apartheid movement. White people had come to understand that "their security required that whites give up the monopoly of power."[3] Intimacies between Black people and white people, such as in places of employment and in white domestic spaces where Black people worked, also helped to enable a shift in consciousness.

The negotiated transition to democracy and the historic 1994 election gave the presidency to Nelson Mandela, an anti-apartheid movement leader and cofounder of its militant wing whom the apartheid government had imprisoned for twenty-seven years for sabotage. But the change in governance did not bring the economic revolution that so many hoped for and that was envisioned in the anti-apartheid movement's Freedom Charter because the new government was forced to adapt to the neoliberal order that had become globally hegemonic after the collapse of state communism. Consequently, little changed after the transition for most South Africans: while white people were allowed to keep their wealth and property and a wealthy multiracial elite benefited from new economic opportunities, Black poverty deepened.[4] And South Africa today grapples with horrific xenophobic violence against other Africans who have sought refuge and/or economic futures there. While the end of apartheid brought to a close a shameful chapter of South African history, it did not bring a nonracial democratic utopia into being.

What might the demise of apartheid in South Africa suggest about the future of militarized global apartheid? Whereas neoliberal capitalism outlived South African apartheid, it is unlikely that militarized global apartheid can end without an end to capitalism as we know it. The entire system of militarized global apartheid depends on racial capitalism's entwinement with security imperialism. The system ensures capitalist profitability through various forms of containment, plunder, and security carcerality at different scales through expropriation and exploitation mechanisms that turn risk into profit. The axis on which militarized global apartheid turns is racism—a global logic with local expressions justified through security rhetorics (counterterrorism, counterinsurgency, crime) with origins in white supremacy. We have reviewed the benefits of this system for capitalists and governments, especially those with authoritarian inclinations, and populist right-wing victories at the polls indicate that citizens in the global north benefit from feelings of racialized entitlement to belonging and from the pleasure of seeing racialized minorities criminalized.[5] Racism's affect is powerful.

But it is clear that this system of extraordinary inequality, expense, damage, and immorality cannot last. Militarized global apartheid is unsustainable for several reasons. Those who are mobile because home has become unlivable or because they are in search of economic opportunities or a different future than what is imaginable at home will not stop moving. Environmental collapse precipitated by extractive and exploitive petro-capitalism threatens the homes of hundreds of millions of people, mostly in the global south, over the next few decades, ensuring that the number of people on the move will only continue to grow. Because risk has been made into profitability, risk logics will continue to expand to include ever-greater numbers of people, including across the global north, which will translate into growing movements against security carceralities that are based on dividing and containing populations labeled as risky. The combination of insistent mobility, environmental collapse, and expanding risk logics that ensnare growing numbers of people will mean that precarity will continue to spread through the globe as a normal condition of life. Precarity demands struggle, and struggle is the means through which political consciousness is forged.

Nevertheless, "expulsion and precaritization are not in themselves politically unifying developments," Jeff Maskovsky reminds us, because security imperialism fragments and hierarchizes as it separates, surveils, and expels. Writing about the securitization of urban Philadelphia in the interests of financial elites, Maskovsky continues, "We cannot assume that this massive social, economic, and political dislocation will catalyze mass counterpolitics." And yet he finds in this context that the very securitization practices that fragment and subject people also enable the emergence of a Black insurgent politics with the potential for building an antiracist commons movement.[6]

I suggest the same potential exists on a global scale. At the moment, mobility from the global south is being met with a range of counterinsurgency operations by the global north, which suggests that it might be important to recognize migrants as insurgents, with political power as an insurgency.[7] "If Western societies are feeling besieged, it might be because they are," Ghassan Hage suggests, arguing that the old colonial order is under siege by migrants in a way that should interest anticolonial scholars.[8] The relentlessness with which people are continuing to move, despite the walls, migrant camps, detention centers, offshore holding facilities, deportations, drones, weapons, patrols, marine cordons, threats, deaths, drownings, and other bureaucratic and militarized means of containing and killing them does indeed suggest the emergence of a political movement we might identify as an insurgency: an insurgency against containment, against being treated as waste by capitalism, against authoritarianism, against racism. If the recent history of other sorts of counterinsurgency efforts are any indication, counterinsurgency operations are especially successful at motivating even more insurgencies. If migrants are besieging the inherited colonial order of racialized hierarchies and racial capitalism, maybe their movement has the capacity to contribute to the creation of a new global order.

Widespread global precarity precipitated and promoted by capitalism, compounded by insistent mobility in the face of environmental collapse, may hold the key to the undoing of contemporary capitalism and of militarized apartheid. The question is whether an emergent political consciousness forged in the struggle for mobility and against security carcerality can gain the force, cohesion, and vision to effect a revolution. Thinking of mobility as insurgency does not mean that migrant insurgency is uncomplicated or free of contradictions, of course—migrants as workers often do accept exploitative conditions, they do get stuck in encampments, and many are on the move because they aspire to obtain the consumption-based lifestyle enjoyed by the world's middle and wealthy classes. Their insurgency is the insistence that they too should have access to the things people want and need to live a fulfilled life, including economic opportunities, adventure, exploration, consumption, and liberty. They don't always get it as a result of their efforts, but that doesn't mean that they aren't trying, or that their struggles lack the stuff of revolution. Migrant insurgencies may be the only movement that contains a basis for alternatives to the security paradigm, for emergent counter-movements and imaginaries that might herald a post-security turn. Migrant insurgencies might be the only movement that carries effective resistance to imperial projects of whiteness, global Islamophobia, class privilege, capitalist extraction, authoritarian governance, and the military occupations that support them.

I leave these possibilities here, dangling, with a vigorous and hopeful nod to the many efforts emerging from coalitions of activists, scholars, artists, and others who are working to prefigure what an alternative future might look like and how we might get there. Antiracist, Indigenous, anti-imperialist, anticapitalist, alter-globalization, immigrant, feminist, worker, and poor people's movements have been doing this work for generations, and their movements, in conjunction with migrant insurgencies, are gaining greater momentum, membership, and attention as the unsustainability of our current global order becomes clearer.[9] We all need to be paying close attention to their efforts, because they probably hold the keys to the best possible future we can collectively hope for.

+ + + + +

It is interesting to look back at the world a hundred years ago, emerging from the horrors of World War I, permeated by European imperialism yet resonating with internationalist calls for global peace, equity, and mutuality. With the postwar "great unweaving" of multilingual, multireligious societies, the newly created League of Nations began with an intent to create a liberal global order of nation-states built on nationalism and sovereignty to ensure world peace.[10] But the overwhelming force of racism poisoned their efforts and ensured their demise. As detailed in the opening chapters, white supremacy was hard at work in shaping race- and ethnicity-based nationalisms, sovereignties, and new national borders in parts of the global north in the aftermath of the war. The emergent postwar world order of nation-states envisioned by Europeans and Americans relied on mutual recognition among states as well as collective recognition of the overarching system of states, an order that had absorbed peoples throughout the world through the extension of European imperialism. As colonization ended over the course of the twentieth century, replaced by a world entirely made up of sovereign nation-states, citizenship became "a universal human condition" even as the new states remained subject to the hierarchical international regulatory regime originally set up by European state-making.[11] Citizenship thus became "part of a supranational governmental regime in which the international system of states plays a fundamental role," a regime characterized by a "grossly unequal" international order because the new states had to bend to the desires of international development and financial institutions.[12]

This international order remains in place today, but throughout this history the mobile—both voluntary and involuntary—have been at the forefront of struggles against its inequalities. Cedric Robinson has argued that Black radicalism and resistance by enslaved people, much more than the English working class of Marx's theorizing, were crucially important in infecting capitalism with its contradictions.[13] Through much of the twentieth century, international coalitions of the working classes, which included many immigrants, fought capitalism and the political exclusions engineered by liberal states. "Thus, it was migrants of all kinds throughout history, not states, who were the true agents of political inclusion and cosmopolitanism."[14]

The global institutions set up during the twentieth century to protect sovereignty through regulating the movement of displaced people are increasingly incapable of doing so. The sheer number of refugees prompted Giorgio Agamben to call the refugee the global vanguard of an emerging world order, one marked by the replacement of citizens with denizens and the disarticulation of "the old trinity of state/nation/territory."[15] Agamben was writing before 9/11 and the global security turn to the war on terror, but since then displacement has only grown more spectacular. Just as resistance to the slave trade and colonialism was led by the enslaved and the colonized, and just as resistance to capitalism was led during the twentieth century by the working classes, resistance today to militarized global apartheid is being led by the mobile and people of color. There are a number of indications that insurgent mobilities are cohering a political consciousness toward the creation of a new global order, articulated with antiracist, anticapitalist, decolonial, and abolitionist efforts. The migrant caravans moving north from Central America, insisting on their right to seek safety, like the refugees moving en masse during 2015 and 2016 toward Europe, form "a collective project through walking together," writes Shahram Khosravi. "Refugees and migrants, by marching along the rails and occupying train stations, resurrected the political and collective project of railway stations as shared social spaces. Furthermore, the Refugees Welcome social movement in the main train stations throughout Europe in 2015 and 2016 brought the idea of a collective political life and a shared public space back to train stations, which otherwise have been depoliticised and dehistoricised, reduced to being viewed as a passage, a corridor or a place for consumption."[16] The mobile across the global south are mobilizing and organizing themselves to travel, as individuals and in groups, finding collaborators in the global north in those who share their visions of a more just, free world, released from the grip of capitalist exploitation, racist supremacy, and security carcerality.

+ + + + +

I will not detail the strategies and tactics of the mobile—as Heath Cabot and Shahram Khosravi have argued so convincingly, the torrent of resources directed at studying refugees and other migrants on the presumption that they constitute a crisis for the global north has been good business for anthropology while exposing refugees and migrants to the probing eyes of the security state and migration regulators.[17] Rather, I will conclude by offering, far too briefly, some examples of movements spreading across the global north in solidarity with migrants that, through collaborative political projects built by the mobile together with those who support them, contain visions of possible alternative futures.

These movements range from organized forms of solidarity and accompaniment that flout laws against offering care to unauthorized migrants to resistance movements that aim to reform borders to revolutionary movements that aim to destroy borders. They all share the belief that borders kill, that exclusionary birthright citizenship is unfair, that mobility is a human right, and that mobility is a form of reparations that the global north owes the global south for centuries of imperialism, colonialism, and capitalist extraction.[18] They diverge in the particulars of their vision for a world of free mobility.

Sanctuary and solidarity movements have a long history. Offering sanctuary to the displaced is recorded throughout human history, but in the contemporary period it is used by communities that refuse to cooperate with immigration authorities by reporting the presence of unauthorized residents. Refusal can mean that local police and municipal employees are forbidden from providing information to deportation agencies, like ICE in the U.S., or it can mean active solidarity such as the Sans-Papiers movement in France in the 1990s, when French citizens mobilized to protect unauthorized fellow residents against deportations and new anti-immigrant laws. Solidarity movements work in explicit support of migrants, such as migrant houses that offer safe protection, activists who assist migrant mobility despite laws against "crimes of solidarity," or cities that pledge to offer active support to migrants (issuing IDs, equal access to city services, and directed assistance) rather than just a refusal to report them to immigration authorities. No More Deaths in Arizona, for example, offers care and protection to migrants attempting to cross the Sonoran Desert, as do activist collectives along the Balkan route and independent rescue organizations in the Mediterranean.[19] The No One Is Illegal (NOII) migrant justice group in Canada provides support for migrants facing deportation and agitates for the regularization of all migrants and the end of deportation and detention.[20]

The Open Borders movement calls for the free movement of people in line with the free movement of capital and goods that is at the heart of the neoliberal economy, or as John Washington put it in *The Nation*, "Schengen, CA-4 [Central America-4 Free Mobility Agreement] and the USA writ globally."[21] Arguing that open borders would still rely on states to enact equitable protections for migrants and might benefit capitalists more than migrants through compelling movement for the benefit of capital, the No Borders movement refuses borders altogether, calling for their eradication, along with national citizenship, which is to be replaced by co-membership in a global society. "No Borders politics can be seen as part of a broader, reinvigorated struggle for the commons" that relies on local ecological knowledges that support sustainable lifestyles, avoid exploitative labor relations, and emphasize collective social practice and decision making.[22] Various models circulate, from "*le droit de la cité*" promoted by Étienne Balibar, who calls for a democratization of borders through representative institutions of mobile people who design mechanisms and policies for free movement, to Achille Mbembe's call for an "Africa-based philosophy of movement" modeled on precolonial African political structures that treated borders as porous intersections for exchange rather than rigid, mutually exclusive boundaries.[23] These movements are growing, their voices getting louder as convergences with other movements for antiracist justice and freedom become more potent.

+ + + + +

The political philosopher Wendy Brown asks, "When do walls become like the confining walls of a prison, rather than the comforting walls of a house?"[24] Walls, marine cordons, and biometric security technologies do not just keep people out, they also pen people in. Concerns about the self-destructive and authoritarian potentialities of the surveillance society have been noted, but, as Wendy Brown asks, "When does the fortress become a penitentiary?"[25]

A short story by the Nobel Prize–winning South African author Nadine Gordimer, one of the most acute observers of the apartheid condition in white communities, offers a chilling object lesson. Gordimer was asked for a contribution to an anthology of children's stories but refused on the grounds that she didn't write for children. When the requester persisted, Gordimer cheekily provided a horror story of modern apartheid life. In the story, a small loving family of husband, wife, and son live "happily ever after" in a nice house with a pool and a garden in the suburbs, their comfort assured by a trustworthy household staff and economic security. Their life is dreamy. But rumors of growing unrest, riots (albeit distant from their tony suburb), crime, and homelessness unsettle them, so they begin investing in security technology to guard their little estate from people of another color causing problems in other locations. Beginning with electronically controlled gates, Neighborhood Watch signs, a fenced perimeter, and a speakerphone, they install burglar bars on the windows and doors and an alarm system (often set off by their cat, or by other alarm systems in the neighborhood). Still feeling insecure, they decide to raise the height of the perimeter wall and inspect their neighbors' security perimeters for additional ideas. They finally settle on "the ugliest, but the most honest in its suggestion of the pure concentration-camp style, no frills, all evident efficiency" security technology: a continuous coil of serrated metal, with blades sharp enough to shred anyone or anything upon contact. For someone ensnared in the blades, "there would be no way out, only a struggle getting bloodier and bloodier, a deeper and sharper hooking and tearing of flesh."

Whereas for the parents the security perimeter communicated safety, the little boy saw the security perimeter through the lens of fantasy, playing cops and robbers with the speakerphone and seeing the serrated coil as a thicket through which he could squiggle to find Sleeping Beauty. One day, playing alone in the garden, he dragged a ladder to the wall and tried to climb through the thicket, only to become impaled on its blades. A ghastly scene concludes the story: "Then the man and his wife burst wildly into the garden and for some reason (the cat, probably) the alarm set up wailing against the screams while the bleeding mass of the little boy was hacked out of the security coil with saws, wire-cutters, choppers."[26]

Apartheid ensnares everyone, promising only destruction as its conclusion.

+ + + + +

Charles Piot's advice, offered in a different context, resonates: "If our interlocutors are tired of being incarcerated by local categories and cultures, and long for the new horizons of global citizenship, it behooves us to do what we have always done best and follow their lead, even if it means giving up all for an unknown future."[27] Piot's challenge to abandon incarcerating epistemic anthropological categories brings to mind Ursula Le Guin's famous, and dark, short story "The Ones Who Walk Away from Omelas." The story tells of the joyous city of Omelas, "bright towered by the sea" and backed by snow-capped mountains, whose residents enjoy a life of leisure, contentment, grace, and beauty. After describing Omelas's charming Festival of Summer, Le Guin reveals that the city's prosperity depends upon the brute misery of a child kept locked in a filthy, tiny, dark, dank basement chamber, whose presence is known to all citizens older than eight. They know that the child's incarceration and cruel treatment is the price of Omelas's comfort; that the child's freedom would come at the cost of Omelas's prosperity. Omelas's residents accept that their collective affluence is worth the exchange. And yet,

> At times one of the adolescent girls or boys who go to see the child does not go home to weep or rage, does not, in fact, go home at all. Sometimes also a man or woman much older falls silent for a day or two, and then leaves home. These people go out into the street, and walk down the street alone. They keep walking, and walk straight out of the city of Omelas,

through the beautiful gates. They keep walking across the farmlands of Omelas. Each one goes alone, youth or girl, man or woman. Night falls; the traveler must pass down village streets, between the houses with yellow-lit windows, and on out into the darkness of the fields. Each alone, they go west or north, towards the mountains. They go on. They leave Omelas, they walk ahead into the darkness, and they do not come back. The place they go towards is a place even less imaginable to most of us than the city of happiness. I cannot describe it at all. It is possible that it does not exist. But they seem to know where they are going, the ones who walk away from Omelas.

People in the global north need to begin to imagine how to walk away. My goal in this book has been to make visible the global system of militarized apartheid that has spread misery and carcerality for some in the name of comfort and prosperity for others. This short concluding chapter offers only a glimpse of the possibilities promoted by those who are actively urging apartheid's beneficiaries to begin walking away. Let's start walking.

This book originated in a paper I prepared for the 2017 "Cultures of Militarism" Wenner-Gren conference in Sintra, Portugal. The conference participants offered critiques that greatly expanded my thinking and forced me to consider additional lines of analysis. Enormous thanks to Leslie Aiello, Ayse Altinay, Andy Bickford, Faisal Devji, Alex Fattal, Francisco Ferrándiz, Daniel Goldstein, Hugh Gusterson, Rema Hammami, Danny Hoffman, Cathy Lutz, Diane Nelson, Laurie Obbink, María Clemencia Ramírez, Danilyn Rutherford, Erica Weiss, and anonymous reviewers for *Current Anthropology*. Even earlier, my comrades in the Network of Concerned Anthropologists charted a course toward creative, political, collaborative thinking about and action against militarization, and I am beholden to them as mentors: Andy Bickford, Greg Feldman, Roberto Gonzalez, Hugh Gusterson, Gustaaf Houtman, Jean Jackson, Cathy Lutz, Kate McCaffrey, David Price, and David Vine.

For intellectual nourishment in specific and general ways, words of encouragement, inspiration, and insight, I am grateful to Samar Al-Bulushi, Philippe Bourgois, Ori Burton, Heath Cabot, Bridget Conley, Jane Cowan, Jennifer Curtis, Anila Daulatzai, Jason De León, John Gilmour, Zoltán Glück, Ruth Gomberg-Muñoz, Charles Gore, Sarah Green, Inderpal Grewal, Michael Hardt, Laurie Kain Hart, Barak Kalir, Shahram Khosravi, Setha Low, Daniel Magaziner, Jeffrey Maskovsky, Achille Mbembe, Charlie Piot, Georgina Ramsay, Katerina Rozakou, Stephanie Savell, Sarah Shields, Scott Straus, Janelle Taylor, Daniel Van Lehman, Bianca Williams, Al Witten, Bev Witten, and anonymous reviewers. Gisela Fosado at Duke University Press has championed this project from its inception, motivating me through low moments when I felt it was boring, derivative, or too depressing to pursue. The professionals at Duke University Press are a joy to work with, and I thank the anonymous reviewers for their careful reading and incisive suggestions.

Audiences and colleagues who heard bits, pieces, sections, and/or confusions on this theme over the past few years pushed me hard in welcome ways. Thanks to audiences at Brown, CUNY Graduate Center, Franklin and Marshall College, Harvard, Pennsylvania State University, PLACE, the University of New England, and Yale University. Sustained conversations during small workshops are a beautiful gift of intellectual life. I am grateful for time shared with colleagues at the 2018 University of the Aegean Summer Program on Cultures, Migrations, and Borders on Lesbos; the 2017 Wenner-Gren conference on militarism; conferences on borders and displacement at the University of Amsterdam, Duke, and the University of Pittsburgh; with the International Panel on Exiting Violence working group on memory and history; and at the University of Stellenbosch's Institute for Advanced Study.

At home in Maine I learn so much from engaging with my smart colleagues Chandra Bhimull, Julie De Sherbinin, Nadia El-Shaarawi, David Gordon, Jill Gordon, Britt Halvorson, Reza Jalali, Vaishali Mamgain, Suzanne Menair, Mary Beth Mills, Lydia Moland, Maple Razsa, Julie Poitras Santos, David Stroll, and Winifred Tate. Tarlan Ahmadov, Pious Ali, Gloria Aponte Clark, Micky Bondo, Xavier Botana, Lelia D'Andrade, Hannah De Angelis, Deqa Dhelac, Muhidin Libah, Rilwan Osman, and Sue Roche fight every day for a better and more just world, inspiring me to aspire harder.

Most of all I love engaging with my thoughtful, critical, funny, intense, brilliant family. I'm so grateful to Laurie Besteman, John Besteman, Jack Lauderbaugh, and Kay Besteman for our wide-ranging political debates. My daughter Gabriela, a self-described empath, always points toward other possible points of view. My son Darien, a self-described commoner, always searches for the abolitionist, antiracist perspective. My husband Jorge, a self-described outsider, always challenges prefigured assumptions. Darien refused to allow me to abandon this project, and he, Gabriela, and Jorge offer nurturing and nourishment in life-sustaining ways that show humanity's best potential. I know this book will be only the starting point for another round of debates and discussions about how to imagine an alternative to our present reality and the kind of work it will take us to move in that direction. I embrace it, and them, in this struggle.

INTRODUCTION THE ARGUMENT

1. Besteman 2019 presents a short version of this argument.

2. First circulated as a PowerPoint, the argument later became the basis for an *Esquire* article and a book of the same name (2003, 2004). Barnett also includes in the Functioning Core some of South America, India, and South Africa. He does not include the Gulf states, which are presumably lumped into the Middle East, placed within the Non-Integrating Gap.

3. Comaroff and Comaroff 2012: 45.

4. Comaroff and Comaroff 2012: 46.

5. Trouillot 2001: 128.

6. For details, see Besteman 1999, 2016, 2017.

7. A large literature exists analyzing Somalia's collapse. See Adam 1995; Besteman 1999; Besteman and Cassanelli 1996; Harper 2012; Kaptiejns 2013; Menkhaus 2009; Samatar 1992; Warah 2014.

8. Hammond 2013.

9. Anderson 2009; BBC News 2008; Fergusson 2013; Foreign Policy 2008, 2009; Garvelink and Tahir 2011; Menkhaus 2010; Minter and Volman 2009; Refugees International 2009; Transparency International 2015.

10. See, e.g., Elmi 2010; Harper 2012; Menkhaus 2009.

11. New America Foundation (n.d.). According to New America's International Security Data website, these strikes killed an estimated 1,265–1,443 people, with a marked uptick in strikes over the past few years, from five in 2015 to 52 in 2019 (Bureau of Investigative Journalism 2018, 2019).

12. See Steinberg 2015; see also Abdi 2015; Rawlence 2016.

13. On the proliferation of border walls, see Brown 2010; Miller 2017.

14. Friedman 1999.

15. For anthropological critiques of Thomas Friedman's *The Lexus and the Olive Tree*, see Haugerud 2005 and Nordstrom 2005.

16. See Balibar 1999; Booker and Minter 2001; Bowling 2013; Feldman 2012: 115; Hage 2016, 2017: 38; Harrison 2002, 2008; Jacobs and Soske 2015; Lloyd

2015; Marable 2008; Mills 1997; Mullings 2009; Nevins 2008; Richmond 1994; Van Houtum 2010. Booker and Minter define global apartheid as "an international system of minority rule whose attributes include: differential access to basic human rights; wealth and power structured by race and place; structural racism, embedded in global economic processes, political institutions and cultural assumptions; and the international practice of double standards that assume inferior rights to be appropriate for certain 'others,' defined by location, origin, race or gender" (2001: n.p.). Klein (2007: 513) writes of "disaster apartheid" emplaced in zones of militarized occupation, such as the Green Zone in Iraq, where some bodies are offered protection while others are excluded. Kalir (2019) suggests the term *departheid* as an apt name for policies in Western states that illegalize migrants and cause them to be subjected to violence and mortal danger. Walia uses the phrase *border imperialism* to capture the processes I explore in this book: "Border imperialism is characterized by the entrenchment and reentrenchment of controls against migrants, who are displaced as a result of the violences of capitalism and empire, and subsequently forced into precarious labor as a result of state illegalization and systemic social hierarchies" (2013: 38).

17. Sanjek 1994: 1.

18. Robinson 2000: 1.

19. Robinson 2000: 26.

20. Mills 1997: 1.

21. Mills 1997: 11, emphasis in the original.

22. Mills 1997: 27, 29.

23. Farmer 2004.

24. Losurdo 2011: 219; see also James [1938] 1963; Lowe 2015; Thomas and Clarke 2006; Wilder 2005.

25. Lowe 2015.

26. Lowe 2015: 136.

27. Lake and Reynolds 2008: 23.

28. Lake and Reynolds 2008: 4.

29. Lake and Reynolds 2008: 72.

30. Mongia 2018: 110.

31. Mongia 2018: 113.

32. Mongia 2018: 139.

33. In his revisionist reading of the history of European liberalism, philosopher Domenico Losurdo (2011) offers hundreds of examples from period writings of leading European liberals whose words demonstrate their belief that those outside the white settler world—enslaved people, Indigenous peoples, contract laborers, indentured workers, the colonized—were barbarians over whom a system of white supremacy was justified. The writers tracked by Lake and Reynolds (2008) in the late nineteenth and early twentieth centuries drew on a long history of liberal discourse that presumed the necessity of racial hierarchy and white superiority.

34. Thomas and Clarke 2013: 306. This point is also echoed by Ann Laura Stoler in her discussion of varied explanations offered by students of colonial history, empire, and modernity about the origins of racialism and racism: that the social and political crafting of racial differences betrays its "capacity and potential to work through sedimented and familiar cultural representations and relations of subjugation that simultaneously tap into and feed the emergence of new ones. Thus, the very 'relevance' of racial distinctions, what makes them speakable, common sense, comfortably incorporated, and ready to be heard, may derive from the dense set of prior representations and practices on which they build and that they in turn recast" (2017: 249).

35. Thomas and Clarke 2006: 7.

36. On the efforts by Chinese revolutionaries and reformists "to mold the nation into a homogeneous, cohesive, monoracial body politic" in reaction against Western imperialists and the Manchu Qing rulers who had colluded with them, see Duara (1997: 52). See also Chan's (2018) nuanced study of the relationship between Chinese migrants and Chinese nationalism, sovereignty, and identity over the past 150 years.

37. Hage 2017: 8–9.

38. Rana 2007: 149. See also Rana (2016) and Selod and Embrick (2013) on the racialization of Muslims.

39. In South Africa, "Black" has historically been used to include people defined as ethnically Black African, Indian, and Coloured, a legal category created for everyone else who does not qualify as "White" (such as people with Khoi, Malay, Chinese, and mixed-race ancestry).

40. The literature on South African apartheid is voluminous. See Frederickson 1981; Mamdani 1996; Thompson 2014; Wolpe 1972. Gordon (2017) offers a very useful and succinct historical overview plus excerpts of the most important documents of the apartheid era. Beinart and Dubow (1995) include key papers explaining the rise of apartheid.

41. Posel 2011.

42. Posel 2011: 319.

43. Michigan State University n.d.

44. The South African government removed people categorized as Indians and Coloureds to separate residential zones, not homelands.

45. This statement is not intended to imply that the homelands did not carry emotional and affective meaning for those who lived there. See Dlamini 2009.

46. Frederickson 1981: 244.

47. Posel 2011: 324.

48. On plunder, see Clarke 2010: 59.

49. Englund 2002.

50. The large literature on Blackness is evidence of this, but see in particular Makalani's argument about intradiasporic racial differences and the essays in Thomas and Clarke (2006).

51. Khosravi 2018.

1. Gupta and Ferguson 1997; see also Malkki 1992, 1995.

2. Salazar and Smart 2011: iii.

3. Lowe 2015: 8.

4. Harrison 2002; Mills 1997; Pierre 2013; Thomas 2009.

5. Torpey 2000. See Sassen (1999) on how World War I refugee flows produced new, interlinked conceptions of state sovereignty and nationalism in Europe, a conception that became globally hegemonic. See Gatrell (2013) on post–World War I population movements in Europe that pushed people into areas that "matched" their nationalities as new nation-states consolidated.

6. There is a huge literature on this point. See, for example, Frederickson 1981; Gregory 2004; Losurdo 2011; Lowe 2015; Mills 1997; Shamir and Mundlak 2013; Wolfe 1999, 2016. Stoler and Cooper (1997: 6) offer a reminder that "colonial regimes were neither monolithic nor omnipotent" but were shaped in relation to a wide variety of shifting sociopolitical formations in the metropole and in the colony.

7. "Europe was made by its imperial projects," write Ann Stoler and Frederick Cooper (1997: 1).

8. Frederickson 1981: 145; see also S. Johnson 2015.

9. The barrier to entry for Chinese immigrants was replaced with a quota of 105 for Chinese people regardless of where in the world they lived; the quota was thus racial and not national (Ngai 2004: 203). See also Lake and Reynolds 2008: 266.

10. See Calavita's (2007) discussion of court cases that determined if an applicant qualified as a white person for naturalization.

11. Lake and Reynolds 2008; Nevins 2008; Ngai 2004.

12. Ngai 2004; see also Immerwahr 2019.

13. Ngai 2004: 125.

14. Grandin 2019a.

15. Nevins 2008: 111.

16. Ngai 2004: 58.

17. Fox and Bloemraad 2015; Ngai 2004.

18. See Calavita 2007; Frederickson 1981; King 2001; Lake and Reynolds 2008; Losurdo 2011; Ngai 2004; Omi and Winant 2015; Pessar 2003.

19. Ngai 2004: 27.

20. There is huge literature documenting these points. See, for example, Alexander 2012; Brodkin 1999; Hinton 2016; Massey and Denton 1993; Middlemass 2019; Wang 2018; Williams 2009.

21. See Calavita 2007; de Genova 2005; Foner 2005; Hintzen and Rahier 2003; Itzigsohn 2009; Ong 2003; Tang 2015; Waters 1994.

22. J. Johnson 2015. On Islamophobia as a form of racism, see Hage, who argues that Islamophobia took shape historically through a series of "othering" moves and ideologies in Western Europe, Australia, and the U.S. that grouped together people from widely varied backgrounds into a generalized "Muslim"

category. The post-9/11 treatment of Muslims across this geographic spread pre-figures Muslims as "uncontainable others" who are impossible to integrate (2017: 17). See also Grewal 2017.

23. Stoler 2002: 64.

24. Lake and Reynolds 2008: 138.

25. Lake and Reynolds 2008: 317, 318.

26. Saul 2010: 136.

27. Chin 2017: 27.

28. Chin 2017: 27.

29. Chin 2017: 96. See also Losurdo 2011; Mills 1997: 29; Richmond 1995; Silverstein 2005; Stolcke 1999; and Torpey 2000: 150; as well as Wilder's (2005) discussion of the ongoing debates in France about the extension of various forms of citizenship to colonial subjects in West Africa and the Caribbean.

30. Fassin 2001.

31. See Mbembe 2011.

32. As of December 2018, the EU includes twenty-eight countries, two of which are not signatories to the Schengen Agreement (Ireland and the UK, although the UK is a signatory to the Dublin Agreement, which assigns re-sponsibility to member states for reviewing asylum claims). Iceland, Norway, Switzerland, and Liechtenstein are signatories to the Schengen Agreement but are not members of the EU.

33. Piot (2019) offers a fascinating and globally relevant close ethnography of how the visa lottery is managed in Togo, showing how the U.S. border is realized at the U.S. embassy in Lomé.

34. Shields 2015.

35. Van Houtum 2010. Van Houtum writes that the lists inscribe "an apartheid geopolitics" (2010: 964).

36. Shields 2015: 88.

37. See Cabot's (2014) ethnography of the enormous burden faced by Greek asylum lawyers dedicated to evaluating the asylum claims of migrants seeking to enter the EU.

38. De Genova 2017a: 2, citing Balibar 2004: 43–45 and Balibar 2001. See also Feldman 2012: 125.

39. Andersson 2014b; Scheel 2017; Soto-Bermant 2017.

40. Andersson 2014b.

41. Andersson 2014b: 6.

42. Andersson 2014b: 19.

43. Cabot 2015.

44. Soto-Bermant 2017: 133; see also Andersson 2014b.

45. De Genova 2017b: 12.

46. De Genova 2017a, b.

47. Stolcke 1995: 12, 8.

48. Hage 2000.

49. Benedicto and Brunet 2018.

50. Perlstein 2017: 39.

51. Feldman (2012) offers a particularly nuanced explanation of the post–Cold War rhetorical slide from neo-nationalism, based on a premise of cultural integrity and moral incommensurability with outsiders, to xenophobic racism targeting immigrants for exclusion in Western Europe. See Brown (2010) on the contemporary proliferation of border walls as an expression of xenophobic nationalism, although she does not address the specific issue of white supremacy.

52. Khosravi 2011.

53. Gans 2008; Mundlak 2007; Shamir and Mundlak 2013.

54. This policy was first enacted as a temporary amendment in 2003, but was later renewed (Barak-Erez 2008; Gans 2008).

55. Barak-Erez 2008; Berda 2018; Gans 2008; Willen 2010. See also the essays in Jacobs and Soske (2015) assessing the ways in which Israel is an apartheid state.

56. Shipper 2010.

57. Tatlow 2016.

58. Shipper 2010: 23.

59. Suzuki 2010.

60. Chen 2010: 56.

61. Shipper 2010.

62. Koo 2018.

63. Ong 2009: 160.

64. Constable 1997: 39.

65. Duara 1997: 52; see also Chan 2018; Nonini and Ong 1997.

66. Pieke 2012.

67. Pieke 2012: 43.

68. Pieke 2012: 46.

69. Pieke 2012: 56.

70. Pieke 2014.

71. Gardner 2015: 3.

72. Gardner 2015: 2–3.

73. AlShehabi 2015; Gardner 2010, 2015; Longva 2005; Mahdavi 2016; Vora 2013. Vora (2013) analyzes how middle-class and elite Indians in Dubai engineer pathways to political belonging, even while lacking a path to official citizenship status. Kanna (2010) discusses how contemporary neoliberal understandings of citizenship in Dubai relate to its colonial past.

74. AlShehabi 2015; Flynn and Grange 2015; Gardner 2010; Kinninmont 2013; Longva 2005.

75. Robinson 2000.

CHAPTER TWO PLUNDER

1. Of course, in the Wallersteinian sense the global north did create the global south as a racialized underclass through the extractive and exploitative extension of imperialism and colonialism.

2. See Coutin 1993; García 2006; Grandin 2006; Manz 2004; Nelson 2019.

3. See Besteman 1999; Caplan 2006; Harrison 2002; Klein 2007: 74; Rodriguez 2010; Weissman 2014.

4. Shane 2017.

5. See Caplan 2006; García 2006; Morgan 1990; Nordstrom 1997; Tang 2015.

6. Geglia 2018.

7. Main 2018; see also Schneider and Ioris 2017.

8. Geglia 2016: 354.

9. Londoño 2019.

10. Tate 2015.

11. Crawford 2018a.

12. Crawford 2018a; University Collaborative Iraq Mortality Study 2013.

13. Turse 2019; see also Smith 2010.

14. Kumar 2010.

15. See, for example, Kaldor 2001; Nordstrom 2004.

16. Of the many accounts that explain and critique SAPS, see in particular Grandin 2006; Ferguson 2006; Harvey 2005; Klein 2007; Pfeiffer and Chapman 2010; Stiglitz 2002. For some specific examples, see Finnegan (2003) and Postero (2005) on Bolivia, Edelman (1990) on Costa Rica, Quesada (1999) on Central America, Gregory (2007) on the Dominican Republic, Gordillo (2014) on Argentina, Zamosc (2004) on Ecuador, Richards (2010) on Chile, Postero and Zamosc (2004) and Vilas (1996) on Latin America, Ferguson (2006) on Zambia, Gardner (2012) on South Asia, and Klein (2007) on Indonesia, the Philippines, South Korea, and Sri Lanka.

17. Caplan 2006; Clark 2005; Ferguson 2006; Goldman 2005.

18. Africa Action 2005; Caplan 2006; Ferguson 2006.

19. Richards 1996; Uvin 1998.

20. Harrison 2002: 60.

21. Clarke 2010; Watts 2006: n.p.

22. Caplan 2006; Clarke 2013; Ferguson 2006; Jackson 2002, 2003; Lucht 2011; Nordstrom 2004; Reno 2000; Richards 1996; Watts 2006.

23. Hedges and Sacco 2012: xi.

24. Tsing 2003.

25. Aparicio 2017.

26. Grandin 2006; Soluri 2005; Striffler and Moberg 2003; Tabuchi, Rigby, and White 2017.

27. Brown 2015: 142.

28. Gudynas 2010.

29. Bauman 2004; Ramsay 2019; Sassen 2014.

30. Anderson 2017.

31. On NAFTA, see Gomberg-Muñoz (2011), Holmes (2013), Marcos (1997), Nevins (2008: 138), Stephen (2007). On the U.S. complaint to the WTO about the Lomé Convention, see Black (2001), Raynolds (2003).

32. Sassen 2014.

33. Li 2010: 10.

34. Li 2018: 330; see also Li 2010, 2017.

35. Dowie 2009.

36. Johns Hopkins China Africa Research Initiative 2019.

37. Larmer 2017b.

38. Larmer 2017a.

39. Casey and Krauss 2018.

40. Londoño 2019.

41. Heiduk and Sakaki 2019.

42. Berda 2018; Gregory 2004.

43. McSweeney et al. 2018.

44. Mbembe 2000: 284.

45. Grandin and Oglesby 2018.

46. Miller 2017: 88.

47. Human Rights Council 2019; IOM 2017; Miller 2017.

48. Miller 2017: 89, citing a report by Germanwatch.

49. Walia 2013.

50. Miller 2017: 221.

51. Crawford 2019; Miller 2017: 97.

52. Miller 2017: 27.

53. Constable 1997: 33; Coutin 2007.

54. Lucht 2011.

55. Lucht 2011: 93.

56. Lucht 2011: 104, quoting from Cole and Booth 2007: 2.

57. Hochschild 2002: 22; see also Ehrenreich and Hochschild 2002.

58. Povinelli 2011; see also Bauman 2004; Harrison 2002; Marcos 1997; Sassen 2014. Lutz and Nonini (1999: 75) use the phrase *refuse regions* to describe areas made superfluous to the global economy.

CHAPTER THREE CONTAINMENT

1. Alekseyeva 2013; Davis 2005: 90; Haugen 2015; Hing 2009; Kalir 2015; Vasquez 2015. Davis argues that the EU border regime emplaced since the 1990s is aimed at voters fearful of "dark-skinned and usually Muslim hordes" of invaders in order to lure them away from turning to far-right politicians.

2. Khosravi 2011: 70.

3. The UNHCR annual Global Trends reports show the pattern of housing refugees in poorer countries in the global south.

4. Trilling 2015.

5. UNHCR 2018.

6. IOM 2017. The figure is for 2016.

7. Hyndman 2000: 17; see also Gatrell 2013; Legomsky 2006; Verdirame and Harrell-Bond 2005.

8. Albahari 2015: 90; see also Trilling 2015.

9. Davis 2005: 90.

10. Kalir 2015; Shamir and Mundlak 2013.

11. Pan 2016.

12. For ethnographic discussions of these points, see Agier (2005, 2010), Bauman (2004), Hyndman (2000), Nyers (2006), Turner (2010), Verdirame and Harrell-Bond (2005). On the narrowing of opportunities for asylum, see Fassin (2005) and Bohmer and Schuman (2008).

13. Ann Stoler provocatively argues that the colony and the camp are closely related political forms because the basis of both is containment. Reading across various iterations of colonial forms of containment (settler colonies, agricultural colonies, work camps, prisons, penal colonies), she writes, "A 'colony' as a political concept is not a place but a principle of managed mobilities, mobilizing and immobilizing populations according to a set of changing rules and hierarchies that orders social kinds: those eligible for recruitment, for resettlement, for disposal, for aid, or for coerced labor and those who are forcibly confined" (2017: 117). Both camp and colony are about managing mobility, security, hierarchy, and the molding of populations as part of imperial projects.

14. Walters 2015: 7.

15. On border thickening, see Rosas (2016).

16. Fassin 2011: 214.

17. See Shahram Khosravi's (2011) description of his experiences of being constantly profiled during his flight as a refugee from Iran to Sweden and, most especially, after settling permanently in Sweden.

18. Berda 2018: 9.

19. Berda 2018: 12.

20. Berda 2018: 36, 37.

21. Lloyd 2015: 13.

22. See Abrego et al. 2017; Andreas 2009; Coutin 2007; Gomberg-Muñoz 2017.

23. Coutin 2007: 21.

24. Dorsey and Díaz-Barriga 2015.

25. Abrego et al. 2017.

26. Gomberg-Muñoz 2016: 3.

27. For more detailed discussions of these policies, see De León (2015), García (2006), Menjívar (2014), Nevins (2008), Ong (2009), Vasquez (2015).

28. Abrego et al. 2017: 704.

29. Griffiths 2017.

30. Shantz 2019.

31. The list of offenses that can lead to automatic deportation includes such innocuous things as incorrectly filling out a form, missing a filing deadline, and even minor traffic violations.

32. Abrego et al. 2018.

33. Gomberg-Muñoz 2016: 5.

34. Vasquez 2015: 604, 650.

35. Abrego et al. 2017: 699.

36. Miller 2014: 18, 2017. The financial resources are equally staggering: the Border Patrol budget has tripled since 9/11, reaching $3.8 billion in 2015 within a CBP budget of $12.8 billion, within a DHS budget of $61 billion (U.S. Department of Homeland Security 2016).

37. American Immigration Council 2019.

38. Kalir 2019: 6, quoting a Migration Policy Institute report, available at https://www.migrationpolicy.org/article/obama-record-deportations-deporter -chief-or-not (Chishti, Pierce, and Bolter 2017). See also Andreas (2009).

39. American Immigration Council 2019.

40. See Miller 2017: 123.

41. American Immigration Council 2019.

42. Andersson 2014a: 120; see also Feldman 2012.

43. Scheel 2017: 43.

44. Benedicto and Brunet 2018; Milivojevic 2013.

45. See Andersson 2017; Scheel 2017.

46. Quoted in Rigo 2005: 14.

47. Kalir 2019: 4.

48. Albahari 2015; Carter and Merill 2007.

49. Tazzioli 2015; see also Albahari 2015.

50. Andersson 2014b; Trilling 2015.

51. Trilling 2015.

52. See Benedicto and Brunet 2018; Kalir 2019.

53. Cabot 2015; Cantat 2016.

54. Kalir 2019: 4.

55. Heller, Pezzani, and Stierl 2019: 54; Heller et al. 2018; Povoledo and Pérez-Peña 2018.

56. Kalir (2019: 1) asks, "How can thousands of people drown each year in the Mediterranean Sea or dehydrate to death in the Arizona desert without it leading to a serious reevaluation of the policies that regulate killing borders?"

57. Heller et al. 2018; Povoledo and Pérez-Peña 2018.

58. Cetti 2015; see also Carr 2012.

59. Penney 2018. Niger also has been pressured to criminalize those who assist migrants.

60. Segantini 2018; see also Albahari 2015; Andersson 2014a; Carter and Merrill 2007; Cetti 2015; Lucht 2011; Trilling 2015.

61. Cobarrubias 2019.

62. Andersson 2014a. Andersson (2017) reports that Europe pressures Morocco to treat migrants so badly that they agree to IOM voluntary repatriation opportunities.

63. Carasik 2015; see also Vogt 2018.

64. Frank-Vitale 2015.

65. Hyndman and Mountz 2008.

66. Amin and Kwai 2018; Flynn 2014a,b; see also Amnesty International 2016; Davis 2005; Greenwood 2012; Legomsky 2006; *New York Times* 2015b; Smith 2018.

67. Fassin 2011.

68. Very little information is available about the treatment of detainees in Canadian prisons and holding facilities in the Gulf states.

69. Detention Watch Network n.d.; Fleischner 2016; Gavett 2011; Gonzalez-Barrera and Krogstad 2014; Miller 2014; Urbina 2014; https://www .freedomforimmigrants.org/detention-statistics).

70. Juárez, Gómez-Aguiñaga, and Bettez 2018: 78; see also Gilman and Romero 2018.

71. Mountz et al. 2012: 526.

72. Bowling 2013: 298; Stumpf 2013.

73. Hall 2012.

74. Ugelvik 2013.

75. Chishti, Pierce, and Bolter 2017; Kalir 2019; Marshall 2016. *Mother Jones* (2014) reports that in 2013, the top five countries to which people were deported were Mexico, Guatemala, Honduras, El Salvador, and the Dominican Republic. The Migration Policy Institute (Chishti, Pierce, and Bolter 2017) puts the number of people deported under Obama at 3.1 million.

76. Gonzalez-Barrera and Krogstad 2014; see also Stumpf 2013.

77. Santos 2014.

78. Kalir 2019: 4.

79. Kalir 2017.

80. Benedicto and Brunet 2018.

81. Coutin 2010: 206; see also Coutin 2007; Peutz 2006. Rodkey (2016) offers an account of how those deported to the Dominican Republic from the U.S. for petty crimes constitute a disposable labor force repurposed abroad, where they are hired to work in call centers servicing U.S. customers. Because their stigmatized status as deportees hinders their entry into the Dominican economy, they become an exploitable labor force for U.S. companies operating there. See also Blitzer 2017.

82. Albahari 2015; Australian Border Deaths Database 2016; BBC News 2014; De León 2015; *New York Times* 2015b; Povoledo and Pérez-Peña 2018. The International Organization for Migration reports that even though border apprehensions at the U.S.-Mexico border dropped by 44 percent in 2017, more migrants died trying to cross than in the previous year (415 in 2017 compared with 398 in 2016) (IOM 2018).

83. Amoore 2006.

84. Vukov 2016.

85. Andersson 2016: 10.

86. Andersson 2014b; Scheel 2017: 43.

87. Annibale 2018; De Genova 2017b: 5.

CHAPTER FOUR LABOR

1. Razsa and Kurnik 2012.

2. Hahamovitch 2011.

3. IOM 2017, 2018; see also Levush 2013.

4. As of 2013, of the OECD countries, Japan, New Zealand, Germany, Australia, Finland, and Mexico all admitted more temporary workers than legal immigrants (Wilson 2013).

5. Hahamovitch 2011.

6. Castles 2006.

7. Chin 2017.

8. Feldman 2012.

9. Feldman 2012.

10. Dreby 2015; Gomberg-Muñoz 2011; Nevins 2008; Ngai 2004; Southern Poverty Law Center 2013.

11. Ngai (2004: 128) borrows the term *imported colonialism* from Andrew Biemiller, lobbyist for the AFL-CIO. The second quote is from Ngai (2004: 136).

12. Hahamovitch 2011: 49.

13. Unlike the situation for agricultural workers, for whom there is no cap on visas, the U.S. caps the number of nonagricultural worker visas offered every year, causing consternation among employers, who compete for limited short-term worker visas and clamor every year for the cap to be raised. Another temporary visa category, the H-1B visa, is for skilled workers who have a minimum of a college degree, whose contracts are owned by their employers and last from one to three years. The U.S. issued 1.8 million H-1B visas between 2001 and 2015, half of which went to immigrants from India who work in computer-related occupations (Ruiz 2017; Wilson 2013).

14. Binford 2013; Feldman 2012.

15. Binford 2013: 50. The Mexican and Caribbean governments maintain offices to support their workers in Canada, but because of low staffing and a desire to maintain good relations with Canada, the beneficial presence of a support staff is fairly insignificant.

16. Binford 2013: 141.

17. Figures are reported in the Migration Data Portal, maintained by the International Organization for Migration, available at https://migrationdataportal.org/themes/remittances.

18. Coutin 2007.

19. Caraballo 2019.

20. Xiang and Lindquist 2014: 125, 131.

21. Constable 2014; Shipper 2010.

22. Benson 2008; Binford 2013; Brennan 2014; Hahamovitch 2011; International Labor Recruitment Working Group 2013; Southern Poverty Law Center 2013.

23. Holmes 2013: 101; Southern Poverty Law Center 2013: 2.

24. Southern Poverty Law Center 2013; Stoll 2013.

25. Menjívar 2014: 361.

26. See, for example, Coe 2013; Fellmeth et al. 2018; Hochschild 2002; Menjívar 2014; Parreñas 2005, 2008.

27. See AlShehabi 2015; Dito 2015; Gardner 2010, 2012; Kelly and Thompson 2015; Longva 2005; Mahdavi 2016.

28. Parreñas 2008: 43.

29. Mahdavi 2016.

30. Recent reports estimate the number of foreign domestic workers in 2019 in Hong Kong at 385,000, or about 10 percent of the city's working population (Experian n.d.). In 2015, about 38 percent of Singapore's population of 3.66 million—nearly 1.4 million—were foreign workers. Domestic workers accounted for over a quarter million of those, and their numbers are predicted to rise by another third of a million over the next decade. Taiwan began importing foreign caregivers and domestic workers in 1992, and their number reached a quarter of a million by 2015, making up just over a third of the foreign blue-collar labor force (Wang et al. 2018). It is unclear whether these statistics include undocumented foreign workers. Malaysia, with a population of 30 million, has an estimated 4 million foreign workers, half of whom lack authorization (Aw 2016).

31. Constable 2014; also Constable 1997.

32. Ong 2009: 160.

33. Rich 2018.

34. Ong 2009.

35. Raijman and Kemp 2007; Shamir and Mundlak 2013: 128; Willen 2007, 2010. See also Flynn and Grange (2015) on mass deportations in the Gulf states.

36. Mundlak 2007: 67.

37. Shamir and Mundlak 2013: 128; Willen 2007, 2010.

38. Berda 2018.

39. Li 2015.

40. Li 2015.

41. Li 2015: 171.

42. Thomas 2017. See also Hannah Appel's (2018) description of the wage differentials between workers who carry U.S. passports and Filipino workers who do the same jobs in the oil extraction industry in Equatorial Guinea. Quoting a skilled Filipino worker who explained, "You are paid according to your passport," Appel describes how employment companies that source international labor for the oil industry in Equatorial Guinea operate "a form of national and racial arbitrage."

43. Kirkpatrick 2018.

44. Castles 2006: 746.

45. Dreby 2015.

46. Holmes 2013.

47. Gomberg-Muñoz 2017: 144.

48. Wilson 2013.

49. Gomberg-Muñoz 2017: 40, 147; see also Gomberg-Muñoz 2011.

50. See Boehm 2012; Dreby 2015; Gomberg-Muñoz 2017; Hing 2009; Vasquez 2015.

51. Boehm 2012.

52. Urbina 2014.

53. Chuang 2014; IOM says, "China's National Statistics Bureau estimates that almost 269 million internal migrant workers are moving from rural areas to the country's growing cities" (https://www.iom.int/countries/china). Compare this figure with the estimated 50–60 million Chinese living overseas in 2015.

54. Alexander and Chan 2004: 626; see also Chuang 2014.

55. Benson 2008.

56. Brennan 2014: 44; see also Boehm 2016: 136; Gomberg-Muñoz 2011.

57. Anderson 2000: 149.

CHAPTER FIVE MILITARIZATION

1. Lutz 2002: 723.

2. Batchelor, Dunne, and Lamb 2002; Steinberg 2014.

3. Von Schnitzler 2016: 49.

4. Kershner 2017. On Israel's successful self-promotion as the global leader in homeland security technology and models, see Machold 2015.

5. Benedicto and Brunet 2018.

6. Benedicto and Brunet 2018; Garella, Sciurba, and Tazzioli 2018; see also https://www.operationsophia.eu/.

7. Reece Jones calls the militarization of border enforcement through such efforts "the most significant change in the Mediterranean region" since 2006 (2016: 17).

8. Grandin 2019b.

9. Andreas 2009; Dunn 2001; Heyman 2008; Palafox 2001; Rosas 2007.

10. Dunn 2001.

11. Andreas 2009.

12. Grandin 2019b.

13. Andreas 2009; Dorsey and Díaz-Barriga 2015; Dunn 2001; Jones 2012, 2016; Miller 2014; Nevins 2001.

14. Miller 2014: 21.

15. Jones 2016. The Tohono O'odhom reservation along the U.S.-Mexico border offers an acutely painful glimpse of thoroughly militarized civilian space, where border patrol and military units operate with impunity against both the people who live there and the environment that local residents have nurtured for generations. "For the O'odham, the result is similar to living under occupation, a term used often in their communities," observes Todd Miller (2017: 153).

16. Miller 2017: 58.

17. Miller 2012.

18. Low 2019.

19. Brown 2010.

20. Miller 2017: 126.

21. Miller 2014.

22. Jones 2009. Jones (2016) also reports on how the global war on terror offered legitimacy to India's expansion of state security practices and laws modeled on the U.S. Patriot Act.

23. Jones 2016.

24. See Brown 2010.

25. See the revealing ethnographic descriptions of checkpoint crossings for Palestinians in Israel in Hammami (2015, 2019) and in India/Bangladesh in Ghosh (2011).

26. Miller 2012; see also Andreas 2009.

27. Rosas 2007: 97.

28. Amoore, Marmura, and Salter 2008.

29. Apuzzo and Schmidt 2014.

30. Breckenridge 2014: 12.

31. Breckenridge 2014: 96.

32. Breckenridge 2014: 20.

33. Browne 2015: 24, 67. Browne also calls the *Book of Negroes* "one of the earliest passports issued for crossing the Canada-U.S. border that identified race, gender, and other markers" (2015: 162).

34. See Amoore 2006, 2009; Ceyhan 2008; Côté-Boucher 2008; Maguire, Rao, and Zurawski 2018; Wilson and Weber 2008.

35. Amoore 2011: 26–27; see also Allen and Vollmer 2017; Amoore 2006, 2009.

36. Amoore 2011.

37. Bowling 2013: 296.

38. Côté-Boucher 2008, 2015.

39. Wilson and Weber 2008.

40. Aus 2013; Vukov 2016.

41. Amoore 2009: 50.

42. Cassiano 2019; Mitchell and Diamond 2018.

43. Roberts 2018a.

44. Buckley and Mozer 2019.

45. Buckley 2019; Buckley and Mozer 2019.

46. Cassiano 2019.

47. Maguire 2018. Decisions about prison sentences in some districts are now subject to secretive algorithms that assess the risk of recidivism, despite studies showing the racial bias built into some programs that wrongly identified defendants of color as twice as likely as white defendants to commit future crimes (Middlemass 2019).

48. Muñiz 2015; Dreier 2018.

49. Masco 2014, 2019.

50. Graham 2019: 210.

51. Amoore 2007: 218.

52. Grewal 2017.

53. Ogasawara 2017: 480.

54. Klaus 2017: 525.

55. Maguire 2012; Monroe 2017.

56. Ahmad and Mehmood 2017.

57. Ahmad and Mehmood 2017: 509.

58. On Kenya, see Glück (2019), who draws a connection between the counter-terror state in Kenya and the British counterinsurgency state of the colonial era. On Kashmir, see Junaid (2013, 2017).

59. Shah 2019: 154; see also Sundar 2016.

60. Roberts 2018b.

61. Lutz 2017: 424.

62. Glück and Low 2017: 284.

63. On the securitization of the body, home, and neighborhood, see Bickford (2020), Low (2010), Schull (2016).

64. Klein 2007: 381.

65. Crawford 2018b.

66. Karlin 2014.

67. Klein 2007.

68. Klein 2007: 381.

69. Klein 2007: 393.

70. Todd Miller quotes this figure from a brochure handed out at the 2014 Milipol, the world's biggest homeland security expo (2017: 110).

71. Machold 2015; Walia 2013.

72. Press 2017.

73. Maguire, Frois, and Zurawski 2014.

74. Lauterbach 2017.

75. There is a robust literature on U.S. empire, much of which emphasizes U.S. imperialism in the form of militarism and military bases around the world, the role of the U.S. in promoting neoliberal economics through austerity regimes and trade, and U.S. claims to territorial control around the world. Hardt and Negri (2000) argue that while the U.S. is a globally hegemonic power and operates as the global police force, it is not itself an empire but rather a component of a new, supranational form of sovereign power they call Empire. John Torpey argues that the U.S. is not an empire because its military strength is increasingly privatized and its economy threatened by its ballooning trade deficit. Noting the U.S. interest in policing mobility, Torpey further notes that controlling mobility is "not a characteristic typically associated with empires" (2005: 169). Collins and McGranahan (2019) argue the opposite in their edited collection of essays about U.S. empire, intended as a corrective to what they claim has been the absence of the term in anthropological discussions of U.S. military action around the world. In line with my own thinking, they write, "There is no single modality of U.S. empire"; rather, it has a plurality of "forms, strategies, justifications, and disguises" (2019: 10). Cathy Lutz and David Vine have provided groundbreaking work about the manifestation of U.S. empire through its 1,000 military bases around the world (Lutz 2006, 2009; Vine 2015, 2019). David Immerwahr (2019) also draws attention to the territorial reach of U.S. empire through its claims to Guam, Puerto

Rico, American Samoa, the Northern Marianas Islands, the U.S. Virgin Islands, and several other islands. Maskovsky and Susser's (2009) volume on the U.S. imperial homeland offers a collection of essays that closely inspect the domestic implications of U.S. imperial efforts following 9/11.

76. There is a plethora of literature about how apartheid practices contained within European colonialism and U.S. history have now extended throughout the globe while also structuring life within the U.S., Europe, and Australia for immigrants from the global south, some of which has been cited in previous chapters. See Calavita 2007; Hage 2000; Harrison 2008; Heyman 2008; Hintzen and Rahier 2003; Marable 2008; Menjívar 2014; Nevins 2008; Pierre 2013; Selod and Embrick 2013.

77. Lutz 2009: 24.

78. Stoler 2017: 193.

79. Stoler 2017: 31.

80. As states shrink to their security functions, security empires are built on the management of security in place of other forms of engagement. As an AFRICOM staff member told anthropologist Danny Hoffman, all AFRICOM cares about is fighting Boko Haram, Al-Shabaab, and Al-Qaeda in the Maghreb—not climate change, disease, or other environmental disasters (Hoffman 2017). The U.S. investment in training African militaries and elite commando units is about counterinsurgency, fighting "terrorism," and containing threats within African borders, using African soldiers to carry out the desires of the U.S., while U.S. collaboration with African governments on African priorities for economic and health security withers and disappears. See also McGovern (2010) on the Sahel.

81. Li 2019: 456.

82. Li 2019: 469.

83. Li 2019: 469.

84. Li 2019: 463.

85. Working through the relationship between national security states, counterterror states, and security imperialism affords a broader perspective on global security as an empire than is normally the case in the field of critical security studies. The first two terms draw attention to the laws, policies, and interventions of the counterterror state, but are less focused on tracking how these affect other spaces that are drawn into imperial security projects. Security empire as a concept directs attention toward those spaces—southern Somalia, northern Niger, Xinjian Autonomous Region, the Mexico-Guatemala border, the ZEDES of Honduras, the new Pakistan-China corridor, migrant camps in Libya, and elsewhere as security spaces produced through empire. The concept responds to the critiques that counterterror and critical security studies emerge from and respond to security projects of the global north, and have been insufficiently attentive to the ways in which security has been shifting across the global south. Howell and Richter-Montpetit (2019), for example, argue that securitization theory, marked in particular by theorists associated with the "Copenhagen School," is racist, marked by three forms of Eurocentrism: civilizationalism, methodological

whiteness, and antiblack racism. Civilizationalism defines Europe as the location of the sort of "normal politics" that securitization is meant to uphold, while
ignoring the racism at the heart of normal politics in Europe. Methodological
whiteness privileges a white liberal status quo, and antiblack racism is apparent in
the use of Africa as a foil, a place to stand in for anarchy, tribalism, and stateless-
ness, in contrast to Europe. See also the contributions in Salter (2019).

CHAPTER SIX FUTURES

1. South African History Online n.d.
2. See, for example, Gobodo-Madikizela (2003) and evidence collected by the
South African Truth and Reconciliation Commission.
3. Mamdani 2015: 159.
4. See Besteman 2008; von Schnitzler 2016; Wilson 2001.
5. Writing about mass incarceration in the U.S., Jackie Wang (2018) argues that
we cannot explain mass incarceration by only attending to its benefits for capital,
but must also acknowledge the power and pleasures of racism that run through
white American society.
6. Maskovsky 2017: 44, 45.
7. I am grateful to Michael Hardt for helping to articulate this argument.
8. Hage 2016: 45.
9. There are literatures and online syllabi on each of these movements as well
as on their intersections. A sampling of relevant recent scholarship includes CR10
Publications Collective (2008), Davis (2003), de Sousa Santos (2018), Escobar
(2019), Jones (2019), Walia (2013), Wang (2018).
10. Bloxham 2009.
11. Hindness 2005: 247.
12. Hindness 2005: 251, 253.
13. Robinson 2000.
14. Nail 2019: 26–27; see also Hardt and Negri 2000.
15. Agamben 1995.
16. Khosravi 2019: 416.
17. Cabot 2019; Khosravi 2018.
18. Washington 2019.
19. No More Deaths website, https://nomoredeaths.org/en/; El-Shaarawi and
Razsa 2018; Smith 2019; Webber 2019.
20. Nail 2019: 31; Smith 2017; Walia 2013.
21. Washington 2019; see also Jones 2019.
22. Anderson, Sharma, and Wright 2009: 12; see also Walia 2013.
23. Balibar 2004; Mbembe 2017b; see also Mbembe 2017a, 2018.
24. Brown 2010: 41.
25. Brown 2010: 41.
26. Gordimer 1989: 72–73. I am grateful to John Gilmour for the gift of this story.
27. Piot 2010: 170.

Abdi, Cawo. 2015. *Elusive Jannah: The Somali Diaspora and a Borderless Muslim Identity*. Minneapolis: University of Minnesota Press.

Abrego, Leisy, Mat Coleman, Daniel E. Martínez, Cecilia Menjívar, and Jeremy Slack. 2017. "Making Immigrants into Criminals: Legal Processes of Criminalization in the Post-IIRIRA Era." *Journal on Migration and Human Security* 5, no. 3: 694–715.

Adam, Hussein 1995. "Somalia: A Terrible Beauty Being Born?" In *Collapsed States: The Disintegration and Restoration of Legitimate Authority*, edited by William Zartman, 69–90. Boulder, CO: Lynne Rienner.

Africa Action. 2005. "Africa Action Statement on 100% Debt Cancellation." Washington, DC, September 23.

Agamben, Giorgio. 1995. "We Refugees." *Symposium* 49, no. 2: 114–19.

Agier, Michael. 2005. *On the Margins of the World: The Refugee Experience Today*. Cambridge: Polity.

Agier, Michel. 2010. "Humanity as an Identity and Its Politics Effects (A Note on Camps and Humanitarian Government)." *Humanity* 1, no. 1: 29–45.

Ahmad, Mahvish, and Rabia Mehmood. 2017. "Surveillance, Authoritarianism and 'Imperial Effects' in Pakistan." *Surveillance and Society* 15, nos. 3–4: 506–13.

Ahmed, Ali Jimale. 2017. "African Solutions for African Problems: Limning the Contours of a New Form of Connectivity." Comments delivered at the tenth anniversary of the Hargeysa International Book Fair, July.

Albahari, Maurizio. 2015. *Crimes of Peace: Mediterranean Migrations at the World's Deadliest Border*. Philadelphia: University of Pennsylvania Press.

Alekseyeva, Anna. 2013. "Russia's War on Foreigners." *Foreign Policy*, September 5. Accessed December 31, 2018. https://foreignpolicy.com/2013/09/05/russias -war-on-foreigners/.

Alexander, Michelle. 2012. *The New Jim Crow: Mass Incarceration in an Age of Colorblindness*. New York: New Press.

Alexander, Peter, and Anita Chan. 2004. "Does China Have an Apartheid Pass System?" *Journal of Ethnic and Migration Studies* 30, no. 4: 609–29.

Allen, William L., and Bastian A. Vollmer. 2017. "Clean Skins: Making the e-Border Security Assemblage." *Environment and Planning D: Society and Space* 36, no. 1: 23–39.

AlShehabi, Omar. 2015. "Histories of Migration to the Gulf." In *Transit States: Labour, Migration and Citizenship in the Gulf,* edited by Abdulhadi Khalaf, Omar AlShehabi, and Adam Hanieh, 3–38. London: Pluto.

American Immigration Council. 2019. "The Cost of Immigration Enforcement and Border Security: Fact Sheet." Washington, DC, May 17. https://www.americanimmigrationcouncil.org/research/the-cost-of-immigration-enforcement-and-border-security.

Amin, Mridula, and Isabella Kwai. 2018. "The Nauru Experience: Zero-Tolerance Immigration and Suicidal Children." *New York Times,* November 5.

Amnesty International. 2016. "Island of Despair: Australia's 'Processing' of Refugees on Nauru." October 17. https://www.amnesty.org/en/documents/asa12/4934/2016/en/.

Amoore, Louise. 2006. "Biometric Borders: Governing Mobilities in the War on Terror." *Political Geography* 25: 336–51.

Amoore, Louise. 2007. "Vigilant Visualities: The Watchful Politics of the War on Terror." *Security Dialogue* 38, no. 2: 215–32.

Amoore, Louise. 2009. "Algorithmic War: Everyday Geographies of the War on Terror." *Antipode* 41, no. 1: 49–69.

Amoore, Louise. 2011. "Data Derivatives: On the Emergence of a Security Risk Calculus for Our Times." *Theory, Culture and Society* 28, no. 6: 24–43.

Amoore, Louise, Stephen Marmura, and Mark B. Salter. 2008. "Editorial: Smart Borders and Mobilities: Spaces, Zones, Enclosures." *Surveillance and Society* 5, no. 2: 96–101.

Anderson, Bridget. 2000. *Doing the Dirty Work? The Global Politics of Domestic Work.* London: Zed.

Anderson, Bridget, Nandita Sharma, and Cynthia Wright. 2009. "Why No Borders." *Refuge* 26, no. 2: 5–18.

Anderson, Jon Lee. 2009. "The Most Failed State: Is Somalia's New President a Viable Ally?" *New Yorker,* December 7.

Anderson, Jon Lee. 2017. "Boundary Issues: Can Mexico Come to Terms with Trump?" *New Yorker,* October 9, 28.

Andersson, Ruben. 2014a. "Hunter and Prey: Patrolling Clandestine Migration in the Euro-African Borderlands." *Anthropological Quarterly* 87, no. 1: 110–49.

Andersson, Ruben. 2014b. *Illegality, Inc.: Clandestine Migration and the Business of Bordering Europe.* Berkeley: University of California Press.

Andersson, Ruben. 2016. "The Global Front against Migration." *Anthropology of This Century* 15 (January). http://aotcpress.com.articles/global-front-migration/.

Andersson, Ruben. 2017. "Rescued and Caught: The Humanitarian-Security Nexus at Europe's Frontiers." In *The Borders of "Europe": Autonomy of*

Migration, Tactics of Belonging, edited by Nicholas de Genova, 64–94. Durham, NC: Duke University Press.

Andreas, Peter. 2009. *Border Games: Policing the U.S.-Mexico Divide*. Ithaca, NY: Cornell University Press.

Annibale, Federico. 2018. "The New Balkan Route." *Jacobin*, July 25. https://www.jacobinmag.com/2018/07/eu-migrants-refugees-balkan-route-frontex-dublin-schengen.

Aparicio, Juan Ricardo. 2017. "Affective Capitalism, Humanitarianism and Extractivism in Colombia: Old and New Borders for Future Times." *Cultural Studies* 31, nos. 2–3: 331–52.

Appel, Hannah. 2018. "Race Makes Markets: Subcontracting in the Transnational Oil Industry." Social Science Research Council, December 18. https://items.ssrc.org/race-capitalism/race-makes-markets-subcontracting-in-the-transnational-oil-industry/.

Apuzzo, Matt, and Michael S. Schmidt. 2014. "U.S. to Continue Racial, Ethnic Profiling in Border Policy." *New York Times*, December 5. https://www.nytimes.com/2014/12/06/us/politics/obama-to-impose-racial-profiling-curbs-with-exceptions.html.

Aus, Katja Franko. 2013. "The Ordered and Bordered Society: Migration Control, Citizenship, and the Northern Penal State." In *The Borders of Punishment: Migration, Citizenship, and Social Exclusion*, edited by Katja Franko Aus and Mary Bosworth, 21–39. Oxford: Oxford University Press.

Australian Border Deaths Database. Accessed December 30, 2016. https://www.monash.edu/arts/border-crossing-observatory/research-agenda/australian-border-deaths-database.

Aw, Tash. 2016. "Malaysia's Immigrant Worker Debate." *New York Times*, March 28.

Balibar, Étienne. 2001. "Outlines of a Topography of Cruelty: Citizenship and Civility in the Era of Global Violence." *Constellations* 8, no. 1: 15–29.

Balibar, Étienne. 2004. "Droit de Cité or Apartheid?" In *We, the People of Europe? Reflections on Transnational Citizenship*, edited by É. Balibar, 31–50. Princeton, NJ: Princeton University Press.

Barak-Erez, Daphne. 2008. "Israel: Citizenship and Immigration Law in the Vise of Security, Nationality, and Human Rights." *International Journal of Constitutional Law* 6, no. 1: 184–92.

Barnett, Thomas P. M. 2003. "The Pentagon's New Map." *Esquire*, March.

Barnett, Thomas P. M. 2004. *The Pentagon's New Map: War and Peace in the Twenty-First Century*. New York: G. P. Putnam's Sons.

Batchelor, Peter, Paul Dunne, and Guy Lamb. 2002. "The Demand for Military Spending in South Africa." *Journal of Peace Research* 39, no. 3: 339–54.

Bauman, Zygmunt. 2004. *Wasted Lives: Modernity and Its Outcasts*. Cambridge: Polity.

BBC News. 2008. "Somalia Is 'Most Ignored Tragedy.'" October 6. Accessed August 14, 2017. http://news.bbc.co.uk/2/hi/africa/7653928.stm.

BBC News. 2014. "Mapping Mediterranean Migration." September 15. Accessed April 1, 2015. http://www.bbc.com/news/world-europe-24521614.

Beinart, William, and Saul Dubow, eds. 1995. *Segregation and Apartheid in Twentieth-Century South Africa*. London: Routledge.

Benedicto, Ainhoa Ruiz, and Pere Brunet. 2018. *Building Walls: Fear and Securitization in the European Union*. Barcelona: Centre Delàs d'Estudis per la Pau. https://www.tni.org/files/publication-downloads/building_walls_-_full_report_-_english.pdf.

Benson, Peter. 2008. "El Campo: Faciality and Structural Violence in Farm Labor Camps." *Cultural Anthropology* 23, no. 4: 589–629.

Berda, Yael. 2018. *Living Emergency: Israel's Permit Regime in the Occupied West Bank*. Stanford, CA: Stanford University Press.

Besteman, Catherine. 1999. *Unraveling Somalia: Race, Violence, and the Legacy of Slavery*. Philadelphia: University of Pennsylvania Press.

Besteman, Catherine. 2008. *Transforming Cape Town*. Berkeley: University of California Press.

Besteman, Catherine. 2016. *Making Refuge: Somali Bantu Refugees and Lewiston, Maine*. Durham: NC: Duke University Press.

Besteman, Catherine. 2017. "Experimenting in Somalia: The New Security Empire." *Anthropological Theory* 17, no. 3: 404–20.

Besteman, Catherine. 2019. "Militarized Global Apartheid." *Current Anthropology* 60, Supplement 19: S26–S38.

Besteman, Catherine, and Lee V. Cassanelli. 1996. *The Struggle for Land in Southern Somalia: The War behind the War*. Boulder, CO: Westview.

Bickford, Andrew. 2020. *Chemical Heroes: Pharmacological Supersoldiers in the US Military*. Durham NC: Duke University Press.

Binford, Leigh. 2013. *Tomorrow We're All Going to the Harvest: Temporary Foreign Worker Programs and Neoliberal Political Economy*. Austin: University of Texas Press.

Black, Stephanie. 2001. *Life and Debt*. Tuff Gong Pictures.

Blitzer, Jonathan. 2017. "The Deportees Taking Our Calls: How American Immigration Policy Has Fueled an Unlikely Industry in El Salvador." *New Yorker*, January 23.

Bloxham, Donald. 2009. "The Great Unweaving: The Removal of Peoples in Europe, 1875–1949." In *Removing Peoples: Forced Removal in the Modern World*, edited by Richard Bessel and Claudia B. Haake. Oxford: Oxford University Press.

Boehm, Deborah A. 2012. *Intimate Migrations: Gender, Family, and Illegality among Transnational Mexicans*. New York: New York University Press.

Boehm, Deborah A. 2016. *Returned: Coming and Going in an Age of Deportation*. Berkeley: University of California Press.

Bohmer, Carol, and Amy Shuman. 2008. *Rejecting Refugees: Political Asylum in the 21st Century*. London: Routledge.

Booker, Salih, and William Minter. 2001. "Global Apartheid." *The Nation*, June 21.

Bowling, Ben. 2013. "Epilogue: The Borders of Punishment: Towards a Criminology of Mobility." In *The Borders of Punishment: Migration, Citizenship, and Social Exclusion*, edited by Katja Franko Aas and Mary Bosworth, 291–305. Oxford: Oxford University Press.

Breckenridge, Keith. 2014. *Biometric State: The Global Politics of Identification and Surveillance in South Africa, 1850 to the Present*. Cambridge: Cambridge University Press.

Brennan, Denise. 2014. *Life Interrupted: Trafficking into Forced Labor in the United States*. Durham, NC: Duke University Press.

Brodkin, Karen. 1999. *How Jews Became White Folks and What That Says about Race in America*. New Brunswick, NJ: Rutgers University Press.

Brown, Wendy. 2010. *Walled States: Walled Sovereignty*. Brooklyn, NY: Zone.

Brown, Wendy. 2015. *Undoing the Demos: Neoliberalism's Stealth Revolution*. Cambridge, MA: MIT Press.

Browne, Simone. 2015. *Dark Matters: On the Surveillance of Blackness*. Durham, NC: Duke University Press.

Buckley, Chris. 2019. "China's Prisons Swell after Deluge of Arrests Engulfs Muslims." *New York Times*, August 31.

Buckley, Chris, and Paul Mozur. 2019. "How China Uses High-Tech Surveillance to Subdue Minorities." *New York Times*, May 22.

Bureau of Investigative Journalism. 2018. "Somalia: Reported US Actions 2018." https://www.thebureauinvestigates.com/drone-war/data/somalia-reported-us-actions-2018.

Bureau of Investigative Journalism. 2019. "Somalia: Reported US Actions 2019." https://www.thebureauinvestigates.com/drone-war/data/somalia-reported-us-actions-2019-strike-logs.

Cabot, Heath. 2014. *On the Doorstep of Europe: Asylum and Citizenship in Greece*. Philadelphia: University of Pennsylvania Press.

Cabot, Heath. 2015. "Crisis and Continuity: A Critical Look at the European Refugee Crisis." Allegra Lab, November 10.

Cabot, Heath. 2019. "The Business of Anthropology and the European Refugee Regime." *American Ethnologist* 46, no. 3: 261–75.

Calavita, Kitty. 2007. "Immigration Law, Race, and Identity." *Annual Review of Law and Social Science* 3: 1–20.

Cantat, Celine. 2016. "Rethinking Mobilities: Solidarity and Migrant Struggles beyond Narratives of Crisis." *Intersections: East European Journal of Society and Politics* 2, no. 4: 11–32.

Caplan, Gerald. 2006. "The Conspiracy against Africa." *International Affairs*, November.

Caraballo, Mayvelin U. 2019. "OFW Remittances Hit All-Time High in 2018." *Manila Times*, February 16. https://www.manilatimes.net/ofw-remittances-hit-all-time-high-in-2018/512476/.

Carasik, Lauren. 2015. "Brutal Borders: Mexico's Immigration Crackdown—And How the United States Funds It." *Foreign Affairs*, November 4.

Carr, Matthew. 2012. *Fortress Europe: Dispatches from a Gated Continent*. New York: New Press.

Carter, Donald, and Heather Merrill. 2007. "Bordering Humanism: Life and Death on the Margins of Europe." *Geopolitics* 12: 248–64.

Casey, Nicholas, and Clifford Krauss. 2018. "It Doesn't Matter if Ecuador Can Afford This Dam. China Still Gets Paid." *New York Times*, December 24.

Cassiano, Marcella Siqueira. 2019. "China's Hukou Platform: Windows into the Family." *Surveillance and Society* 17, nos. 1–2: 232–39.

Castles, Stephen. 2006. "Guestworkers in Europe: A Resurrection." *International Migration Review* 40, no. 4: 741–66.

Cetti, Fran. 2015. "Fortress Europe: The War against Migrants." *International Socialism* 148. http://isj.org.uk/fortress-europe-the-war-against-migrants/.

Ceyhan, Ayse. 2008. "Technologization of Security: Management of Uncertainty and Risk in the Age of Biometrics." *Surveillance and Society* 5, no. 2: 102–23.

Chan, Shelly. 2018. *Diaspora's Homeland: Modern China in the Age of Global Migration*. Durham, NC: Duke University Press.

Chen, Sealing. 2010. *On the Move for Love: Migrant Entertainers and the U.S. Military in South Korea*. Philadelphia: University of Pennsylvania Press.

Chin, Rita. 2017. *The Crisis of Multiculturalism in Europe: A History*. Princeton, NJ: Princeton University Press.

Chishti, Muzaffar, Sarah Pierce, and Jessica Bolter. 2017. "The Obama Record on Deportations: Deporter in Chief or Not?" Migration Policy Institute, January 26. https://www.migrationpolicy.org/article/obama-record-deportations-deporter-chief-or-not.

Chuang, Julia. 2014. "Chains of Debt: Labor Trafficking as a Career in China's Construction Industry." In *Human Trafficking Reconsidered: Rethinking the Problem, Envisioning New Solutions*, edited by Kimberly Kay Hoang and Rhacel Salazar Parreñas, 58–68. New York: International Debate Education Association.

Clark, Gracia. 2005. "The Permanent Transition in Africa." *Voices* 7, no. 1: 6–9.

Clarke, Kamari. 2010. "New Spheres of Transnational Formations: Mobilizations of Humanitarian Diasporas." *Transforming Anthropology* 18, no. 1: 48–65.

Clarke, Kamari. 2013. "Treat Greed in Africa as a War Crime." *New York Times*, January 29.

Cobarrubias, Sebastian. 2019. "Mapping Illegality: The i-Map and the Cartopolitics of 'Migration Management' at a Distance." *Antipode* 51, no. 3: 770–94.

Coe, Catie. 2013. *The Scattered Family: Parenting, African Migrants, and Global Inequality*. Chicago: University of Chicago Press.

Cole, Jeffrey, and Sally Booth. 2007. *Dirty Work: Immigrants in Domestic Service, Agriculture, and Prostitution in Sicily*. Lanham, MD: Lexington.

Collins, John F., and Carole McGranahan. 2019. "Ethnography and U.S. Empire." In *Ethnographies of U.S. Empire*, edited by Carole McGranahan and John F. Collins, 1–24. Durham, NC: Duke University Press.

Comaroff, Jean, and John L. Comaroff. 2012. *Theory from the South, or, How Euro-America Is Evolving toward Africa*. Boulder, CO: Paradigm.

Constable, Nicole. 1997. *Maid to Order in Hong Kong: Stories of Filipina Workers*. Ithaca, NY: Cornell University Press.

Constable, Nicole. 2014. *Born Out of Place: Migrant Mothers and the Politics of International Labor*. Berkeley: University of California Press.

Costs of War. n.d. "Iraqi Refugees." Brown University. http://watson.brown.edu /costsofwar/costs/human/refugees/iraqi.

Costs of War. 2019. "U.S. Spending for War in Afghanistan FY2001–2019." Brown University. https://watson.brown.edu/costsofwar/figures/2019/us-war -spending-afghanistan-2001.

Côté-Boucher, Karine. 2008. "The Diffuse Border: Intelligence-Sharing, Control and Confinement along Canada's Smart Border." *Surveillance and Society* 5, no. 2: 142–65.

Côté-Boucher, Karine. 2015. "Bordering Citizenship in 'an Open and Generous Society': The Criminalization of Migration in Canada." In *The Routledge Handbook on Crime and International Migration*, edited by Sharon Pickering and Julie Ham, 75–90. London: Routledge.

Coutin, Susan Bibler. 1993. *The Culture of Protest: Religious Activism and the U.S. Sanctuary Movement*. Boulder, CO: Westview.

Coutin, Susan Bibler. 2007. *Nations of Emigrants: Shifting Boundaries of Citizenship in El Salvador and the United States*. Ithaca, NY: Cornell University Press.

Coutin, Susan Bibler. 2010. "Confined Within: National Territories as Zones of Confinement." *Political Geography* 29, no. 4: 200–208.

Crawford, Neta C. 2018a. "Human Cost of the Post-9/11 Wars: Lethality and the Need for Transparency." November. Costs of War Project, Brown University. https://watson.brown.edu/costsofwar/files/cow/imce/papers/2018 /Human%20Costs%2C%20Nov%208%202018%20CoW.pdf.

Crawford, Neta C. 2018b. "United States Budgetary Costs of the Post-9/11 Wars through FY2019: $5.9 Trillion Spent and Obligated." November 14. Costs of War Project, Brown University. https://watson.brown.edu/costsofwar/files /cow/imce/papers/2018/Crawford_Costs%20of%20War%20Estimates%20 Through%20FY2019.pdf.

Crawford, Neta C. 2019. "Pentagon Fuel Use, Climate Change, and the Costs of War." June 12. Costs of War Project, Brown University. https://watson .brown.edu/costsofwar/files/cow/imce/papers/2019/Pentagon%20Fuel%20 Use%2C%20Climate%20Change%20and%20the%20Costs%20of%20 War%20Final.pdf.

CR10 Publications Collective. 2008. *Abolition Now! Ten Years of Strategy and Struggle against the Prison Industrial Complex*. Oakland, CA: AK Press.

Davis, Angela. 2003. *Are Prisons Obsolete?* New York: Seven Stories Press.

Davis, Mike. 2005. "The Great Wall of Capital." In *Against the Wall*, edited by Michael Sorkin, 88–99. New York: New Press.

De Genova, Nicolas. 2005. *Working the Boundaries: Race, Space, and "Illegality" in Mexican Chicago*. Durham, NC: Duke University Press.

De Genova, Nicholas. 2017a. "Introduction: The Borders of 'Europe' and the European Question." In *The Borders of "Europe": Autonomy of Migration, Tactics of Belonging*, edited by Nicholas de Genova, 1–35. Durham, NC: Duke University Press.

De Genova, Nicholas. 2017b. "The 'Migrant Crisis' as Racial Crisis: Do Black Lives Matter in Europe?" *Ethnic and Racial Studies* 42, no. 10: 1765–82.

De León, Jason. 2015. *The Land of Open Graves: Living and Dying on the Migrant Trail*. Berkeley: University of California Press.

De Sousa Santos, Boaventura. 2018. *The End of the Cognitive Empire: The Coming of Age of Epistemologies of the South*. Durham, NC: Duke University Press.

Detention Watch Network. n.d. http://www.detentionwatchnetwork.org/.

Dhillon, Jaskiran, and Nick Estes, eds. 2019. *Standing with Standing Rock: Voices from the #NoDAPL Movement*. Minneapolis: University of Minnesota Press.

Dito, Mohammed. 2015. "Kafala: Foundations of Migrant Exclusion in GCC Labour Markets." In *Transit States: Labour, Migration and Citizenship in the Gulf*, edited by Abdulhadi Khalaf, Omar AlShehabi, and Adam Hanieh, 79–99. London: Pluto.

Dlamini, Jacob. 2009. *Native Nostalgia*. Auckland Park, South Africa: Jacana Media.

Dorsey, Margaret, and Miguel Díaz-Barriga. 2015. "The Constitution-Free Zone in the United States: Law and Life in a State of Carcelment." *PoLAR* 38, no. 2: 204–25.

Dowie, Mark. 2009. *Conservation Refugees: The Hundred-Year Conflict between Global Conservation and Native Peoples*. Cambridge, MA: MIT Press.

Dreby, Joanna. 2015. *Everyday Illegal: When Policies Undermine Immigrant Families*. Berkeley: University of California Press.

Dreier, Hannah. 2018. "How a Crackdown on MS-13 Caught Up Innocent High School Students." *New York Times*, December 27. https://www.nytimes.com/2018/12/27/magazine/ms13-deportation-ice.html.

Duara, Prasenjit. 1997. "Nationalists among Transnationals: Overseas Chinese and the Idea of China." In *Ungrounded Empires*, edited by Aihwa Ong and Donald M. Nonini, 44–68. New York: Routledge.

Dunn, Timothy J. 2001. "Border Militarization via Drug and Immigration Enforcement: Human Rights Implications." *Social Justice* 28, no. 2: 7–30.

Edelman, Marc. 1990. "When They Took the 'Muni': Political Culture and Anti-Austerity Protest in Rural Northwestern Costa Rica." *American Ethnologist* 19, no. 4: 736–57.

Ehrenreich, Barbara, and Arlie Russell Hochschild. 2002. "Introduction." In *Global Woman: Nannies, Maids, and Sex Workers in the New Economy*, edited by Barbara Ehrenreich and Arlie Russell Hochschild, 1–13. New York: Metropolitan.

Elmi, Afyare Abdi. 2010. "Revisiting United States Policy toward Somalia." In *Securing Africa: Post 9/11 Discourses on Terrorism*, edited by Malinda S. Smith, 173–92. New York: Taylor and Francis.

El-Shaarawi, Nadia, and Maple Razsa. 2018. "Movements upon Movements: Refugee and Activist Struggles to Open the Balkan Route to Europe." *History and Anthropology* 30, no. 1: 91–112.

Englund, Harri. 2002. "Ethnography after Globalism: Migration and Emplacement in Malawi." *American Ethnologist* 29, no. 2: 261–86.

Escobar, Arturo. 2019. *Designs for the Pluriverse: Radical Interdependence, Autonomy, and the Making of Worlds*. Durham, NC: Duke University Press.

Experian. n.d. "The Value of Care: Key Contributions of Migrant Domestic Workers to Economic Growth and Family Well-Being in Asia." Study commissioned by Experian, in partnership with Enrich. http://www.enrichhk.org/wp-content/uploads/2019/02/Final_The-Value-of-Care_Full-Report.pdf.

Farmer, Paul. 2004. "An Anthropology of Structural Violence." *Current Anthropology* 45, no. 3: 305–25.

Fassin, Didier. 2001. "The Biopolitics of Otherness: Undocumented Foreigners and Racial Discrimination in French Public Debate." *Anthropology Today* 17, no. 1: 3–7.

Fassin, Didier. 2005. "Compassion and Repression: The Moral Economy of Immigration Policies in France." *Cultural Anthropology* 20, no. 3: 362–87.

Fassin, Didier. 2011. "Policing Borders, Producing Boundaries: The Governmentality of Immigration in Dark Times." *Annual Review of Anthropology* 40: 213–26.

Feldman, Gregory. 2012. *The Migration Apparatus: Security, Labor, and Policy-Making in the European Union*. Palo Alto, CA: Stanford University Press.

Fellmeth, Gracia, Kelly Rose-Clarke, Chenyue Zhao, Laura K. Busert, Yunting Zheng, Alessandro Massazza, Hacer Sonmez, Ben Eder, Alice Blewitt, Wachiraya Lertgrai, Miriam Orcutt, Katharina Ricci, Olaa Mohamed-Ahmed, Rachel Burns, Duleeka Knipe, Sally Hargreaves, Therese Hesketh, Charles Opondo, and Delan Devakumar. 2018. "Health Impacts of Parental Migration on Left-Behind Children and Adolescents: A Systematic Review and Meta-Analysis." *The Lancet* 392: 2567–82.

Ferguson, James. 2006. *Global Shadows: Africa in the Neoliberal World Order*. Durham, NC: Duke University Press.

Fergusson, James. 2013. *The World's Most Dangerous Place: Inside the Outlaw State of Somalia*. Boston: Da Capo.

Finnegan, William. 2003. "The Economics of Empire: Notes on the Washington Consensus." *Harpers*, May.

Fleischner, Nicki. 2016. "Weekly Chart: The Cost of U.S. Immigration Detention Centers." Americas Society/Council of the Americas, September 8. http://www.as-coa.org/articles/weekly-chart-cost-us-immigrant-detention-centers.

Flynn, Michael. 2014a. "How and Why Immigration Detention Crossed the Globe." Global Detention Project, Working Paper no. 8. April. Geneva: Global Migration Centre.

Flynn, Michael. 2014b. "There and Back Again: On the Diffusion of Immigration Detention." *Journal on Migration and Human Security* 2, no. 3: 165–97.

Flynn, Michael, and Mariette Grange. 2015. "Immigration Detention in the Gulf." Special Report. Geneva: Global Detention Project.

Foner, Nancy. 2005. *In a New Land: A Comparative View of Immigration.* New York: New York University Press.

Foreign Policy. 2008. "The 2008 Failed States Index."

Foreign Policy. 2009. "The 2009 Failed States Index." Accessed August 14, 2017. http://foreignpolicy.com/2009/06/21/the-2009-failed-states-index/.

Fox, Cybelle, and Irene Bloemraad. 2015. "Beyond 'White by Law': Explaining the Gulf in Citizenship Acquisition between Mexican and European Immigrants, 1930." *Social Forces* 94, no. 1: 181–207.

Frank-Vitale, Amelia. 2015. "Looming Crisis: What the United States Must Do to Address the Plight of Migrants from Central America." Institute of Current World Affairs, Washington, DC, December 21. https://www.icwa.org/looming-crisis-what-the-united-states-must-do-to-address-the-plight-of-migrants-from-central-america/.

Frederickson, George. 1981. *White Supremacy: A Comparative Study in American and South African History.* Oxford: Oxford University Press.

Friedman, Thomas. 1999. *The Lexus and the Olive Tree: Understanding Globalization.* New York: Farrar, Straus and Giroux.

Gans, Chaim. 2008. "Nationalist Priorities and Restrictions in Immigration: The Case of Israel." *Law and Ethics of Human Rights* 2, no. 1: article 12.

García, María Cristina. 2006. *Seeking Refuge: Central American Migration to Mexico, the United States, and Canada.* Berkeley: University of California Press.

Gardner, Andrew. 2012. "Why Do They Keep Coming? Labor Migrants in the Gulf States." In *Migrant Labor in the Persian Gulf,* edited by Mehran Kamrava and Zahra Babar, 41–58. London: Hurst.

Gardner, Andrew M. 2010. *City of Strangers: Gulf Migration and the Indian Community in Bahrain.* Ithaca, NY: Cornell University Press.

Gardner, Andrew M. 2015. "Migration, Labor and Business in the Worlding Cities of the Arabian Peninsula." Institute of Developing Economies, Discussion Paper no. 513. Chiba, Japan: IDE-JETRO.

Garella, Glenda, Alessandra Sciurba, and Martina Tazzioli. 2018. "Introduction: Mediterranean Movements and the Reconfiguration of the Military Humanitarian Border in 2015." *Antipode* 50, no. 3: 662–72.

Garvelink, William J., and Farha Tahir. 2011. "Somalia Remains the Worst Humanitarian Crisis in the World." Center for Strategic and International Studies, December 16. Accessed August 14, 2017. http://csis.org/publication/somalia-remains-worst-humanitarian-crisis-world.

Gatrell, Peter. 2013. *The Making of the Modern Refugee.* Oxford: Oxford University Press.

Gavett, Gretchen. 2011. "Lost in Detention." *Frontline*, October 18. http://www.pbs
.org/wgbh/pages/frontline/race-multicultural/lost-in-detention/map-the-u
-s-immigration-detention-boom/.

Geglia, Beth. 2016. "Honduras: Reinventing the Enclave." NACLA *Report on the
Americas* 48, no. 4: 353–60.

Geglia, Beth. 2018. "Life Laid Bare in Honduras: How the Migrant Caravan Makes
Neoliberal Dictatorship Visible." *Toward Freedom*, October 25. https://
towardfreedom.org/archives/americas/life-laid-bare-in-honduras-how-the
-migrant-caravan-makes-neoliberal-dictatorship-visible/.

Ghosh, Sahana. 2011. "Cross-Border Activities in Everyday Life: The Bengal Bor-
derland." *Contemporary South Asia* 19, no. 1: 49–60.

Gilman, Denise, and Luis A. Romero. 2018. "Immigration Detention, Inc." *Journal
on Migration and Human Security* 6, no. 2: 145–60.

Glück, Zoltán. 2019. "Security Urbanism and the Counterterror State in Kenya."
In *Spaces of Security: Ethnographies of Securityscapes, Surveillance, and Con-
trol*, edited by Setha Low and Mark Maguire, 31–56. New York: New York
University Press.

Glück, Zoltán, and Setha Low. 2017. "A Sociospatial Framework for the Anthropology of Security." *Anthropological Theory* 17, no. 3: 281–96.

Gobodo-Madikizela, Pumla. 2003. *A Human Being Died That Night*. New York:
Houghton Mifflin.

Goldman, Michael. 2005. "Tracing the Roots/Routes of World Bank Power." *International Journal of Sociology and Social Policy* 25, nos. 1–2: 10–25.

Gomberg-Muñoz, Ruth. 2011. *Labor and Legality: An Ethnography of a Mexican
Immigrant Network*. Oxford: Oxford University Press.

Gomberg-Muñoz, Ruth. 2016. "Criminalized Workers: Introduction to Special
Issue on Migrant Labor and Mass Deportation." *Anthropology of Work
Review* 37, no. 1: 3–10.

Gomberg-Muñoz, Ruth. 2017. *Becoming Legal: Immigration Law and Mixed-Status
Families*. Oxford: Oxford University Press.

Gonzalez-Barrera, Ana, and Jens Manuel Krogstad. 2014. "US Deportations of
Immigrants Reach Record High in 2013." Pew Research Center, October 2.
http://www.pewresearch.org/fact-tank/2014/10/02/u-s-deportations-of
-immigrants-reach-record-high-in-2013/.

Gordillo, Gaston. 2014. *Rubble: The Afterlife of Destruction*. Durham, NC: Duke
University Press.

Gordimer, Nadine. 1989. "Once upon a Time." *Salmagundi* 81: 67–73.

Gordon, David M. 2017. *Apartheid in South Africa: A Brief History with Documents*. Boston: Bedford/St. Martin's.

Graham, Stephen. 2019. "Enigmatic Presence: Satellites and the Vertical Spati-
alities of Security." In *Spaces of Security: Ethnographies of Securityscapes,
Surveillance, and Control*, edited by Setha Low and Mark Maguire, 206–30.
New York: New York University Press.

Grandin, Greg. 2006. *Empire's Workshop: Latin America, the United States, and
the Rise of the New Imperialism*. New York: Henry Holt.

Grandin, Greg. 2019a. *The End of the Myth: From the Frontier to the Border Wall in the Mind of America*. New York: Metropolitan.

Grandin, Greg. 2019b. "The Militarization of the Southern Border Is a Long-Standing American Tradition." *The Nation*, January 14.

Grandin, Greg, and Elizabeth Oglesby. 2018. "Who Killed Jakelin Caal Maguín at the US Border?" *The Nation*, December 17.

Greenwood, Phoebe. 2012. "Huge Detention Centre to Be Israel's Latest Weapon in Migration Battle." *The Guardian*, April 17. https://www.theguardian.com/world/2012/apr/17/detention-centre-israel-migration.

Gregory, Derek. 2004. *The Colonial Present: Afghanistan, Palestine, Iraq*. Oxford: Blackwell.

Gregory, Steven. 2007. *The Devil behind the Mirror: Globalization and Politics in the Dominican Republic*. Berkeley: University of California Press.

Grewal, Inderpal. 2017. *Saving the Security State: Exceptional Citizens in Twenty-First-Century America*. Durham, NC: Duke University Press.

Griffiths, Melanie. 2017. "Foreign, Criminal: A Doubly Damned Modern British Folk-Devil." *Citizenship Studies* 21, no. 5: 527–46.

Gudynas, Eduardo. 2010. "The New Extractivism of the 21st Century: Ten Urgent Theses about Extractivism in Relation to Current South American Progressivism." Americas Policy Program, Americas Program Report, January 21.

Gupta, Akhil, and James Ferguson. 1997. *Anthropological Locations: Boundaries and Grounds of a Field Science*. Berkeley: University of California Press.

Hage, Ghassan. 2000. *White Nation: Fantasies of White Supremacy in a Multicultural Society*. New York: Routledge.

Hage, Ghassan. 2016. "État de Siège: A Dying Domesticating Colonialism?" *American Ethnologist* 43, no. 1: 38–49.

Hage, Ghassan. 2017. *Is Racism an Environmental Threat?* Cambridge: Polity.

Hahamovitch, Cynthia. 2011. *No Man's Land: Jamaican Guestworkers in America and the Global History of Deportable Labor*. Princeton, NJ: Princeton University Press.

Hall, Alexandra. 2012. *Border Watch: Cultures of Immigration, Detention, and Control*. London: Pluto.

Hammami, Rema. 2015. "On (Not) Suffering at the Checkpoint: Palestinian Narrative Strategies of Surviving Israel's Carceral Geography." *Borderlands* 14, no. 1. http://www.borderlands.net.au/vol14no1_2015/hammami_checkpoint.pdf.

Hammami, Rema. 2019. "Destabilizing Mastery and the Machine: Palestinian Agency and Gendered Embodiment at Israeli Military Checkpoints." *Current Anthropology* 60, Supplement 19: S87–S97.

Hammond, Laura. 2013. "History, Overview, Trends and Issues in Major Somali Refugee Displacements in the Near Region (Djibouti, Ethiopia, Kenya, Uganda and Yemen)." *Bildhaan* 13: 55–79.

Hardt, Michael, and Antonio Negri. 2000. *Empire*. Cambridge, MA: Harvard University Press.

Harper, Mary. 2012. *Getting Somalia Wrong? Faith, War and Hope in a Shattered State*. London: Zed.

Harrison, Faye. 2002. "Global Apartheid, Foreign Policy, and Human Rights." *Souls: Journal of Black Politics, Culture, and Society* 4, no. 3: 48–68.

Harrison, Faye. 2008. "Global Apartheid, Foreign Policy, and Human Rights." In *Transnational Blackness: Navigating the Global Color Line*, edited by Manning Marable and Vanessa Agard-Jones, 19–39. New York: Palgrave Macmillan.

Harvey, David. 2005. *The New Imperialism*. Oxford: Oxford University Press.

Haugen, Heidi Østbø. 2015. "Destination China: The Country Adjusts to a New Migration Reality." Migration Policy Institute, March 4. https://www.migrationpolicy.org/article/destination-china-country-adjusts-its-new-migration-reality.

Haugerud, Angelique. 2005. "Globalization and Thomas Friedman." In *Why America's Top Pundits Are Wrong*, edited by Catherine Besteman and Hugh Gusterson, 102–20. Berkeley: University of California Press.

Hedges, Chris, and Joe Sacco. 2012. *Days of Destruction, Days of Revolt*. New York: Nation.

Heiduk, Felix, and Alexandra Sakaki. 2019. "China's Belt and Road Initiative: The View from East Asia." *East Asia* 36: 93–113.

Heller, Charles, Lorenzo Pezzani, Itamar Mann, Violeta Moreno-Lax, and Eyal Weizman. 2018. "It's an Act of Murder: How Europe Outsources Suffering as Migrants Drown." *New York Times*, December 26.

Heller, Charles, Lorenzo Pezzani, and Maurice Stierl. 2019. "Toward a Politics of Freedom of Movement." In *Open Borders: In Defense of Free Movement*, edited by Reece Jones, 51–76. Athens: University of Georgia Press.

Heyman, Josiah M. 2008. "Constructing a Virtual Wall: Race and Citizenship in U.S.-Mexico Border Policing." *Journal of the Southwest* 50, no. 3: 305–33.

Hindness, Barry. 2005. "Citizenship and Empire." In *Sovereign Bodies: Citizens, Migrants, and States in the Postcolonial World*, edited by Thomas Blom Hansen and Finn Stepputat, 241–56. Princeton, NJ: Princeton University Press.

Hing, Bill Ong. 2009. "Institutional Racism, ICE Raids, and Immigration Reform." *University of San Francisco Law Review* 44: 1–49.

Hinton, Elizabeth. 2016. *From the War on Poverty to the War on Crime: The Making of Mass Incarceration in America*. Cambridge, MA: Harvard University Press.

Hintzen, Percy C., and Jean Muteba Rahier, eds. 2003. *Problematizing Blackness: Self-Ethnographies by Black Immigrants to the United States*. London: Routledge.

Hochschild, Arlie Russell. 2002. "Love and Gold." In *Global Woman: Nannies, Maids, and Sex Workers in the New Economy*, edited by Barbara Ehrenreich and Arlie Russell Hochschild, 15–30. New York: Metropolitan.

Hoffman, Danny. 2017. "Military Humanitarianisms and Africa's Troubling 'Forces for Good.'" *Items: Bulletin of the Social Science Research Council,*

May 16. https://items.ssrc.org/from-our-fellows/military-humanitarianism
-and-africas-troubling-forces-for-good/.

Holmes, Seth. 2013. *Fresh Fruit, Broken Bodies: Migrant Farmworkers in the United States*. Berkeley: University of California Press.

Howell, Alison, and Melanie Richter-Montpetit. 2019. "Is Securitization Theory Racist? Civilisationism, Methodological Whiteness, and Antiblack Thought in the Copenhagen School." *Security Dialogue*, 1–20. https://journals .sagepub.com/doi/10.1177/0967010619862921.

Human Rights Council. 2019. "Climate Change and Poverty: Report of the Special Rapporteur on Extreme Poverty and Human Rights." June 25. https:// www.ohchr.org/Documents/Issues/Poverty/A_HRC_41_39.pdf.

Hyndman, Jennifer. 2000. *Managing Displacement: Refugees and the Politics of Humanitarianism*. Minneapolis: University of Minnesota Press.

Hyndman, Jennifer, and Alison Mountz. 2008. "Another Brick in the Wall? Neo-Refoulement and the Externalization of Asylum by Australia and Europe." *Government and Opposition* 43, no. 2: 249–69.

Immerwahr, Daniel. 2019. *How to Hide an Empire*. New York: Farrar, Straus and Giroux.

International Labor Recruitment Working Group. 2013. "The American Dream Up for Sale: A Blueprint for Ending International Labor Recruitment Abuse." February.

International Organization for Migration. 2017. *World Migration Report 2018*. Geneva: IOM.

International Organization for Migration. 2018. *Global Migration Indicators*. Berlin: Global Migration Data Analysis Center, IOM.

Itzigsohn, José. 2009. *Encountering American Faultlines: Race, Class, and the Dominican Experience in Providence*. New York: Russell Sage Foundation.

Jackson, Stephen. 2002. "Making a Killing: Criminality and Coping in the Kivu War Economy." *Review of African Political Economy* 29: 93–94.

Jackson, Stephen. 2003. "Fortunes of War: The Coltan Trade in the Kivus." In *Power, Livelihoods and Conflict: Case Studies in Political Economy Analysis for Humanitarian Action*, edited by Sarah Collinson, 21–36. London: Humanitarian Policy Group.

Jacobs, Sean, and Jon Soske, eds. 2015. *Apartheid Israel: The Politics of an Analogy*. Chicago: Haymarket.

James, C. L. R. [1938] 1963. *The Black Jacobins: Toussaint L'Ouverture and the San Domingo Revolution*. New York: Vintage.

Johns Hopkins China Africa Research Initiative. 2019. "Loan Database." http:// www.sais-cari.org/data.

Johnson, Jennifer. 2015. "Trump Calls for a 'Total and Complete Shutdown of Muslims Entering the United States.'" *Washington Post*, December 7.

Johnson, Sylvester. 2015. "Monstrosity, Colonialism and the Racial State." *J19: The Journal of Nineteenth-Century Americanists* 3, no. 1: 173–81.

Jones, Reece. 2009. "Geopolitical Boundary Narratives, the Global War on Terror and Border Fencing in India." *Transactions* 34: 290–304.

Jones, Reece. 2012. *Border Walls: Security and the War on Terror in the United States, India, and Israel*. London: Zed.

Jones, Reece. 2016. *Violent Borders: Refugees and the Right to Move*. New York: Verso.

Jones, Reece, ed. 2019. *Open Borders: In Defense of Free Movement*. Athens: University of Georgia Press.

Juárez, Melina, Bárbara Gómez-Aguiñaga, and Sonia P. Bettez. 2018. "Twenty Years after IIRIRA: The Rise of Immigrant Detention and Its Effects on Latinx Communities across the Nation." *Journal on Migration and Human Security* 6, no. 1: 74–96.

Junaid, Mohamad. 2013. "Death and Life under Occupation: Space, Violence and Memory in Kashmir." In *Everyday Occupations: Experiencing Militarism in South Asia and the Middle East*, edited by Kamala Visweswaran, 158–90. Philadelphia: University of Pennsylvania Press.

Junaid, Mohamad. 2017. "Internal Insecurity: Ikhwan, Elections, and the State of Emergency in Kashmir." Conference paper, American Anthropology Association meeting.

Kaldor, Mary. 2001. *New and Old Wars: Organized Violence in a Global Era*. Palo Alto, CA: Stanford University Press.

Kalir, Barak. 2015. "The Jewish State of Anxiety: Between Moral Obligation and Fearism in the Treatment of African Asylum Seekers in Israel." *Journal of Ethnic and Migration Studies* 41, no. 4: 580–98.

Kalir, Barak. 2017. "Between 'Voluntary' Return Programs and Soft Deportation: Sending Vulnerable Migrants in Spain Back 'Home.'" In *Return Migration and Psychosocial Wellbeing: Discourses, Policy-Making and Outcomes for Migrants and Their Families*, edited by Zana Vathi and Russell King, 56–71. New York: Routledge.

Kalir, Barak. 2019. "Departheid: The Draconian Governance of Illegalized Migrants in Western States." *Conflict and Society: Advances in Research* 5: 1–22.

Kanna, Ahmed. 2010. "Flexible Citizenship in Dubai: Neoliberal Subjectivity in the Emerging 'City-Corporation.'" *Cultural Anthropology* 25, no. 1: 100–129.

Kapteijns, Lidwien. 2013. *Clan Cleansing in Somalia: The Ruinous Legacy of 1991*. Philadelphia: University of Pennsylvania Press.

Karlin, Mark. 2014. "James Risen: The Post-9/11 Homeland Security Industrial Complex Profiteers and Endless War." Interview, *Truthout*, November 16. https://truthout.org/articles/james-risen-the-post-9-11-homeland-security-industrial-complex-profiteers-and-endless-war/.

Kelly, Annie, and Hazel Thompson. 2015. "The Vanished: The Filipino Domestic Workers Who Disappear behind Closed Doors." *The Guardian*, October 24.

Kershner, Isabel. 2017. "Trump Cites Israel's 'Wall' as Model. The Analogy Is Iffy." *New York Times*, January 27. https://www.nytimes.com/2017/01/27/world/middleeast/trump-mexico-wall-israel-west-bank.html.

Khosravi, Shahram. 2011. *"Illegal" Traveler: An Auto-Ethnography of Borders.* London: Palgrave Macmillan.

Khosravi, Shahram. 2018. "Afterword: Experiences and Stories along the Way." *Geoforum.* https://doi.org/10.1016/j.geoforum.2018.05.021.

Khosravi, Shahram. 2019. "What Do We See if We Look at the Border from the Other Side?" *Social Anthropology* 27, no. 3: 409–24.

King, Desmond. 2001. "Making Americans: Immigration Meets Race." In *E Pluribus Unum? Contemporary and Historical Perspectives on Immigrant Political Incorporation,* edited by Gary Gerstle and John Mollenkopf, 143–72. New York: Russell Sage Foundation.

Kinninmont, Jane. 2013. *"Citizenship in the Gulf": The Gulf States and the Arab Uprisings.* Edited by Ana Echagüe. London: Chatham House.

Kirkpatrick, David D. 2018. "On the Front Line of the Saudi War in Yemen: Child Soldiers from Darfur." *New York Times,* December 28.

Klaus, Witold. 2017. "Security First: New Right-Wing Government in Poland and Its Policy towards Immigrants and Refugees." *Surveillance and Society* 15, nos. 3–4: 523–28.

Klein, Naomi. 2007. *The Shock Doctrine: The Rise of Disaster Capitalism.* New York: Picador.

Koo, Se-Woong. 2018. "South Korea's Enduring Racism." *New York Times,* July 1.

Kumar, Amitava. 2010. *A Foreigner Carrying in the Crook of His Arm a Tiny Bomb.* Durham, NC: Duke University Press.

Lake, Marilyn, and Henry Reynolds. 2008. *Drawing the Global Colour Line: White Men's Countries and the International Challenge of Racial Equality.* Cambridge: Cambridge University Press.

Larmer, Brook. 2017a. "Is China the World's New Colonial Power?" *New York Times Magazine,* May 2.

Larmer, Brook. 2017b. "What the World's Emptiest Airport Says about Chinese Influence." *New York Times Magazine,* September 13.

Lauterbach, Claire. 2017. "No-Go Zones: Ethical Geographies of the Surveillance Industry." *Surveillance and Society* 15, nos. 3–4: 557–66.

Legomsky, Stephen H. 2006. "The USA and the Caribbean Interdiction Program." *International Journal of Refugee Law* 18, nos. 3–4: 677–95.

Levush, Ruth. 2013. "Guest Worker Programs: Comparative Analysis." Law Library of Congress, February. http://www.loc.gov/law/help/guestworker /comparative_analysis.php.

Li, Darryl. 2015. "Offshoring the Army: Migrant Workers and the U.S. Military." UCLA *Law Review* 62, no. 124: 126–74.

Li, Darryl. 2019. "From Exception to Empire: Sovereignty, Carceral Circulation, and the 'Global War on Terror.'" In *Ethnographies of U.S. Empire,* edited by Carole McGranahan and John F. Collins, 456–75. Durham, NC: Duke University Press.

Li, Tania M. 2010. "To Make Live or Let Die? Rural Dispossession and the Protection of Surplus Populations." *Antipode* 41, no. 1: 66–93.

Li, Tania M. 2017. "The Price of Un/Freedom: Indonesia's Colonial and Contemporary Plantation Labor Regimes." *Comparative Studies in Society and History* 59, no. 2: 245–76.

Li, Tania M. 2018. "After the Land Grab: Infrastructural Violence and the 'Mafia System' in Indonesia's Oil Palm Plantation Zones." *Geoforum* 96: 328–37.

Lloyd, Jenna M. 2015. "Carceral Citizenship in an Age of Global Apartheid." *Occasion* 8: 1–15.

Londoño, Ernesto. 2019. "U.S. Interests and China's Money Collide in El Salvador." *New York Times*, September 22.

Longva, Anh Nga. 2005. "Neither Autocracy nor Democracy but Ethnocracy: Citizens, Expatriates, and the Socio-Political System in Kuwait." In *Monarchies and Nations: Globalisation and Identity in the Arab States of the Gulf*, edited by Paul Dresch and James Piscatori, 114–35. London: I. B. Tauris.

Losurdo, Domenico. 2011. *Liberalism: A Counter-History*. London: Verso.

Low, Setha. 2010. "A Nation of Gated Communities." In *The Insecure American: How We Got Here and What We Should Do about It*, edited by Hugh Gusterson and Catherine Besteman, 27–44. Berkeley: University of California Press.

Low, Setha. 2019. "Domesticating Security: Gated Communities and Cooperative Apartment Buildings in New York City and Long Island, New York." In *Spaces of Security: Ethnographies of Securityscapes, Surveillance, and Control*, edited by Setha Low and Mark Maguire, 141–62. New York: New York University Press.

Lowe, Lisa. 2015. *The Intimacies of Four Continents*. Durham, NC: Duke University Press.

Lucht, Hans. 2011. *Darkness before Daybreak: African Migrants Living on the Margins in Southern Italy Today*. Berkeley: University of California Press.

Lutz, Catherine. 2002. "Making War at Home in the United States: Militarization and the Current Crisis." *American Anthropologist* 104, no. 3: 723–35.

Lutz, Catherine. 2006. "Empire Is in the Details." *American Ethnologist* 33, no. 4: 593–611.

Lutz, Catherine. 2009. "U.S. Foreign Military Bases: The Edge and Essence of Empire." In *Rethinking America: The Imperial Homeland in the 21st Century*, edited by Jeff Maskovsky and Ida Susser, 15–30. Boulder, CO: Paradigm.

Lutz, Catherine. 2017. "Afterward: Producing States of Security." *Anthropological Theory* 17, no. 3: 421–25.

Lutz, Catherine, and Donald Nonini. 1999. "The Economies of Violence and the Violence of Economies." In *Anthropological Theory Today*, edited by Henrietta L. Moore, 73–113. Cambridge: Polity Press.

Machold, Rhys. 2015. "Mobility and the Model: Policy Mobility and the Becoming of Israeli Homeland Security Dominance." *Environment and Planning A* 47: 816–32.

Maguire, Mark. 2012. "Biopower, Racialization and New Security Technology." *Social Identities* 18, no. 5: 593–607.

Maguire, Mark. 2018. "Policing Future Crimes." In *Bodies as Evidence: Security, Knowledge, and Power,* edited by Mark Maguire, Ursula Rao, and Nils Zurawski, 137–58. Durham, NC: Duke University Press.

Maguire, Mark, Catarina Frois, and Nils Zurawski, 2014. "Introduction: The Anthropology of Security: Prospects, Retrospects and Aims." In *Anthropology of Security: Perspectives from the Frontline of Policing, Counter-Terrorism and Border Control,* edited by Mark Maguire, Catarina Frois, and Nils Zurawski, 1–23. London: Pluto.

Maguire, Mark, Ursula Rao, and Nils Zurawski, eds. 2018. *Bodies as Evidence: Security, Knowledge, and Power.* Durham, NC: Duke University Press.

Mahdavi, Pardis. 2016. *Crossing the Gulf: Love and Family in Migrant Lives.* Stanford, CA: Stanford University Press.

Main, Alexander 2018. "Dirty Elections in Honduras, with Washington's Blessing." NACLA, January 11.

Malkki, Liisa 1992. "National Geographic: The Rooting of Peoples and the Territorialization of National Identity among Scholars and Refugees." *Cultural Anthropology* 7, no. 1: 24–44.

Malkki, Liisa 1995. "Refugees and Exile: From 'Refugee Studies' to the National Order of Things." *Annual Review of Anthropology* 24: 495–523.

Mamdani, Mahmood. 1996. *Citizen and Subject: Contemporary Africa and the Legacy of Late Colonialism.* Princeton, NJ: Princeton University Press.

Mamdani, Mahmood. 2015. "The South African Moment." In *Apartheid Israel: The Politics of an Analogy,* edited by Sean Jacobs and Jon Soske, 153–59. Chicago: Haymarket.

Manz, Beatriz. 2004. *Paradise in Ashes: A Guatemalan Journey of Courage, Terror, and Hope.* Berkeley: University of California Press.

Marable, Manning. 2008. "Introduction: Blackness beyond Boundaries: Navigating the Political Economics of Global Inequality." In *Transnational Blackness: Navigating the Global Color Line,* edited by Manning Marable and Vanessa Agard-Jones, 1–8. New York: Palgrave Macmillan.

Marcos, Subcomandante. 1997. "The Fourth World War Has Begun." *Nepantla: Views from the South* 2, no. 3: 559–72.

Marshall, Serena. 2016. "Obama Has Deported More People than Any Other President." *ABC News,* August 29. http://abcnews.go.com/Politics/obamas -deportation-policy-numbers/story?id=41715661.

Masco, Joseph P. 2014. *Theater of Operations: National Security Affect from the Cold War to the War on Terror.* Durham, NC: Duke University Press.

Masco, Joseph P. 2019. "The Secrecy/Threat Matrix." In *Bodies as Evidence: Security, Knowledge, and Power,* edited by Mark Maguire, Ursula Rao, and Nils Zurawski, 175–200. Durham, NC: Duke University Press.

Maskovsky, Jeff. 2017. "Reclaiming the Street: Black Urban Insurgency and Antisocial Security in Twenty-First Century Philadelphia." *Focaal* 79: 39–53.

Maskovsky, Jeff, and Ida Susser, eds. 2009. *Rethinking America: The Imperial Homeland in the 21st Century.* Boulder, CO: Paradigm.

Massey, Norman, and Nancy Denton. 1993. *American Apartheid: Segregation and the Making of the Underclass*. Cambridge, MA: Harvard University Press.

Mbembe, Achille. 2000. "At the Edge of the World: Boundaries, Territoriality, and Sovereignty in Africa." *Public Culture* 12, no. 1: 259–84.

Mbembe, Achille. 2011. "Provincializing France?" *Public Culture* 23, no. 1: 85–119.

Mbembe, Achille. 2017a. "Africa Needs Free Movement." *Mail and Guardian*, March 24. https://mg.co.za/article/2017–03–24–00-africa-needs-free -movement.

Mbembe, Achille. 2017b. "Scrap the Borders That Divide Us." *Mail and Guardian*, March 17. https://mg.co.za/article/2017–03–17–00-scrap-the-borders-that -divide-africans.

Mbembe, Achille. 2018. "The Idea of a Borderless World." *Africa Is a Country*. November 11. https://africasacountry.com/2018/11/the-idea-of-a-borderless -world.

McGovern, Mike. 2010. "Chasing Shadows in the Dunes: Islamist Practice and Counterterrorist Policy in West Africa's Sahara-Sahel Zone." In *Securing Africa: Post-9/11 Discourses on Terrorism*, edited by Malinda S. Smith, 79–98. New York: Taylor and Francis.

McSweeney, Kendra, David J. Wrathall, Erik A. Nielsen, and Zoe Pearson. 2018. "Grounding Traffic: The Cocaine Commodity Chain and Land Grabbing in Eastern Honduras." *Geoforum* 95: 122–32.

Menjívar, Cecilia 2014. "Immigration Law beyond Borders: Externalizing and Internalizing Border Control in an Era of Securitization." *Annual Review of Law and Social Science* 10: 353–69.

Menkhaus, Kenneth. 2009. "Somalia: 'They Created a Desert and Called It Peace(Building).'" *Review of African Political Economy* 36, no. 120: 223–33.

Menkhaus, Kenneth. 2010. "Stabilisation and Humanitarian Access in a Collapsed State: The Somali Case." *Disasters* 34, no. S3: 1–22.

Michigan State University. n.d. "South Africa: Overcoming Apartheid, Building Democracy." http://overcomingapartheid.msu.edu/multimedia.php?id =65–259–6.

Middlemass, Keesha. 2019. "A Felony Conviction as a Roboprocess." In *Life by Algorithms: How Roboprocesses Are Remaking Our World*, edited by Catherine Besteman and Hugh Gusterson. Chicago: University of Chicago Press.

Milivojevic, Sanja. 2013. "Borders, Technology and (Im)mobility: 'Cyber-Fortress Europe' and Its Emerging Southeast Frontier." *Australian Journal of Human Rights* 19, no. 3: 101–23.

Miller, Todd. 2012. "Fortress USA: The Wild World of Border Security and Boundary Building in Arizona." *The Nation*, June 7.

Miller. Todd. 2014. *Border Patrol Nation: Dispatches from the Front Lines of Homeland Security*. San Francisco: City Lights.

Miller, Todd. 2017. *Storming the Wall: Climate Change, Migration, and Homeland Security*. San Francisco: City Lights.

Mills, Charles. 1997. *The Racial Contract*. Ithaca, NY: Cornell University Press.

Minter, William, and Daniel Volman. 2009. "The Somalia Crossroads: Piracy and an Insurgency Tempt Washington to Get It Wrong—Again." *These Times*, June 29. Accessed August 14, 2017. http://inthesetimes.com/article/4520/the _somalia_crossroads.

Mitchell, Anna, and Larry Diamond. 2018. "China's Surveillance State Should Scare Everyone." *The Atlantic*, February 2.

Mongia, Radhika. 2018. *Indian Migration and Empire: A Colonial Genealogy of the Modern State*. Durham, NC: Duke University Press.

Monroe, Kristin V. 2017. "Tweets of Surveillance: Traffic, Twitter, and Securitization in Beirut, Lebanon." *Anthropological Theory* 17, no. 3: 322–37.

Morgan, Glenda. 1990. "Violence in Mozambique: Towards an Understanding of Renamo." *Journal of Modern African Studies* 28, no. 4: 603–19.

Mother Jones. 2014. "The Obama Administration's 2 Million Deportations, Explained." April 4.

Mountz, Alison, Kate Coddington, R. Tina Catania, and Jenna M. Loyd. 2012. "Conceptualizing Detention: Mobility, Containment, Bordering, and Exclusion." *Progress in Human Geography* 37, no. 4: 522–41.

Mullings, Leith. 2009. *New Social Movements in the African Diaspora: Challenging Global Apartheid*. New York: Palgrave Macmillan.

Mundlak, Gary. 2007. "Litigating Citizenship beyond the Law of Return." In *Transnational Migration to Israel in Global Comparative Perspective*, edited by Sarah S. Willen, 51–70. Lanham, MD: Lexington.

Muñiz, Ana. 2015. *Police, Power, and the Production of Racial Boundaries*. New Brunswick, NJ: Rutgers University Press.

Nail, Thomas. 2019. "Sanctuary, Solidarity, Status!" In *Open Borders: In Defense of Free Movement*, edited by Reece Jones, 23–33. Athens: University of Georgia Press.

Nelson, Diane. 2019. "Low Intensities." *Current Anthropology* 60, Supplement 19: S122–S133.

Nevins, Joseph. 2001. "Searching for Security: Boundary and Immigration Enforcement in an Age of Intensifying Globalization." *Social Justice* 28, no. 2: 132–48.

Nevins, Joseph. 2008. *Dying to Live: A Story of U.S. Immigration in an Age of Global Apartheid*. San Francisco: Open Media/City Lights.

New America Foundation. n.d. "America's Counterterrorism Wars: Drone Strikes: Somalia." Accessed May 29, 2019. https://www.newamerica.org/in-depth /americas-counterterrorism-wars/somalia/.

New York Times. 2015a. "Australia's Brutal Treatment of Migrants." Editorial Board, September 3.

New York Times. 2015b. "Migrant Deaths on the Mediterranean." Editorial Board, January 5.

Ngai, Mae. 2004. *Impossible Subjects: Illegal Aliens and the Making of Modern America*. Princeton, NJ: Princeton University Press.

Nonini, Donald M., and Aihwa Ong. 1997. "Introduction: Chinese Transnationalism as an Alternative Modernity." In *Ungrounded Empires*, edited by Aihwa Ong and Donald M. Nonini, 3–35. New York: Routledge.

Nordstrom, Carolyn. 1997. *A Different Kind of War Story*. Philadelphia: University of Pennsylvania Press.

Nordstrom, Carolyn. 2004. *Shadows of War: Violence, Power, and International Profiteering in the Twenty-First Century*. Berkeley: University of California Press.

Nordstrom, Carolyn. 2005. "Extrastate Globalization of the Illicit." In *Why America's Top Pundits Are Wrong*, edited by Catherine Besteman and Hugh Gusterson, 138–53. Berkeley: University of California Press.

Nyers, Peter. 2006. *Rethinking Refugees: Beyond States of Emergency*. New York: Routledge.

Ogasawara, Midori. 2017. "Surveillance at the Roots of Everyday Interactions: Japan's Conspiracy Bill and Its Totalitarian Effects." *Surveillance and Society* 15, nos. 3–4: 477–85.

Omi, Michael, and Howard Winant. 2015. *Racial Formation in the United States*, 3rd ed. New York: Routledge.

Ong, Aihwa. 2003. *Buddha Is Hiding: Refugees, Citizenship, and the New America*. Berkeley: University of California Press.

Ong, Aihwa. 2009. "A Bio-Cartography: Maids, Neo-Slavery, and NGOs." In *Migrations and Mobilities: Citizenship, Borders, and Gender*, edited by Seyla Benhabib and Judith Resnick, 157–86. New York: New York University Press.

Palafox, José. 2001. "Border Games and Border Thinking: A Review of Border Games: Policing the US-Mexican Divide." *Social Justice* 28, no. 2: 149–52.

Pan, Liang. 2016. "Why China Isn't Hosting Syrian Refugees." *Foreign Policy*, February 26.

Parreñas, Rhacel Salazar. 2005. *Children of Global Migration: Transnational Families and Gendered Woes*. Stanford, CA: Stanford University Press.

Parreñas, Rhacel Salazar. 2008. *The Force of Domesticity: Filipina Migrants and Globalization*. New York: New York University Press.

Penney, Joe. 2018. "Europe Benefits by Bankrolling an Anti-Migrant Effort. Niger Pays a Price." *New York Times*, August 25.

Perlstein, Rick. 2017. "I Thought I Understood the American Right. Trump Proved Me Wrong." *New York Times Magazine*, April 11, 36–41.

Pessar, Patricia. 2003. "Transnationalism and Racialization with Contemporary U.S. Immigration." In *Problematizing Blackness: Self-Ethnographies by Black Immigrants to the United States*, edited by Percy C. Hintzen and Jean Muteba Rahier, 21–34. New York: Routledge.

Peutz, Natalie. 2006. "Embarking on an Anthropology of Removal." *Current Anthropology* 47, no. 2: 217–41.

Pfeiffer, James, and Rachel Chapman. 2010. "Anthropological Perspectives on Structural Adjustment and Public Health." *Annual Review of Anthropology* 39: 149–65.

Pieke, Frank N. 2012. "Immigrant China." *Modern China* 38, no. 1: 40–77.

Pieke, Frank N. 2014. "Anthropology, China, and the Chinese Century." *Annual Review of Anthropology* 43: 123–38.

Pierre, Jemima. 2013. *The Predicament of Blackness: Postcolonial Ghana and the Politics of Race*. Chicago: University of Chicago Press.

Piot, Charles. 2010. *Nostalgia for the Future: West Africa after the Cold War*. Chicago: University of Chicago Press.

Piot, Charles. 2019. *The Fixer: Visa Lottery Chronicles*. Durham, NC: Duke University Press.

Posel, Deborah. 2011. "The Apartheid Project." In *The Cambridge History of South Africa*, edited by Robert Ross, Anne Kelk Mager, and Bill Nasson, 319–68. Cambridge: Cambridge University Press.

Postero, Nancy. 2005. "Indigenous Responses to Neoliberalism: A Look at the Bolivian Uprising of 2003." *PoLAR* 28, no. 1: 73–92.

Postero, Nancy Grey, and Leon Zamosc. 2004. "Indigenous Movements and the Indian Question in Latin America." In *The Struggle for Indigenous Rights in Latin America*, edited by Nancy Grey Postero and Leon Zamosc, 1–32. Brighton, UK: Sussex Academic.

Povinelli, Elizabeth. 2011. *Economies of Abandonment*. Durham, NC: Duke University Press.

Povoledo, Elisabetta, and Richard Pérez-Peña. 2018. "After Migrants Drowned at Sea, Debate over Who Should Have Saved Them." *New York Times*, September 11.

Press, Gil. 2017. "6 Reasons Israel Became a Cybersecurity Powerhouse Leading the $82 Billion Industry." *Forbes*, July 18. https://www.forbes.com/sites /gilpress/2017/07/18/6-reasons-israel-became-a-cybersecurity-powerhouse -leading-the-82-billion-industry/#20e59882420a.

Quesada, James. 1999. "From Central American Warriors to San Francisco Day Laborers: Suffering and Exhaustion in a Transnational Context." *Transforming Anthropology* 8, nos. 1–2: 162–85.

Raijman, Rebeca, and Adriana Kemp. 2007. "Labor Migration, Managing the Ethno-National Conflict, and Client Politics in Israel." In *Transnational Migration to Israel in Global Comparative Perspective*, edited by Sarah S. Willen, 31–50. Lanham, MD: Lexington.

Ramsay, Georgina. 2019. "Time and the Other in Crisis: How Anthropology Makes Its Displaced Object." *Anthropological Theory*. https://doi.org/10.1177 /1463499619840464.

Rana, Junaid. 2007. "The Story of Islamophobia." *Souls* 9, no. 2: 148–61.

Rana, Junaid. 2016. "The Racial Infrastructure of the Terror-Industrial Complex." *Social Text 129* 34, no. 4: 111–38.

Rawlence, Ben. 2016. *City of Thorns: Nine Lives in the World's Largest Refugee Camp*. New York: Picador.

Raynolds, Laura T. 2003. "The Global Banana Trade." In *Banana Wars: Power, Production, and History in the Americas*, edited by Steve Striffler and Mark Moberg, 23–47. Durham, NC: Duke University Press.

Razsa, Maple, and Andrej Kurnik. 2012. "The Occupy Movement in Žižek's Hometown: Direct Democracy and a Politics of Becoming." *American Ethnologist* 39, no. 2: 238–58.

Refugees International. 2009. "Somalia: Political Progress, Humanitarian Stalemate." April 3. Accessed August 14, 2017. http://refugeesinternational.org /policy/field-report/somalia-political-progress-humanitarian-stalemate.

Reno, William. 2000. "Clandestine Economies, Violence and States in Africa." *Journal of International Affairs* 53, no. 2: 433–59.

Rich, Motoko. 2018. "Bucking a Global Trend, Japan Seeks More Immigrants. Ambivalently." *New York Times*, December 7.

Richards, Patricia. 2010. "Of Indians and Terrorists: How the State and Local Elites Construct the Mapuche in Neoliberal Multicultural Chile." *Journal of Latin American Studies* 42, no. 1: 59–90.

Richards, Paul. 1996. *Fighting for the Rain Forest: War, Youth, and Resources in Sierra Leone*. Portsmouth, NH: Heineman.

Richmond, Anthony H. 1994. *Global Apartheid: Refugees, Racism, and the New World Order*. Oxford: Oxford University Press.

Richmond, Anthony H. 1995. "Citizenship, Naturalization, and Asylum: The Case of Britain." *Refuge* 22, no. 2: 59–66.

Rigo, Enrica. 2005. "Citizenship at Europe's Borders: Some Reflections on the Post-Colonial Condition of Europe in the Context of EU Enlargement." *Citizenship Studies* 9, no. 1: 3–22.

Roberts, Sean R. 2018a. "The Biopolitics of China's 'War on Terror' and the Exclusion of the Uyghurs." *Critical Asian Studies* 50, no. 2: 232–58.

Roberts, Sean R. 2018b. "Self-Perpetuating Conflict: How the Global War on Terror Has Supported Autocrats and Created More Terrorists." Center for a Public Anthropology. https://www.publicanthropology.org/self -perpetuating-conflict-how-the-global-war-on-terror-has-supported -autocrats-and-created-more-terrorists-by-sean-roberts-2/.

Robinson, Cedric J. [1983] 2000. *Black Marxism: The Making of the Black Radical Tradition*. Chapel Hill: University of North Carolina Press.

Rodkey, Evin. 2016. "Disposable Labor, Repurposed: Outsourcing Deportees in the Call Center Industry." *Anthropology of Work Review* 37, no. 1: 34–44.

Rodriguez, Robyn Magalit. 2010. *Migrants for Export: How the Philippine State Brokers Labor to the World*. Minneapolis: University of Minnesota Press.

Rosas, Gilberto. 2007. "The Fragile Ends of War: Forging the United States–Mexico Border and Borderlands Consciousness." *Social Text 91* 25, no. 2: 81–102.

Rosas, Gilberto. 2016. "The Border Thickens: In-Securing Communities after IRCA." *International Migration* 54, no. 2: 119–30.

Ruiz, Neil. 2017. "Key Facts about the U.S. H-1B Visa Program." Pew Research Center, April 27. https://www.pewresearch.org/fact-tank/2017/04/27/key -facts-about-the-u-s-h-1b-visa-program/.

Salazar, Noel B., and Alan Smart. 2011. "Anthropological Takes on (Im)Mobility." *Identities: Global Studies in Culture and Power* 18, no. 6: i–ix.

Salter, Mark B., ed. 2019. "Horizon Scan: Critical Security Studies for the Next 50 Years." *Security Dialogue* 59, no. 4S: 9–37.

Samatar, Abdi Ismail. 1992. "Destruction of State and Society in Somalia: Beyond the Tribal Convention." *Journal of Modern African Studies* 30, no. 4: 625–41.

Sanjek, Roger. 1994. "The Enduring Inequalities of Race." In *Race*, edited by Steven Gregory and Roger Sanjek, 1–17. New Brunswick, NJ: Rutgers University Press.

Santos, Fernanda. 2014. "Detainees Sentenced in Seconds in 'Streamline' Justice on Border." *New York Times*, February 11.

Sassen, Saskia. 1999. *Guests and Aliens*. New York: New Press.

Sassen, Saskia. 2014. *Expulsions: Brutality and Complexity in the Global Economy*. Cambridge, MA: Belknap Press.

Saul, John. 2010. "Two Fronts of Anti-Apartheid Struggle: South Africa and Canada." *Transformation: Critical Perspectives on Southern Africa* 74: 135–51.

Scheel, Stephan. 2017. "The Secret Is to Look Good on Paper: Appropriating Mobility within and against a Machine of Illegalization." In *The Borders of "Europe": Autonomy of Migration, Tactics of Belonging*, edited by Nicholas de Genova, 37–63. Durham, NC: Duke University Press.

Schull, Natasha. 2016. "Data for Life: Wearable Technology and the Design of Self-Care." *BioSocieties* 1–17.

Schneider, Aaron, and Rafael R. Ioris. 2017. "Honduras in Flames." NACLA, December 6.

Segantini, Tommaso. 2018. "Keeping Them Out, Killing Them Off." *Jacobin Magazine*, November 28. https://www.jacobinmag.com/2018/11/european-union-migration-borders-criminalization-refugees.

Selod, Saher, and David G. Embrick. 2013. "Racialization and Muslims: Situating the Muslim Experience in Race Scholarship." *Sociology Compass* 7, no. 8: 644–55.

Shah, Alpa. 2019. *Nightmarch: Among India's Revolutionary Guerrillas*. Chicago: University of Chicago Press.

Shamir, Hila, and Guy Mundlak. 2013. "Spheres of Migration: Political, Economic and Universal Imperatives in Israel's Migration Regime." *Middle East Law and Governance* 5: 112–72.

Shane, Scott. 2017. "The Not-So-Secret War: Revisiting American Intervention in Laos." *New York Times Review of Books*, February 5, 12.

Shantz, Jeff. 2019. "The Other North American Border Panic: Detention, Deportation, Death in Canada." *Border Criminologies*, February 22. Accessed August 1, 2019. https://www.law.ox.ac.uk/research-subject-groups/centre-criminology/centreborder-criminologies/blog/2019/02/other-north.

Shields, Peter. 2015. "The Human Cost of the European Union's External Border Regime." *Peace Review* 27: 82–90.

Shipper, Apichai W. 2010. "Politics of Citizenship and Transnational Gendered Migration in East and Southeast Asia." *Pacific Affairs* 83, no. 1: 11–29.

Silverstein, Paul A. 2005. "Immigrant Racialization and the New Savage Slot: Race, Migration, and Immigration in the New Europe." *Annual Review of Anthropology* 34: 363–84.

Smith, David. 2018. "A Lesson in Demonizing Refugees." *New York Times*, July 5.

Smith, Malinda, ed. 2010. *Securing Africa: Post 9-11 Discourses on Terrorism*. New York: Ashgate.

Smith, Sophie, ed. 2017. "Against the Day." *South Atlantic Quarterly* 116, no. 4.

Soluri, John. 2005. *Banana Cultures: Agriculture, Consumption, and Environmental Change in Honduras and the United States*. Austin: University of Texas Press.

Soto-Bermant, Laia. 2017. "The Mediterranean Question: Europe and Its Predicament in the Southern Peripheries." In *The Borders of "Europe": Autonomy of Migration, Tactics of Belonging*, edited by Nicholas de Genova, 120–40. Durham, NC: Duke University Press.

South African History Online. n.d. "Pass Laws in South Africa 1800–1994." https://www.sahistory.org.za/article/pass-laws-south-africa-1800-1994.

South African Truth and Reconciliation Commission. Official website. http://www.justice.gov.za/trc/.

Southern Poverty Law Center. 2013. *Close to Slavery: Guestworker Programs in the United States*. Montgomery, AL: Southern Poverty Law Center.

Steinberg, Jonny. 2014. "Policing, State Power, and the Transition from Apartheid to Democracy: A New Perspective." *African Affairs* 113, no. 451: 173–91.

Steinberg, Jonny. 2015. *A Man of Good Hope*. New York: Alfred A. Knopf.

Stephen, Lynn. 2007. *Transborder Lives: Indigenous Oaxacans in Mexico, California, and Oregon*. Durham, NC: Duke University Press.

Stiglitz, Joseph E. 2002. *Globalization and Its Discontents*. New York: W. W. Norton.

Stolcke, Verena. 1995. "Talking Culture: New Boundaries, New Rhetorics of Exclusion in Europe." *Current Anthropology* 36, no. 1: 1–24.

Stoler, Ann Laura. 2002. *Carnal Knowledge and Imperial Power: Race and the Intimate in Colonial Rule*. Berkeley: University of California Press.

Stoler, Ann Laura. 2017. *Duress: Imperial Durabilities in Our Times*. Durham, NC: Duke University Press.

Stoler, Ann Laura, and Frederick Cooper. 1997. "Between Metropole and Colony: Rethinking a Research Agenda." In *Tensions of Empire: Colonial Cultures in a Bourgeois World*, edited by Ann Laura Stoler and Frederick Cooper, 1–57. Berkeley: University of California Press.

Stoll, David. 2013. *El Norte or Bust! How Migration Fever and Microcredit Produced a Financial Crash in a Latin American Town*. Lanham, MD: Rowman and Littlefield.

Striffler, Steve, and Mark Moberg, eds. 2003. *Banana Wars: Power, Production, and History in the Americas*. Durham, NC: Duke University Press.

Stumpf, Juliet P. 2013. "The Process Is the Punishment in Crimmigration Law." In *The Borders of Punishment: Migration, Citizenship, and Social Exclusion*, edited by Katja Franko Aas and Mary Bosworth, 58–76. Oxford: Oxford University Press.

Sundar, Nandini. 2016. *The Burning Forest: India's War in Bastar*. New Delhi: Juggernaut.

Suzuki, Nobue. 2010. "Outlawed Children: Japanese Filipino Children, Legal Defiance and Ambivalent Citizenships." *Pacific Affairs* 83, no. 1: 31–50.

Tabuchi, Hiroko, Claire Rigby, and Jeremy White. 2017. "Amazon Deforestation, Once Tamed, Comes Roaring Back." *New York Times*, February 24.

Tang, Eric. 2015. *Unsettled: Cambodian Refugees in the New York City Hyperghetto*. Philadelphia: Temple University Press.

Tate, Winifred. 2015. *Drugs, Thugs, and Diplomats: U.S. Policymaking in Colombia*. Palo Alto, CA: Stanford University Press.

Tatlow, Didi Kirsten. 2016. "Hoping to Work in China? If You're a Class c Foreigner, It May Be Tough." *New York Times*, September 21.

Tazzioli, Martina. 2015. "The Politics of Counting and the Scene of Rescue." *Radical Philosophy* 192 (July–August).

Thomas, Deborah A. 2009. "The Violence of Diaspora: Governmentality, Class Culture, and Circulations." *Radical History Review* 103: 83–104.

Thomas, Deborah A., and Kamari Maxine Clarke. 2006. "Introduction: Globalization and the Transformations of Race." In *Globalization and Race: Transformations in the Cultural Production of Blackness*, edited by Kamari Maxine Clarke and Deborah A. Thomas, 1–34. Durham, NC: Duke University Press.

Thomas, Deborah A., and M. Kamari Clarke. 2013. "Globalization and Race: Structures of Inequality, New Sovereignties, and Citizenship in a Neoliberal Era." *Annual Review of Anthropology* 42: 305–25.

Thomas, Kevin J. A. 2017. *Contract Workers, Risk, and the War in Iraq: Sierra Leonean Labor Migrants at a U.S. Military Base*. Montreal: McGill-Queens University Press.

Thompson, Leonard. 2014. *A History of South Africa*, 4th ed. New Haven, CT: Yale University Press.

Torpey, John. 2000. *The Invention of the Passport: Surveillance, Citizenship and the State*. Cambridge: Cambridge University Press.

Torpey, John. 2005. "Imperial Embrace? Identification and Constraints on Mobility in a Hegemonic Empire." In *Global Surveillance and Policing: Borders, Security, Identity*, edited by Elia Zureik and Mark B. Salter, 157–72. Cullompton, UK: Willan.

Transparency International. 2015. "Corruption Perceptions Index." Accessed February 8, 2017. http://www.transparency.org/cpi2015#results-table.

Trilling, Daniel. 2015. "What to Do with the People Who Make It Across?" *London Review of Books*, October 8.

Trouillot, Michel-Rolph. 2001. "The Anthropology of State in the Age of Globalization: Close Encounters of the Deceptive Kind." *Current Anthropology* 42, no. 1: 125–38.

Tsing, Anna. 2003. "Natural Resources and Capitalist Frontiers." *Economic and Political Weekly* 38, no. 48: 5100–106.

Turner, Simon. 2010. *Politics of Innocence: Hutu Identity, Conflict, and Camp Life.* Oxford: Berghahn.

Turse, Nick. 2019. "Violence Has Spiked in Africa since the Military Founded Africom, Pentagon Study Finds." *The Intercept*, July 29. https://theintercept .com/2019/07/29/pentagon-study-africom-africa-violence/.

Ugelvik, Thomas. 2013. "Seeing like a Welfare State: Immigration Control, Statecraft, and a Prison with Double Vision." In *The Borders of Punishment: Migration, Citizenship, and Social Exclusion*, edited by Katja Franko Aas and Mary Bosworth, 183–97. Oxford: Oxford University Press.

UNHCR. 2018. "Global Trends: Forced Displacement in 2017." Geneva: UNHCR. https://www.unhcr.org/en-us/statistics/unhcrstats/5b27be547/unhcr-global -trends-2017.html.

University Collaborative Iraq Mortality Study. 2013. "Mortality in Iraq Associated with the 2003–2011 War and Occupation: Findings from a National Cluster Sample Survey." *PLoS Medicine*, October 15. https://journals.plos.org /plosmedicine/article?id=10.1371/journal.pmed.1001533.

Urbina, Ian 2014. "Using Jailed Migrants as a Pool of Cheap Labor." *New York Times*, May 24.

US Department of Homeland Security. 2016. "Budget-in-Brief." https://www.dhs .gov/sites/default/files/publications/FY_2016_DHS_Budget_in_Brief.pdf.

Uvin, Peter. 1998. *Aiding Violence: The Development Enterprise in Rwanda.* West Hartford, CT: Kumerian.

Van Houtum, Henk. 2010. "Human Blacklisting: The Global Apartheid of the EU's External Border Regime." *Environment and Planning D: Society and Space* 28: 957–76.

Vasquez, Yolanda. 2015. "Constructing Crimmigation: Latino Subordination in a 'Post-Racial' World." University of Cincinnati College of Law, Public Law and Legal Theory, Research Paper no. 15–10, May 26.

Verdirame, Guglielmo, and Barbara Harrell-Bond. 2005. *Rights in Exile: Janus-Faced Humanitarianism.* New York: Berghahn.

Vilas, Carlos. 1996. "Neoliberal Social Policy: Managing Poverty (Somehow)." *NACLA Report on the Americas*, May–June, 16–25.

Vine, David. 2011. *Island of Shame: The Secret History of the U.S. Military Base on Diego Garcia.* Princeton, NJ: Princeton University Press.

Vine, David. 2015. *Base Nation: How U.S. Military Bases Abroad Harm America and the World.* New York: Henry Holt.

Vine, David. 2019. "Islands of Imperialism: Military Bases and the Ethnography of U.S. Empire." In *Ethnographies of U.S. Empire*, edited by Carole McGranahan and John F. Collins, 249–69. Durham, NC: Duke University Press.

Vogt, Wendy A. 2018. *Lives in Transit: Violence and Intimacy on the Migrant Journey.* Berkeley: University of California Press.

Von Schnitzler, Antina. 2016. *Democracy's Infrastructure: Techno-Politics and Protest after Apartheid*. Princeton, NJ: Princeton University Press.

Vora, Neha. 2013. *Impossible Citizens: Dubai's Indian Diaspora*. Durham, NC: Duke University Press.

Vukov, Tamara. 2016. "Target Practice: The Algorithmics and Biopolitics of Race in Emerging Smart Border Practices and Technologies." *Transfers* 6, no. 1: 80–97.

Walia, Harsha. 2013. *Undoing Border Imperialism*. Oakland, CA: AK Press.

Walters, William. 2015. "Reflections on Migration and Governmentality." *Movement: Journal for Critical Migration and Border Regime Studies* 1, no. 1. https://movements-journal.org/issues/01.grenzregime/04.walters-migration.governmentality.html.

Wang, Chieh-Hsuan, Chien-Ping Chung, Jen-Te Hwang, and Chia-yang Ning. 2018. "The Foreign Domestic Workers in Singapore, Hong Kong, and Taiwan: Should Minimum Wage Apply to Foreign Domestic Workers?" *Chinese Economy* 51, no. 2: 154–74.

Wang, Jackie. 2108. *Carceral Capitalism*. Cambridge, MA: MIT Press.

Warah, Rasna. 2014. *War Crimes: How Warlords, Politicians, Foreign Governments and Aid Agencies Conspired to Create a Failed State in Somalia*. Bloomington, IN: AuthorHouse.

Washington, John. 2019. "What Would an Open-Borders World Actually Look Like?" *The Nation*, April 24.

Waters, Mary. 1994. "Ethnic and Racial Identities of Second-Generation Black Immigrants in New York City." *International Migration Review* 28, no. 4: 795–820.

Watts, Michael. 2006. "Empire of Oil: Capitalist Dispossession and the Scramble for Africa." *Monthly Review* 58, no. 4.

Webber, Frances. 2019. "Solidarity Crimes." *Border Criminologies* (blog). https://www.law.ox.ac.uk/research-subject-groups/centre-criminology/centreborder-criminologies/blog/2019/07/solidarity-crimes.

Weissman, Stephen. 2014. "What Really Happened in Congo: The CIA, the Murder of Lumumba, and the Rise of Mobutu." *Foreign Affairs*, July–August.

Wilder, Gary. 2005. *The French Imperial Nation-State: Negritude and Colonial Humanism between the Two World Wars*. Chicago: University of Chicago Press.

Willen, Sarah S. 2007. "Introduction." In *Transnational Migration to Israel in Global Comparative Perspective*, edited by Sarah S. Willen, 1–27. Lanham, MD: Lexington.

Willen, Sarah S. 2010. "Citizens, 'Real' Others, and 'Other' Others: The Biopolitics of Otherness and the Deportation of Unauthorized Migrant Workers from Tel Aviv, Israel." In *The Deportation Regime: Sovereignty, Space, and the Freedom of Movement*, edited by Nicholas de Genova and Nathalie Peutz, 262–94. Durham, NC: Duke University Press.

Williams, Brett. 2009. "Body and Soul: Profits from Poverty." In *The Insecure American*, edited by Hugh Gusterson and Catherine Besteman, 224–37. Berkeley: University of California Press.

Wilson, Dean, and Leanne Weber. 2008. "Surveillance, Risk and Preemption on the Australian Border." *Surveillance and Society* 5, no. 2: 124–41.

Wilson, Jill H. 2013. "Immigration Facts: Temporary Foreign Workers." Brookings Institution, Immigration Facts Series, June 18. http://www.brookings.edu /research/reports/2013/06/18-temporary-workers-wilson.

Wilson, Richard. 2001. *The Politics of Truth and Reconciliation in South Africa: Legitimizing the Post-Apartheid State*. Cambridge: Cambridge University Press.

Wolfe, Patrick. 1999. *Settler Colonialism and the Transformation of Anthropology: The Politics and Poetics of an Ethnographic Event*. London: Cassell.

Wolfe, Patrick. 2006. "Settler Colonialism and the Elimination of the Native." *Journal of Genocide Research* 8, no. 4: 387–409.

Wolpe, Harold. 1972. "Capitalism and Cheap Labour Power in South Africa: From Segregation to Apartheid." *Economy and Society* 1, no. 4: 425–56.

Xiang, Biao, and Johan Lindquist. 2014. "Migration Infrastructure." *International Migration Review* 48, no. S1: S122–S148.

Zamosc, Leon. 2004. "The Indian Movement in Ecuador: From Politics of Influence to Politics of Power." In *The Struggle for Indigenous Rights in Latin America*, edited by Nancy Grey Postero and Leon Zamosc, 131–57. Brighton, UK: Sussex Academic.

asylum: EU asylum shopping surveillance, 110; racialization of, 67; sovereignty and exclusion and restrictions on, 63–65

austerity regimes, insecurity fostered by, 40–42, 46–48

Australia: death linked to immigration restrictions in, 80; detention and deportation in, 76; exclusionary citizenship in, 26–27; immigration restrictions in, 62, 70, 76; Iraq war supported by, 45; smart border technology in, 110–11

Balibar, Étienne, 30, 133

Balkan countries: border wall construction in, 104; immigration restrictions and, 31–32, 75–76; security imperialism and, 123–24

banana oligarchies, trade agreements and, 50–51

Barnett, Thomas, 2–3, 13; Somali case study and, 6–7

Barre, Siyad, 4–8

belonging: detention and deportation and, 79; mobility and, 21–23

Belt and Road Initiative (BRI) (China), 53

Berda, Yael, 66

Binford, Leigh, 87–88

biometric data: border security and, 80–81; smart borders technology and, 108–16

Boehm, Deborah, 96

Boer Wars, 76

Book of Negroes (UK), 109–10

border security: border-thickening and externalization and, 65–67; climate change and, 57–58; death toll from, 79–81; deportable labor force development and, 85–86; in EU, 71–76; in Israel, 64; limitations of, 10; offshoring of borders and, 67–76; smart borders technology and, 108–116; sovereignty and exclusion and, 62–65; in U.S., 66–71, 75–76; wall construc-

tion for, 103–108. See also militarized border security

Bosnia, security imperialism and, 123–24

Bowling, Ben, 78

Bracero program, 86–87

Brennan, Denise, 99

British imperialism: nationalist identity and, 27–33; race and, 10–14

Brown, Wendy, 49, 134

Browne, Simone, 110

Caal Maquín, Jakelin case study, 55–57

Cabot, Heath, 132

Cambodia, U.S. military intervention in, 43

Canada: detention and deportation in, 76; exclusionary citizenship in, 26–28; guest workers in, 87–90, 150n15; immigration restrictions in, 69–70; smart border technology in, 110–11

capitalism: plunder of, 18–19, 48–50; race and, 8–14; security imperialism and, 117–24, 120–24. See also racial capitalism

caravans of migrants, 55–57, 132

care work, as plunder, 34–36, 59

Caribbean: guest workers from, 86–87; U.S. military exercises in, 106

Castles, Stephen, 85

Central America: capture and deportation of migrants from, 75–76; corporate capitalist plunder in, 48–50; land expropriation and narco-economies in, 54–55; land expropriation in, 52; military intervention in, 42–46; refugees from, 64. See also specific countries

Central Intelligence Agency (CIA), military intervention in Central and South America and, 42–46

Cetti, Fran, 74

Chile, CIA intervention in, 42

Chin, Rita, 28–29

China: British imperialism and, 10–14; guest workers from, 88–89; heritage citizenship in, 34–37; immigration restrictions in, 64–65; interventions in Central America by, 44; land expropriation by, 52–53; racist nationalism in, 37–38; security imperialism in, 124; smart border technology in, 111–16; undocumented workers in, 97–98; U.S. restrictions on immigrants from, 23–33, 86, 142n9

Chinese Communist Party, nationalist identity and, 37–38

Chiquita corporation, 49–50

circular carcerality, 123

citizenship: decolonization and, 131; in GCC states, 38; heritage citizenship, 33–39; settler colonialism and definitions of, 39; smart border technology and hierarchies of, 111; undocumented workers and, 96–98; whiteness as qualification for, 23–33

Citizenship Law (Israel), 33–34

civilizationalism, 155n85

Civil Rights Acts, 25–26

Clarke, Kamari, 12–13

climate change, population displacement and, 57–58

Clinton, Bill, 67–68, 105

Collins, John F., 154n75

Colombia: corporate capitalist plunder in, 48–49; U.S. intervention in, 44

colonialism: extraction and plunder during, 41–42; race and, 9–14

Comaroff, Jean, 3

Comaroff, John, 3

conservation efforts, land expropriation and, 51–52

Conspiracy Bill (Japan), 114

Constable, Nicole, 92

Constitution-free zone (U.S.-Mexico border), 70–71, 105–6

containment of migration: border-thickening and externalization and, 65–67; of immigration, 61–62; sovereignty and exclusion and, 62–65

contingent citizenship, undocumented workers and, 96–97

Contras (Nicaragua), 43

Copenhagen School, 155n85

CoreCivic, 77

Corrections Corporation of America, 77

Côté-Boucher, Karine, 111

counterinsurgency operations, limitations of, 129–30

Coutin, Susan, 68, 88

criminalized immigration: border wall construction and, 107–8; regimes of, 19, 78–79; for women workers, 90–94

crimmigration policies, 62, 66–71; detention and deportation and, 78–79

critical security studies, security imperialism and, 155n85

Cuba: detention of immigrants from, 76; racialization of asylum seekers from, 67

cultural integrity, deportable labor force development and, 85–86

cultural logic of apartheid, 16–18; European immigration restrictions and, 30–33

cybersecurity industry, 118

Dadaab refugee camp complex, 5–6

debt burden in global south: austerity regimes and, 46–48; land expropriation and, 53

De Genova, Nicholas, 31–32, 81

Del Monte corporation, 49

Department of Defense (U.S.), venture capitalist research division of, 117–24

Department of Homeland Security (DHS), 69–71, 77, 106

deportation of immigrants, 76–79; guest worker deportations, 92–94; undocumented workers, 96–98

detention policies of global north, 76–79; undocumented workers and, 97–98

Doctors Without Borders, 74

Dole corporation, 49

domestic labor: conditions for women in, 34–37, 59, 151n30; guest worker status of, 90–94

Dominions Land Act (Canada), 27
Dowie, Mark, 51
drug trafficking: border security and role of, 67–68; land expropriation and, 54; U.S. intervention linked to, 44
Dublin Agreement of 2003, 30
Dublin Regulation, 72
Duterte, Rodrigo, 53

economic oligarchy: climate change and, 57–58; intervention in Latin America of, 43–46
Ecuador, Chinese land expropriation in, 52
Ehrenreich, Barbara, 59
Elbit Systems, 107
El Salvador: Chinese intervention in, 44; labor export policies and, 58–59; U.S. military intervention in, 42–43
Emergency Trust Fund for Africa, 75
Ethiopia, Somalian intervention by, 5–8, 45
ethno-racial categorization, apartheid and, 13–18
Eurodac program, 110
Europe: colonial imperative and race in, 10–14; exclusionary citizenship in, 26–29; guest worker programs in, 85–94; immigration restrictions in, 30–33; race and history of, 8–10; refugee flows into, 63–64; Schengen Agreement in, 29–30; security industry in, 118; xenophobic racism in, 144n51
European Asylum Support Office, 73
European Border and Coast Guard, 73
European Border Surveillance System (EUROSUR), 30–31, 73, 110
European Union (EU): border wall construction in, 104–8; detention and deportation regime in, 79; immigration restrictions in, 29–31, 62, 71–76; as security empire, 119–24; Smart Borders program in, 110
exceptionalism, security imperialism and, 121–22

exclusion, refugee policies and philosophy of, 62–65
existential reciprocity, migration and, 59
Export Processing Zones (Honduras), 44

family life: temporary labor impact on, 89–90; undocumented workers' impact on, 96–97
Farmer, Paul, 9–10
Fassin, Didier, 66
Federal Bureau of Investigation (FBI), 69
Ferguson, James, 21
Filipina/o labor: exploitation of, 36–37, 151n42; in U.S., 86; women guest workers, 90–94
"Five Country Conference," 110–11
"Fortress Europe" ideology, 75
fragmented globality, 4
France: detention and deportation in, 76; immigration policies in, 28–29; Sans-Papiers movement in, 133
Frederickson, George, 23
Freedom Party (Austria), 32
Friedman, Thomas, 6–7
Frontex (EU agency), 64, 73–75, 79, 110
Functioning Core: defined, 2–3; Somali case study and, 6–7

Gardner, Andrew, 38
GEO Group, 77
global homeland security market, growth of, 118–24
globalization: deportable labor force and, 85–94; race and mobility and, 4
global north: apartheid practices of, 40–42; border-thickening and externalization and, 65–67; climate change and role of, 57–58; defined, 2–4; guest worker programs in, 83–84, 98–99; heritage citizenship in, 33–39; labor control by, 19, 83–84; land tenure and expropriation by, 51–55; military outsourcing in, 94–95; nationalist identities in, 22–23; plunder by, 18–19; security empires and, 119–24; solidarity

movements with migrants in, 132–34. *See also* specific countries

global south: austerity regimes in, 46–48; climate change impact in, 57–58; defined, 3–4; labor export policies and, 58–59; military intervention and disruption in, 42–46; refugee concentrations in, 63–65; remittances from guest workers in, 88–90; security imperialism impact in, 124–25. *See also* specific countries

global war on terror: legitimization of security imperialism and, 153n22; population displacement and, 44–45; security imperialism and, 155n85

Gomberg-Muñoz, Ruth, 96, 99

Gordimer, Nadine, 134–35

Grandin, Greg, 55

Greece, immigration restrictions and, 75–76

Guatemala: Jakelin Caal Maquín case and, 55–57; U.S. military intervention in, 42–46

guest worker programs, 83–84; in China, 97–98; in Gulf States, 90–91; post-World War II emergence of, 85; remittances by workers in, 88–89; undocumented labor and, 95–98; in U.S., 86–87; women in, 90–94

Gulf States (GCC states): detention and deportation in, 76, 92–93; guest worker programs in, 90–94; heritage citizenship in, 38–39; immigration restrictions in, 64; undocumented labor in, 95–98

Gupta, Akhil, 21

H-1B visa, 150n13

H-2 guest worker visa, 86–87

Hage, Ghassan, 13–14

Haiti: detention of immigrants from, 76; racialization of asylum seekers from, 67; structural violence in, 9–10

Hanson, Pauline, 32

Hardt, Michael, 154n75

Harrison, Faye, 48

Hedges, Chris, 48

heritage citizenship, 33–39

hierarchical integration policies: labor control and, 84; smart border technology and, 111

Hochschild, Arlie, 59

Holmes, Seth, 89, 98–99

Homeland Security Act of 2002, 68–69

homelands policy, South African apartheid and, 16–18, 27–28

Honduras: climate change impact in, 57–58; drug trafficking in, 44; land expropriation for drugs in, 54; security imperialism in, 124; U.S. intervention in, 43–44

Hong Kong: heritage citizenship in, 34, 36; women guest workers in, 90–94, 151n30

hukou system (China), 97–98

identity documentation and management, refugee regimes and, 63–65

Illegal Immigration Reform and Immigrant Responsibility Act (IIRIRA), 68

immcarceration, 78

Immewahr, David, 154n75

immigration: border-thickening and externalization and, 65–67; British imperialism and, 27–28; citizenship and, 23–33; containment of, 61–62; "crimmigration" policies and, 62, 66–76; death rates linked to restrictions on, 79–81; deportable labor force development and, 86–94; detention and deportation policies and, 76–79; heritage citizenship and, 33–39; illegalization of, 67–76; reform of, 25–26

Immigration and Customs Enforcement (ICE), 68–71, 77

imperial governmentality, race and, 10

incarceration: of immigrants, detention and deportation centers for, 76–79; surveillance technology and, 112–16, 153n47; U.S. policies for, 69–71, 156n5

India: border security in, 107, 116; British imperialism and migration from, 11–14; citizenship and belonging in Middle East of, 144n73; security imperialism in, 124
indigenous people: colonialism and removal of, 10; land expropriation from, 51–52; reservation system for, 27–28
Indonesia: Chinese investment in, 53; corporate capitalist plunder in, 48; guest workers from, 88–94; labor export policies and, 58–59; land expropriation in, 51; security imperialism in, 124; U.S. intervention in, 42–43; women guest workers from, 90–94
insecurity, drivers of, 40–42
insurgency as political power, emergence of, 129–30
International Convention on the Protection of the Rights of All Migrant Workers and Members of Their Families, 90
International Monetary Fund (IMF), 46, 52
International Organization for Migration (IOM), 57, 84, 87
international refugee law, sovereignty and exclusion and, 62–65
Iraq: capitalist plunder in, 49; deportation of workers in, 92–93; migrant military labor in, 94–95; U.S. invasion of, 45
ISIS, creation of, 45
Islamic Courts Union (ICU), 5
Islamist groups, military intervention and rise of, 45
Islamophobia: global security initiatives and, 119–24; racist rhetoric concerning, 13–14
Israel: border controls in, 66–67, 104–8; deportation of guest workers in, 93–94; detention and deportation centers in, 76–77; detention centers in, 64; heritage citizenship in, 33–34; land expropriation by, 53–54; as security empire, 119–24; security technology exports by, 118–24

Israeli Defense Forces, 118
Italy, restrictions on immigration in, 73–76

Japan: heritage citizenship in, 34–35; immigration restrictions in, 64–65; security systems in, 114–15; undocumented labor in, 95–98; women guest workers in, 92–94
Johnson Reed Act (1924), 24

Kalir, Barak, 73, 79
Kashmir, smart security systems in, 116
kefala system, 38–39, 90
Kenya: security imperialism and, 122–23; smart security systems in, 116
Khosravi, Shahram, 33, 74, 132
Klein, Naomi, 118
knowledge classification, militarized security policies and, 113–16
Kumar, Amitava, 45

labor: apartheid as control of, 16–18; border-thickening and externalization and, 65–67; deportable labor force construction, 85–94; global north control of, 19, 83–84; heritage citizenship and, 34–39; Israeli border infrastructure and, 66; labor export policies and, 58–59; outsourced military labor, 94–95; undocumented labor, 95–98
Lake, Marilyn, 11–13, 27
land tenure and expropriation: capitalist plunder and, 49–50; by global north, 51–55
Laos, U.S. military intervention in, 43
Latinx communities, U.S. criminalization of immigration and, 69–71
Law of Return (Israel), 33–34
League of Nations, 131
Lebanon, surveillance systems in, 115
Leggeri, Fabrice, 75
Le Guin, Ursula, 135–36
Le Pen, Marine, 32
Li, Darryl, 94, 123–24

Li, Tania, 51
liberalism, race and, 10
Liberia, austerity regime impact in, 47
Libya, restrictions on immigration from, 73–76
Lindquist, Johan, 88–89
Lloyd, Jenna, 67
"logic of incarceration," women guest workers and, 92–94
Lomé Convention, 50–51
Losurdo, Domenico, 10, 140n33
Lowe, Lisa, 10
Lucht, Hans, 59
Lumumba, Patrice, 42–43
Lutz, Cathy, 102, 116–17, 154n75

Mahdavi, Pardis, 91
Malaysia, women guest workers in, 91–94, 151n30
Mamdani, Mahmood, 127
Mandela, Nelson, 128
Marcos, Ferdinand, 43
Mare Nostrum operation, 73
maritime wall construction, 105
Marx, Karl, 131
Masco, Joe, 113
Maskovsky, Jeff, 128
mass migration contingency planning, militarized border protection and, 106–7
Mbembe, Achille, 54, 134
McGranahan, Carole, 154n75
Mexican immigrants: deportable labor force development using, 86–88, 98–99; racialization of, 24–25; as undocumented labor, 96–99
Mexico: criminalization of immigration on U.S. border with, 68, 75–76; NAFTA's impact in, 50–51; refugees in, 64; U.S. border wall with, 104–8, 152n15
Middle East: border wall construction in, 107–8; death linked to immigration restrictions in, 80; land expropriation in, 53–54; restrictions on immigration from, 72–76; smart

security systems in, 115; women guest workers in, 90–94
migration: affect and desire as motivations for, 58–59; austerity regimes and growth of, 47–48; border-thickening and externalization and, 65–67; climate change and, 57–58; containment of, 61–62; criminalization of, 67–76; death rates linked to restrictions on, 79–81; detention and deportation policies and, 76–79; EU restrictions on, 71–76; guest worker programs and, 85–94; heritage citizenship and, 34–39; Jakelin Caal Maquín case study of, 55–57; labor export policies and, 58–59; military intervention and rise of, 42–43; postcolonial patterns of, 132; state regulation of, 109–10; trade agreements and growth of, 50. *See also* refugees
militarized border security: characteristics of, 102–8; criminalization of immigration and, 68–76; global north investment in, 19; guest worker permits and surveillance and, 93–94; smart borders technology and, 108–16; Tohono O'odhom reservation and, 152n15; wall construction, 103–8
militarized global apartheid: apparatus for, 18; definition of, 102–8; evolution of, 1–2, 139n16; immigration control and, 81–82; insecurity fostered by, 40–42; security imperialism and, 120–24; Somalia as case study in, 4–8; unsustainability of, 126–30. *See also* private military contractors
military interventions: capitalist plunder and, 48–50; historical impact of, 42–46; as marine border wall, 105; outsourced temporary labor for, 94–95
Miller, Todd, 57–58, 106
Mills, Charles, 9
mobility: belonging and, 21–23; militarized global apartheid and, 1–2; Schengen Agreement and, 29–30

change dislocations and, 57–58; containment policies and, 61–62; in GCC states, 38; heritage citizenship and, 34–39; Jakelin Caal Maquín case study of, 55–57; land expropriation and, 51–55; military intervention and rise of, 42–43; trade agreements and growth of, 50

Posel, Deborah, 15–16

postcolonial era, military interventions in, 42–46

Povinelli, Elizabeth, 59–60

power inequality, security imperialism and, 121–24

predictive policing technologies, 113

pregnancy restrictions, for women guest workers, 91–94

Prevention Through Deterrence policy (U.S.), 68, 79–80

private military contractors: border control technologies and, 105–8; migrant labor hired by, 94–95; security technology and, 116–24; smart borders technology and, 108–16

Q'eqchi'-Maya migration, 55–57

race and racialization: border security technology and reinvention of, 80–81; citizenship and, 23–33; definitions of, 8–14, 141n34; heritage citizenship and, 33–39; illegalization of immigration and, 67–76; Islamophobia and, 142n22; land expropriation and, 51–52; mobility and, 1–2; refugee restrictions and role of, 64–65; security imperialism and, 120–24; smart border technology and, 110–16; U.S. criminalization of immigration and, 69–71; women guest workers and, 92–94

racial capitalism, citizenship and, 39

Racial Contract, 9

Racial Contract, The (Mills), 9

racialized nativism, creation of, 18

Raytheon, 110

Reagan, Ronald, 67

refugees: belonging and, 21–23; border-thickening and externalization and, 65–67; climate change and, 57; containment of, 61–62; international regime concerning, 62–65; post-World War I flow of, 142n5; in Somalia, 5–6. See also migration; mobility

remittances from guest workers, economic impact of, 88–89

Renamo (Mozambique), 43

resource extraction: as capitalist plunder, 48–50; land expropriation for, 52–53; neo-extraction practices, 49–50

Reynolds, Henry, 11–13, 27

Risen, James, 118

risk logics, global mobility patterns and, 128

Robinson, Cedric, 8–9, 39, 131

"robo-sniper" technology, 107

Russia: counterterrorism systems in, 116; detention and deportation centers in, 76–77; immigration restrictions in, 64

Rwanda, austerity regime impact in, 47

Sacco, Joe, 48

sacrifice zones, corporate capitalist plunder and, 48

Salazar, Noel, 21

sanctuary movements, emergence in global north of, 132–34

Sanjek, Roger, 8

Sans-Papiers movement, 133

Sassen, Saskia, 51

satellite systems, militarized security policies and, 114–16

Scheel, Stephan, 72

Schengen Agreement, 29–30, 72, 110, 143n32

Seam States, defined, 3

Seasonal Agricultural Worker Program (SAWP) (Canada), 87–89

Seasteading Institute, 44

Second Generation Schengen Information System (SIS II), 110

Secrecy Act of 2013 (Japan), 114

Secure Communities, 69